Produced by Independent Publishers for the Independently Minded

PRICE GUIDE 2005/6

MILLER'S

classic
motorcycles

MILLER'S CLASSIC MOTORCYCLES PRICE GUIDE 2005/6

Created and designed by
Miller's Publications
The Cellars, High Street
Tenterden, Kent TN30 6BN
Telephone: 01580 766411
Fax: 01580 766100

General Editor: Mick Walker
Production Co-ordinator: Kari Reeves
Project Co-ordinator & Designer: Philip Hannath
Editorial Co-ordinator: Deborah Wanstall
Editorial Assistants: Melissa Hall, Joanna Hill, Maureen Horner
Advertisement Designer: Simon Cook
Jacket Design: Colin Goody
Advertising Executive: Emma Gillingham
Advertising Administrator & Co-ordinator: Melinda Williams
Production Assistants: June Barling, Caroline Bugeja, Ethne Tragett
Additional Photography: Chris Alty, Bob Masters, Robin Saker, Mick Walker

First published in Great Britain in 2004
by Miller's, a division of Mitchell Beazley,
imprints of Octopus Publishing Group Ltd,
2–4 Heron Quays, London E14 4JP

A CIP catalogue record for this book is
available from the British Library

ISBN 1 84000 962 4

Illustrations and film output by 1.13, Whitstable, Kent
Printed and bound by Toppan Printing Co (HK) Ltd, China

Front cover illustration:

1965 BSA 650 Lightning
£3,000–3,600 / €4,500–5,400 / $5,600–6,600 ⊞ MW

classic motorcycles

GENERAL EDITOR
Mick Walker

FOREWORD
Roy Francis

Contents

Acknowledgments

The publishers would like to acknowledge the great assistance given by our consultants:

Malcolm Barber — Bonhams, Montpelier Street, Knightsbridge, London SW7 1HH Tel: 0207 393 3900

Roy Francis — 4 Haste Hill Road, Boughton Monchelsea, Maidstone, Kent ME17 4IP

James Knight — Bonhams, Montpelier Street, Knightsbridge, London SW7 1HH Tel: 0207 393 3900

Michael Jackson — Cheffins, 49/53 Regent Street, Cambridge CB2 1AF Tel: 01264 810875

Brian Verrall — Caffyns Row, High Street, Handcross, Nr Haywards Heath, West Sussex RH17 6BJ Tel: 01444 400678

Rick Walker — R&M Walker, 45 Caves Close, Terrington St Clement, King's Lynn, Norfolk Tel: 01553 829141

We would like to extend our thanks to all auction houses, their press offices, and dealers who have assisted us in the production of this book, along with the organisers and press offices of the following events:

The International Classic Motor Cycle Show, Stafford

Beaulieu September Autojumble & Automart

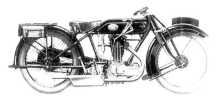

Foreword

Like the turning of the wheel, motorcycling can take you full circle. I have experienced the highs and lows in the motorcycle trade and sport, together with the loss of close friends. I am proud to have assisted in the careers of Bill Ivy and Paul Smart from road racing, Paul Hurry and Martin Goodwin from speedway, grass and long track, and Graham Jarvis from trials.

Together with Paul Smart, I ran a successful dealership in Kent with franchises for Honda, Kawasaki, Triumph and Yamaha. I now follow the classic scene, which maintains its strength with shows, parades, autojumbles and auctions, many of which I attend. Often at these events you hear 'Wish I had kept that', something we may all have wished at times.

For me, in recent years, highlights in classic parades have been the 30-year tribute to Bill Ivy at Brands Hatch, when I rode the Chisholm Honda CR93 and a Kirby G50 Matchless Metisse, after which Bill's family presented me with his 1966 Silver FIM World 125cc Championship Medal.

I have assisted Paul Smart with his machines at the Centennial TT Classic and also at the Goodwood tribute to Barry Sheene. Together we made memorable trips to Montlhéry in France and Misano in Italy.

When the opportunity arises to make a longed-for purchase, you often need to act quickly to ascertain a value. This is where publications such as *Miller's Classic Motorcycles Price Guide* and Mick Walker's contributions are invaluable in your research. In my view confirming the price of a possession that has grown in value is not unlike success in competition.

To those who read and make use of this publication, I hope your motorcycling interest, at whatever level, gives you the same pleasure and fulfilment that it has given me.

How to use this book

I t is our aim to make this Guide easy to use. Motorcycle marques are listed alphabetically and then chronologically. Dirt Bikes, Military Bikes, Mopeds, Police Bikes, Racing Bikes, Scooters, Sidecars and Specials are located after the marques, towards the end of the book. In the Memorabilia section objects are grouped by type. If you cannot find what you are looking for, please consult the index which starts on page 174.

---

82 NORTON

Norton *(British 1902–)*

James Lansdowne Norton built his first motorcycle in 1902, using a French Clement engine. The Energette, as it was called, was soon entered in reliability and speed trials.

In 1907, a Norton ridden by Rem Fowler had the distinction of winning the multi-cylinder class at the very first Isle of Man TT. Then came the first Norton designed engines, and by late 1907, the first of the 490cc (79 x 100mm bore and stroke) long-stroke, single-cylinder engines had been unveiled.

In 1911, following a long illness, James Norton lost control of the company to the Vandervell family, although he remained joint managing director with R. T. Shelley.He died in 1925 at the early age of 56.

Post-war developments included the Roadholder front forks, rigid frame, restored, incorrect fuel tank for year. Dominator overhead-fuel-valve parallel twin (1948) and Featherbed duplex frame (1950). Geoff Duke and sidecar star Eric Oliver gave Norton several world road racing titles in

the immediate post-war period.

However, all was not well, and rival AMC (Associated Motor Cycles) took over Norton in 1953. This signalled the end of the glory days. At the end of the 1954 season, Norton ceased racing factory specials and, from then on, only built the production Manx models.

In 1958, the lightweight twin, the 249cc Jubilee, was launched, followed by the 349cc Navigator (1960) and 400cc Electra (1962).

None of these could really be called successful, and with Norton's larger singles totally outdated in the marketplace, it was left to the Dominator family of big twins to keep the flag flying. Besides the already established 500, there was a 600, which was superseded by a 650 as the 1960s dawned, while the new 750 Atlas (originally for export only) arrived in 1961.

AMC went into receivership in 1966. Then came the Poore era of the Commando.

1930 Norton Model 19, 588cc, overhead-valve vertical single, iron head and barrel, forward-mounted magneto, Webb forks, rigid frame, restored, incorrect fuel tank for year. **£2,700–3,000 / €4,000–4,500 / $5,000–5,500 ⚘ CGC** The Model 19 was essentially a longer-stroke version of the better-known 490cc Model 18. Production ceased at the end of 1932.

1979 Norton 850 Commando Interstate Mk3, 829cc, overhead-valve twin, 73 x 89mm bore and stroke, front and rear disc brakes, indicators, 12 volt electrics, electric start, fork gaiters, left-hand gear-change, original, very good condition. **£3,600–4,000 / €5,400–6,000 / $6,700–7,400 ⊞ NLM**

Miller's Motorcycle Milestones

Norton Commando 750 (1967–73), **850** (1973–78) **Price Range: 750** £2,000–5,000 / €3,000–7,500 / $3,700–9,200 **850** £2,500–5,000 / €3,000–7,500 / $3,700–9,200 The Commando project began with the appointment of Stefan Bauer at Norton Villiers as director of engineering in January, 1967. Boss Dennis Poore wanted Bauer to lead a technical team to develop a new big twin to replace the ageing 750 Atlas.

Bauer was ably assisted by two well-known British engineers, Bernard Hooper and Bob Twigg. Actually, this was just as well, Bauer had no previous two-wheel experience at all, his background being in nuclear physics, and he had spent the previous 12 years with Rolls-Royce. Even so, his team was successful in creating a very marketable machine, which was launched, to much public acclaim, at the Earls Court Motorcycle Show in September, 1967.

The most innovative feature of the newcomer was its frame, the 745cc (73 x 89mm bore and stroke) Atlas engine (albeit with sloping cylinders) and four-speed AMC-type gearbox being retained in rubber mountings by a full-cradle duplex steel assembly.

There is no doubt that the Commando was a clever

commercial design. It gave the appearance of being a very different motorcycle from the machine it replaced, yet actually, except for the frame and bodywork, most components were the same. Even so, it was a huge success, not only in the showroom, but also on the race track. It was voted Machine of the Year by *Motor Cycle News* in 1968, a title it went on to win no fewer than five years in a row, a feat that had never been bettered. The first model year was 1969, when it was sold as the 750 Fastback. The Roadster arrived for 1970, and for 1971 a new version of the Fastback and Roadster appeared, together with the Street Scrambler, Hi Rider and Production Racer; 1972 saw the Interstate, which featured a larger tank and a disc front brake (already used on the Production Racer). All models were fitted with disc brakes from the middle of the year.

Then, for 1973, the 850 (829cc, 77 x 89mm bore and stroke) version was launched in Roadster, Hi Rider and Interstate forms. In 1974, the John Player Norton café racer appeared. Finally, for 1975, the Roadster and Interstate 850s gained electric start, left-hand gear change and a disc rear brake.

In 1978, the final batch of 30 machines (Interstate 850s) was built.

Marque Introduction
provides an overview of the marque including factory changes and in some instances the history of a particular model. Introductions change from year to year and not every section will begin with an introduction.

Caption
provides a brief description of the motorcycle or item, and could include comments on its history, mileage, any restoration work carried out and current condition.

Price Guide
this is based on actual prices realized. Remember that Miller's is a price guide not a price list and prices are affected by many variables such as location, condition, desirability and so on. Don't forget that if you are selling it is quite likely you will be offered less than the price range. Price ranges for items sold at auction tend to include the buyer's premium and VAT if applicable. The exchange rate used in this edition is 1.50 for € and 1.85 for $.

Source Code
refers to the 'Key to Illustrations' on page 167 that lists the details of where the item was sourced. Advertisers are also indicated on this page. The ⚘ icon indicates the item was sold at auction. The ⊞ icon indicates the item originated from a dealer. The ⚙ icon indicates the item originated from a motorcycle club, see Directory of Motorcycle Clubs on page 172.

Bold Footnote
covers relevant additional information about a motorcycle's restoration and/or racing history, designer, riders and special events in which it may have participated.

Miller's Motorcycle Milestones
highlights important historic motorcycle events and the effect they have had on the motorcycle industry.

Understanding Motorcycle Electrics

Electrics is an aspect of motorcycle restoration that gives many people nightmares. Even though this need not be so, as I shall explain, it is true that electrics worries more owners and restorers of motorcycles than any other part of the machine. A major reason for this is that unlike a broken clutch cable, or a siezed piston, an electrical glitch may not always be instantly obvious.

In truth, real electrical problems, or at least those that cannot be solved, are rare. However, if a real problem does exist there is a set of rules which, if followed, will make life easier.

Adopt a sensible planned approach – always have to hand the appropriate workshop manual and wiring diagram for your particular make, model and year of machine; bear in mind that electrical systems, even for the same basic model, may have different wiring diagrams. For example, the late 1970s Ducati 860GTS had two electrical component suppliers – Aprilia and CEV – and two separate warning-light boards, headlamps, looms and the like. In addition, different markets have different systems, American and European specifications often being entirely different.

On older machines, it is often possible to repair components such as magnetos, dynamos and control boxes. However, since the advent of 'sealed-for-life' electronic devices in the early 1970s, replacement is often the only option.

Besides the electrical components themselves, wiring is all-important, and it may be necessary to purchase a new loom, or have one specially made. Trying to get the best out of your system with old, and often damaged, wiring components is simply asking for trouble.

Quite often, an electrical fault can have the simplest of causes. It may be a poor earth, an equally poor connection somewhere in the system or a faulty fuse. Remember always to check the basics first.

You will also need the right tools for the job. The essentials are a set of small (magneto) spanners, electrician's screwdrivers, pliers, wire strippers, cutters, an electrician's soldering iron, a hydrometer (to test the battery cells) and a small avometer. Finally, remember that these tools are best kept apart from the mainstream items of your main (mechanical) toolbox.

Most older machines, certainly larger-capacity motorcycles from the first half of the 20th century, employed magneto ignition. There are several different makes and types. Major manufacturers include BTU and Lucas (Britain), Bosch (Germany), Marelli (Italy) and Splitdorf (USA). The magneto is completely independent of the rest of the electrical system. It guarantees a powerful spark even at high engine speeds and has proved itself to be generally very reliable.

The constituent parts of the magneto are a permanent magnet, which is integral with the camshaft and serves as a rotor; the fixed stator, which comprises the laminated core with the ignition coil; the contact breaker and, where there is automatic advance and retard, a compensator device.

As electric lighting equipment (instead of the gas-type pioneer machines) became popular during the late 1920s, so the dynamo and magneto operated closely together (magdyno). A voltage control regulator also became necessary.

Another form of ignition was by battery/coil. This really became popular after the arrival of the crankshaft-mounted alternator in the early 1960s. With this came the advantage of no touching components to wear. However, there were other difficulties with early alternators such as control problems and boiled batteries, although in time these were largely beaten with the introduction of the zener diode (basically a heat sink), which gave better control, and the switch from six to 12 volt electrical systems.

For a time during the 1960s, British manufacturers (such as BSA and Triumph) employed the energy-transfer set-up. This allowed the motorcycle to run minus lights and battery. Aimed largely at the American off-road market, this had the disadvantages of requiring the rotor to be accurately timed to the engine and of providing a less powerful spark.

Another ignition system found on classic motorcycles is the flywheel magneto. Crankshaft-mounted, this was employed primarily on small-capacity machines, particularly two-strokes. Essentially, the flywheel magneto is precisely what it says, with the rotor (often of brass) keyed to the crankshaft and a stator bolted to the crankcase, the latter containing the coils for both ignition and lighting.

Finally, there came electronic ignition. This promised much, as indicated by a 1981 BMW brochure, which explained, 'The breakerless electronic ignition, which retains its settings for the lifetime of the motorcycle and incurs no wear in operation, is one of the reasons for long running life and low fuel consumption.' BMW also said that it improved starting – so much for the theory. Unfortunately, in practice, the picture was not quite so rosy, as several owners soon found out.

While operating, electronic ignition was, and is, a definite improvement over what had gone before. But if a component malfunctions, there is absolutely nothing the rider can do except push his bike home or call the breakdown services. With the old systems, at least one had the chance of rediscovering ignition by the roadside; with electronics, this is impossible. **Mick Walker**

The Motorcycle Market

The motorcycle world was rocked when the recent fire at the National Motorcycle Museum in Birmingham destroyed hundreds of important, hand-picked motorcycles and severely damaged many others. The speculation that the impact of this would be a significant upturn in the market has not been realized, although the museum is actively sourcing important machines for their re-opening, which is scheduled for later this year.

The stability of the UK economy over the last year has cushioned the motorcycle market from the volatility of the financial markets caused by the current situation in Iraq. However, exceptional motorcycles of quality and rarity, that combine both condition and provenance, have moved strongly forwards.

The classic motorcycle goes from strength to strength and demand for top-quality bikes continues to exceed supply. The movement is supported by an ever expanding list of prestigious motorsport events, including the Goodwood Festival of Speed and the Goodwood Revival, where top bikes are often presented and ridden by their original celebrity riders.

The European motorcycle auction market continues to be dominated by Bonhams, with four specialist sales each year, flagshipped by their Stafford County Showground sales in April and October. Palmer Snell continue their presence in the West Country, Cheffins in the East of England and from their Buxton base, and H&H now include motorcycles in their general motoring sales.

Reflecting the continued popularity in the Sunbeam MCC Epsom to Brighton Run, pre-1915 Pioneer machines have maintained their value, although large horsepower, multi-cylinder models have shown significant increases. 'Barn discovery' machines sold during the year include a 1908 Douglas sold by Bonhams at the East of England Showground at Peterborough for £6,210 / €9,300 / $11,500 against a price guide of £2,500–3,500 / €3,750–5,200 / $4,600–6,500 and at Stafford a 1913 New Hudson realized £5,290 / €7,900 / $9,800 against a price guide of £1,500–2,000 / €2,250–3,000 / $2,800–3,700. The relatively straight-forward restoration of these early machines is the undoubted attraction, along with the challenge of persuading the restored machine to complete the annual Epsom to Brighton run. Cheffins sold a 1914 Alldays & Onions for £5,500 / €8,200 / $10,200 at the Duxford Imperial War Museum in October while an ever-popular 1912 Rudge Multi 3½hp sold for £7,400 / €11,100 / $13,700 at their Old Warden sale in July.

Brough Superiors and Vincents continued to excite on both sides of the Atlantic, Bonhams selling one of the oldest surviving Broughs, a 1922 6½hp model for £27,600 / €41,000 / $51,000 at Stafford in April. A 1933 Brough Superior SS80 achieved £14,200 / €21,300 / $26,300 at Cheffins' April Godmanchester sale. Bonhams' Stafford sale in October generated huge interest when a photographic and literature archive from the Brough Superior factory was offered for sale. George Brough's personal International Travelling Pass issued in 1925 and relating to Brough Superior Reg. No. HP 2122 realized £1,035 / €1,550 / $1,900 against a top estimate of £80 / €120 / $150.

All eyes were on Bonhams' dispersal sale of the Geeson Brothers' Motorcycle Museum Collection, an interesting mix of bikes built up over 40 years or so. Interest came from the USA, Australia, Japan and mainland Europe, resulting in exceptional prices. Two US bidders fought it out over a Douglas Endeavour on which the hammer finally fell at £16,675 / €25,000 / $31,000, a 1934 Sunbeam Model 95R Works Prototype was bought by a UK collector for £15,238 / €22,900 / $28,200 against Japanese bidding and a 1934 Matchless Silver Hawk achieved a massive £19,838 / €29,800 / $37,000.

Run-of-the-mill post-WWII machines remain popular at entry level for Club events but the market in this area has shown no upward movement, with supply tending to exceed demand. Prices for 1950s and early 1960s machines can be misleading as they do not always include the cost of transferable registration numbers. Many collectors will only consider purchasing bikes that retain their original registration number, and fortunately the DVLA continues to be most helpful in allowing registration numbers to be recovered where appropriate.

Among post-war bikes, Manx Nortons and AJS 7Rs are now back above the £10,000 / €15,000 / $18,500 threshold, good examples making significantly more, and the very specialist field of classic racers reflects continued interest. A rare 1964 Honda 125cc CR93, presented as last raced in 1978, achieved a healthy £21,275 / €32,000 / $39,000 at Stafford in April.

In America Bonhams and Butterfields have had recent sales in Brookline, Massachussetts and Los Angeles. Jerry Wood & Co Auctioneers hold an annual motorcycle sale at the Daytona Antique and Classic Motorcycle Auction Meet in Florida, during Daytona Bike Week. This well respected auction has been running for 17 years and this year realized sales of £445,000 / €667,000 / $823,000 plus buyer's premium at eight per cent. The Dick Brown collection, mainly Triumphs, helped boost this result.

Throughout the last year the market has continued to grow in all areas. The recovery of the dollar against the pound is expected to result in stronger interest from the USA in the coming year's European sales, while home buyers are poised to fend off overseas bidding on top quality, top provenance machines.

Malcolm Barber

Aermacchi *(Italian 1950–78)*

1961 Aermacchi Ala Verde, 248cc, overhead-valve horizontal single, alloy head, cast-iron barrel, downdraught Dell'Orto UB carburettor, 20bhp, 4-speed gearbox, beam-type frame, exposed-stanchion Ceriani front forks, full-width alloy hubs, 84mph top speed.
£2,600–2,900 / € 3,900–4,350 / $4,800–5,300 ⊞ MW

1966 Aermacchi Sprint, 246cc, overhead-valve horizontal single, unit construction, 5-speed foot-change gearbox, centre and side stands, original, unrestored.
£1,700–1,900 / € 2,550–2,850 / $3,150–3,500 ⊞ NLM
The Sprint was mainly sold in the USA. It differed from the European Ala Verde in having a touring rather than sports specification, including conventional handlebars, fork gaiters and a large dualseat.

AJS *(British 1909–66)*

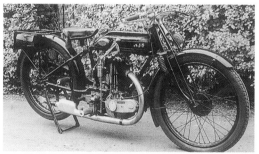

1915 AJS Model D, 6hp, with acetylene lighting kit, bulb horn, luggage rack, restored, near concours condition.
£7,900–9,500 / € 11,900–14,200 / $14,500–17,500 ⚒ B(Kn)
Formerly suppliers of proprietary engines, the Stevens brothers of Wolverhampton diversified into manufacturing complete motorcycles, setting up A. J. Stevens & Co in 1909. The brothers' first machine was a 292cc (2.5hp) single equipped with either direct belt drive (Model A) or a two-speed countershaft gearbox with all-chain drive (Model B), this latter combination being advanced in its day, especially for a lightweight. A 5hp V-twin – the Model D – joined the range in 1912. Intended for sidecar work, the Model D was powered by a 631cc side-valve engine and came with a beefed-up version of the two-speed gearbox. The model D's engine was enlarged to 696cc (6hp) for 1913, while a three-speed gearbox and internal expanding rear brake were additional improvements. A new, smaller V-twin – the 550cc Model A – arrived in November 1914, at which time the Model D was redesigned along 'A' lines and further enlarged to 748cc. One of the most effective and popular sidecar tugs of its day, the AJS Model D continued in production well into the 1920s.

1926 AJS 2¾hp Big Port, 349cc, overhead-valve single, 74 x 81mm bore and stroke, iron head and barrel, exposed valve gear and pushrods, restored.
£3,950–4,750 / € 5,900–7,100 / $7,300–8,750 ⚒ B(Kn)
The AJS company of Wolverhampton was just down the road from rival Sunbeam. In contrast to Sunbeam, the strength of AJS lay in its lightweight 350cc machine in both side-valve and overhead-valve guises. These were renowned for their handling and reliability – many remained in daily service until the 1960s. A feature of the vintage AJS was the overhead-valve 'Big Port' engine, so-called because of its excessive exhaust-pipe diameter.

▶ **1927 AJS Big Port,** 499cc, overhead-valve single, 84 x 90mm bore and stroke, forward-mounted magneto, 3-speed hand-change gearbox, concours condition.
£3,850–4,300 / € 5,800–6,500 / $7,100–7,900 ⊞ MW

AJS Model	ENGINE cc/cyl	DATES	CONDITION		
			1	2	3
16MS	348/1	1949–63	£2,600	£1,800	£1,300
18S	497/1	1949–63	£2,700	£1,900	£1,400
20	498/2	1949–61	£2,900	£2,000	£1,500
30	593/2	1956–58	£2,700	£1,800	£1,500
31CSR	646/2	1958–66	£3,000	£2,200	£1,600

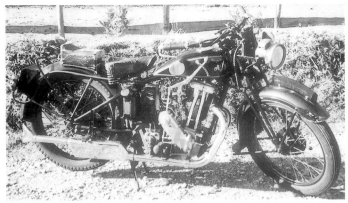

► **1930 AJS R6,** 346cc, overhead-valve twin-port single 74 x 81mm bore and stroke, 4-speed hand-change gearbox, saddle tank, lighting equipment, original, unrestored.
£4,500–5,000 / €6,700–7,400
$8,300–9,200 ⊞ CotC
The 'R' prefix was used to denote 1930 model year AJS machines.

1930 AJS R5, 349cc, side-valve vertical single, 74 x 81mm bore and stroke, hand-change gearbox, side and centre stands, Powell and Hanmer headlamp, all original tinware, needing full cosmetic restoration.
£1,850–2,200 / €2,750–3,300 / $3,400–4,050 ⚲ CGC
The history of AJS can be split into two periods (or three, if considering the two-stroke scramblers produced by Norton Villiers at Andover between 1968 and 1974): the beginning of production at Wolverhampton in 1911, under the Stevens Brothers, and the move to south London, under the Collier Brothers after the 'first' company failed in 1931.

1931 AJS SB6, 349cc, overhead-valve single, 74 x 81mm bore and stroke, all-chain drive, centrally-sprung girder forks, rigid frame.
£3,150–3,500 / €4,700–5,200 / $5,800–6,400 ⊞ BLM
Early in 1931, four new models were listed by AJS, two having the 'Big Port' name. A major change was made to the lubrication systems, which became total loss, but retained their dry-sump appearance. This was because a by-pass was taken from the main delivery so that some oil returned to the tank, but only as an indication that the system was working. These were the three-fifty SB6 and five-hundred SB8.

◄ **1952 AJS Model 20,** 498cc, overhead-valve vertical twin, individual cylinder heads and barrels, one-piece crankshaft with three main bearings, restored to original specification.
£2,800–3,100 / €4,200–4,650
$5,200–5,800 ⊞ BLM
The Model 20 (and its Matchless brother, the G9), was first shown at the London Earls Court show in late 1948, but initial supplies went exclusively for export.

1955 AJS Model 20 de luxe, 498cc, overhead-valve twin, 66 x 72.8mm bore and stroke, 4-speed Burman foot-change gearbox, non-standard rear carrier, front crash bars, good condition.
£2,900–3,200 / €4,350–4,800 / $5,300–5,900 ⊞ MW
Changes for 1955 included full-width hubs front and rear, Amal Monobloc carburettor, frame with hole for air filter tube, deeper headlamp shell carrying speedometer, and new front mudguard without front stay.

1955 AJS 16MS, 348cc, overhead-valve single, alloy head, cast-iron barrel, Amal Monobloc carburettor, Burman gearbox, full-width hubs, 'jampot' rear shocks.
£2,500–2,800 / €3,750–4,200 / $4,600–5,100 ⊞ BLM
For 1955, the AJS (and Matchless) single received auto ignition advance with a bulge on the timing cover, timing-side main and bearing with larger flange, larger inner drive-side main, revised oil tank connections. The 350 was also given the larger fuel tank of the 500.

1955 AJS Model 20 Standard, 498cc, overhead-valve twin, 4-speed foot-change gearbox, Teledraulic front forks, 'jampot' rear shock absorbers, standard specification, very good condition.
£2,500–2,800 / €3,800–4,200 / $4,600–5,100 ⊞ PM

1958 AJS Model 30 CSR, 593cc, overhead-valve vertical twin, 72 x 72.8mm bore and stroke, alloy heads, cast-iron barrels, siamesed exhaust system, 4-speed foot-change gearbox, full-width alloy brake hubs, full-cradle single-downtube frame.
£2,700–3,000 / €4,000–4,500 / $5,000–5,500 ⊶ CMT
The Model 30 (and its Matchless version, the G11) was built between 1956 and the end of 1958. However, the CSR sportster was only offered for the 1958 model year.

A.K.D. *(British 1903–32)*

1911 AKD, 493cc, inlet-over-exhaust single, forward-mounted magneto, belt and chain drive, sprung saddle, carrier, leather side pouches.
£7,700–8,500 / €11,500–12,700 / $14,200–15,700 ⊞ VER
AKD (Abingdon King Dick), or simply Abingdon, sold motorcycles between 1903 and the end of 1932. At first, the company used proprietary engines includin Fafnir, Kerry, Minerva and MMC, but later built its own singles and V-twins. From 1933, AKD concentrated on its core business of making hand tools, notably spanners.

Alldays & Onions *(British 1903–24)*

▶ **1914 Alldays & Onions 3½hp,** 499cc, 4-stroke single, rear-mounted magneto, direct belt drive from crankshaft, hand-change 3-speed Sturmey-Archer gearbox, early Pioneer Certificate No. 160.
£6,000–7,200 / €9,000–10,800 / $11,100–13,300 ⚲ CGC
The Birmingham based Alldays & Onions firm began with de Dion Bouton-engined three-wheelers in 1898. In 1903, it built its first motorcycle. Renamed Allon from 1915, the company built big V-twins (798 and 988cc) and singles (499 and 539cc), plus a 292cc two-stroke. Production ceased in 1924.

Ambassador *(British 1947–65)*

◀ **1962 Ambassador Popular,** 197cc, Villiers 9E engine, 59 x 72mm bore and stroke, 3-speed foot-change gearbox, 5in brakes, 18in wheels, original, unrestored.
£770–850 / €1,150–1,300
$1,450–1,600 ⊞ PM
Located in Ascot, Berkshire, Ambassador was founded by Kaye Don, the former racing car and powerboat driver. Although the first prototype machine, built in 1946, sported a 494cc side-valve JAP engine, all production Ambassador models were powered by Villiers two-stroke engines. In October 1962, the company was acquired by rival DMW.

Anglian *(British 1903–12)*

► **1904 Anglian de Dion Bouton 2¾hp**,
de Dion Bouton single-cylinder engine.
£4,100–4,500 / € 6,000–6,700
$7,400–8,300 ⊞ **MW**
As well as their own 2½hp Anglian motors,
these pioneer machines were available
with 2¾hp engines from de Dion Bouton,
MMC, Fafnir and Saralea, and later
Blumfield and JAP.

Ariel *(British 1902–70)*

Ariel was one of the cornerstones of the once great British motorcycle industry. Its first motorcycle, powered by an imported Belgian Minerva engine, made its debut at the 1901 national show for the 1902 season, and thereafter the Birmingham based marque went on to build a reputation for sound design and excellent finish which was to last until its demise in 1965.

For much of its early history, Ariel was overseen by the Sangster family, who became key figures in the birth and growth of the British motorcycle industry. Some of the greatest designers worked for Ariel over the years – men like Val Page, Edward Turner and Bert Hopwood.

Val Page was with Ariel, off and on, from the mid-1920s until the late 1950s. Having moved from JAP, his first contribution for his new employer was a series of single-cylinder models with overhead- and side-valve engines, the basics of which would endure until the late 1950s, when a brand-new innovative series of 250cc two-stroke twins -– the Leader and, later, the Arrow – came from the pen of the same man.

Edward Turner's most enduring contribution to Ariel was the legendary Square Four. There is little doubt that had this innovative and exciting design not been launched at the beginning of the Depression, which blighted the industrial world during the early 1930s, it would have achieved much greater success. Even so, in many ways the Square Four was a forerunner to the modern four-cylinder super bike.

Another famous Ariel range was the Red Hunter overhead-valve sporting roadster singles, manufactured in 350 and 500cc engine sizes. These ran from the early 1930s until the late 1950s.

Post-WWII, as part of the giant BSA group, Ariel slowly lost its independence, but not before a new range of four-stroke twins of 500 and 650cc engine sizes was introduced.

Ariel also enjoyed notable success in motorcycle sport – in road racing, motocross and, most of all, trials. In the last the performances of Sammy Miller on his lightweight HT5 500cc single are the stuff of legend.

Even though the Ariel name passed into history some 40 years ago (if one discounts the débâcle of the BSA Ariel-badged 50cc trike of 1970), it retains a most enthusiastic and loyal group of followers. This is because the motorcycles the company once produced are seen today as real classics.

◄ **1923 Ariel 8hp**, 994cc, MAG inlet-over-exhaust V-twin engine, 82 x 94mm bore and stroke, Ariel countershaft 3-speed hand-change gearbox with clutch and kickstarter, Cox patent Atmos carburettor, hand-pump lubrication with drip feed, magneto ignition, 20in wheels, 60in wheelbase, restored by the famous frame specialist Ken Sprayston.
£9,400–10,500
€ 14,100–15,700
$17,400–19,400 ⊶ **AOM**

◀ **1927 Ariel Model C,** 346cc, overhead-valve single, 72 x 85mm bore and stroke, 3-speed hand-change gearbox, saddle tank, all chain drive, magdyno ignition, central spring girder forks, rigid frame.
£3,600–4,000
€5,400–6,000
$6,700–7,400 ⊞ MW
The Model C was designed by Val Page after he joined Ariel from JAP.

1932 Ariel Model SG, 498cc, four-overhead-valve single, 60-degree sloping cylinder, iron head and barrel, dry sump lubrication with a centrifugal filter, 4-speed gearbox.
£3,350–3,750 / €5,000–5,600 / $6,200–6,900 ⚙ AOM
This series was built in various engine sizes, from 248 to 557cc, and was introduced in early 1930. All the 498 and 557cc 'sloper engines' featured double-roller bearing big-ends.

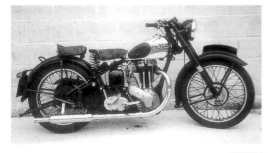

1938 Ariel NH2 Red Hunter, 346cc, overhead-valve single, twin-port head, totally enclosed valve springs, valve guides automatically lubricated, 72 x 85mm bore and stroke, 4-speed Burman foot-change gearbox, top speed 72mph.
£3,200–3,850 / €4,800–5,800 / $5,900–7,100 ⚙ B(Kn)
Considerable changes to the overhead-valve, single-cylinder Ariel engines were introduced for 1938. There were new cylinder heads and revised valve gear. Not only did these make an appreciable difference to the appearance, but they also provided more efficient and oil-tight engines. The NH2 used the twin-port head, the NH1 a single-port version; otherwise, they were largely the same.

◀ **1950 Ariel NH Red Hunter,** 346cc, overhead-valve vertical single, 72 x 85mm bore and stroke, iron head and barrel, forged steel connecting rod, roller-bearing big-end, 13bhp, vertically split aluminium crankcases, Burman 4-speed foot-change gearbox, top speed 71mph, original and unrestored.
£2,250–2,500 / €3,400–3,800 / $4,150–4,600 ⊞ BLM

▶ **1951 Ariel 4G Mk 1,** 497cc, overhead-valve all-alloy square-four engine, 4-speed Burman gearbox, telescopic forks, plunger rear suspension, valanced front mudguard, fully restored.
£4,500–5,000 / €6,700–7,500
$8,300–9,200 ⊞ BLM
When the 1951 Ariel range was announced in September 1950, a number of modifications common to all the company's models were introduced: 'to improve the appearance and ease maintenance tasks.' Several of these concerned the fuel tank. A new die-cast alloy fork bracket was the home for the speedo and a fork-top fascia, as the ammeter had been transferred to the headlamp. This enabled the filler cap to be moved to the centre of the tank, increasing capacity. The oil pressure switch was mounted in a small circular tank insert.

ARIEL Model	ENGINE cc/cyl	DATES	CONDITION 1	2	3
4G Mk 1 Square Four	995/4	1949–53	£4,000+	£3,400	£2,200
VB600	398/1	1945–58	£2,100	£1,600	£1,200
NH350	346/1	1945–59	£2,900	£2,000	£1,600
LH200 Colt	198/1	1954–59	£600	£400	£200
Leader	247/2	1958–65	£1,600	£1,000	£700
Arrow	247/2	1960–64	£1,400	£800	£600
Golden Arrow	247/2	1961–65	£1,800	£1,200	£800

Miller's
Motorcycle Milestones

Ariel Square Four 498cc (1931–32), 601cc (1932–36), 599cc (1937–39), 997cc (1937–59)
Price Range: £3,000–6,000 / €4,500–9,000 / $5,500–11,100

It was extremely unfortunate that Ariel's most prestigious and technically interesting design was born in a world caught in the grip of the worst economic depression in history. As a consequence, sales never reached anything like its innovation deserved. At a time when the term 'superbike' had yet to be coined, the Square Four was one of the few motorcycles of its era that really deserved the title (others would have included the Matchless Silver Hawk V4 and Brough Superior SS100). Although prototypes had been extensively tested (and even ridden by members of the press), the first the public saw of the new Ariel was when production versions were displayed at the Olympia show in London in November, 1930. This was a 498cc (51 x 61mm bore and stroke) machine with overhead camshaft and costing just over £75 / €112 / $140. First deliveries began during 1931, and in that first year a total of 957 were delivered. Then at the 1931 Olympia show, a 601cc (56 x 61mm) version made its debut. Although the original smalle-engined machine was still listed, a mere 45 were subsequently sold and it was soon axed, whereas in 1932 the new 600 sold a total of 1,174 examples.

Between 1932 and 1936, only the 600 ohc version was available and some 5,000 of these were produced. In 1937, a revised model, the 4G, with overhead valves and a displacement of 997cc (65 x 75mm) went on sale; together with an overhead-valve 599cc (50.4 x 75mm bore and stroke) 600. Sales continued in small numbers up to September 1939, and with the Square Four being considered unsuitable for service with the armed forces (although a few machines went to the police and civil defence authorities), production of any significance did not resume until after WWII. The next development in the immediate post-war period was the fitting of telescopic front forks. In 1949, the engine was redesigned (the 600 having not been built post-war) with a light-alloy top end – referred to as the 4G Mark 1. Then 1953 saw the introduction of the Mark 2, or '4-pipe' model. This featured detachable light-alloy exhaust manifolds on each side, with two header pipes neatly siamesed into individual exhaust pipes. Fewer than 4,000 Mark 2s were built, and production came to a halt in 1959, when the last Mk example left the Birmingham Selly Oak works.

◄ 1952 Ariel 4G Mk 1, 497cc, overhead-valve square-four engine, 65 x 75mm bore and stroke, dry sump, plunger-pump lubrication, car-type 4-cylinder distributor, completely restored. **£4,400–5,300 / €6,600–7,900 / $8,100–9,700 ✗ B(Kn)** This is an example of the all-alloy two-pipe 4G Mk 1, which has the Frank Anstey-designed link plunger rear suspension.

1952 Ariel VB600, side-valve vertical single, alloy head, cast-iron cylinder, 86.4 x 102mm bore and stroke, Burman 4-speed foot-change gearbox, plunger rear suspension, dualseat. **£2,350–2,600 / €3,500–3,900 / $4,350–4,800 ⊞ CotC**

1954 Ariel VH Red Hunter, 497cc, overhead-valve vertical single, single-port alloy head, cast-iron barrel, 81.8 x 95mm bore and stroke, Amal 376 Monobloc carburettor, very good original condition. **£3,050–3,400 / €4,600–5,100 / $5,600–6,200 ⊞ BLM**

◀ **1954 Ariel VB600,** 598cc, side-valve vertical single, 17bhp at 4,400rpm, aluminium head, cast-iron barrel, magneto ignition, Burman GB6 4-speed gearbox, top speed 77mph.
£1,250–1,500 / €1,900–2,250 / $2,300–2,750 ⚒ B(Kn)
In common with other British manufacturers, Ariel had listed a side-valve 600 since the 1920s, primarily for the sidecar market. Many solo riders also liked the fuss-free flexibility of such an engine, however, so much so that Ariel's VB machine remained in production until 1959 with only relatively minor changes – telescopic forks appeared in 1947 and a swinging-arm rear end in 1955.

1955 Ariel NH Red Hunter, 346cc, overhead-valve vertical single, 72 x 85mm bore and stroke, magdyno, 4-speed foot-change gearbox, swinging-arm frame, telescopic front forks, single-sided brakes, fluted tank, good original condition.
£2,700–3,000 / €4,000–4,500 / $5,000–5,500 ⌖ WCMC

1956 Ariel NH Red Hunter, 346cc, overhead-valve single, alloy head, cast-iron barrel, 72 x 85mm bore and stroke, Burman 4-speed gearbox, 7in brakes, duplex front downtubes, missing tank chrome flutes.
£2,500–2,800 / €3,750–4,200 / $4,600–5,100 ⊞ MW
Full-width alloy brake hubs, rear chain enclosure, and a combined headlamp cowl and instrument panel were among a raft of new features unveiled when the 1956 Ariel range was launched at the beginning of September 1955. Another innovation for the Red Hunter 350 was the use of a cylinder barrel employing cast-in pushrod tunnels instead of the separate pushrod tubes formerly used (already seen on the 500).

▶ **1959 Ariel Leader,** 247cc, 2-stroke parallel twin, 54 x 54mm bore and stroke, 8:25:1 compression ratio, 16bhp at 6,400rpm, top speed 70mph, many optional extras, including panniers, indicators, rear carrier, chrome bumper and parking light.
£1,450–1,600 / €2,200–2,450 $2,700–3,000 ⊞ BLM

Aspes *(Italian 1967–82)*

◀ **1976 Aspes Jumo,** 124cc, 2-stroke Hiro engine, radial-fin aluminium head, alloy cylinder, 5-speed gearbox, duplex cradle frame, Grimeca hydraulic 2-piston caliper and single front disc brake, 7-spoke wheels, matching speedometer and rev-counter.
£1,800–2,000
€2,700–3,000
$3,350–3,700 ⊞ MW
The Aspes Jumo was designed as a sports roadster/clubman's racer. It could do 80+ mph with silencer attached, and 90+ mph without it.

Banshee *(British 1921–24)*

▶ **1922 Banshee,** 269cc, Villiers single-cylinder 2-stroke engine with deflector piston, 3-speed hand-change gearbox, belt drive, footboards.
£2,300–2,750 / €3,450–4,100 / $4,250–5,100 ⚒ B(Kn)
Banshee was a Birmingham marque that produced motorcycles between 1921 and 1924, mainly fitted with Villiers 269cc two-stroke engines. 'Banshee' suggests a howling noise, which is reportedly like the exhaust note of these machines. Very few examples of Banshee motorcycles are known to exist.

Benelli *(Italian 1911–)*

◀ **1936 Benelli 250 Super Sport,** 246cc, overhead-camshaft single, 67 x 70mm bore and stroke, twin-port cylinder head, 4-speed foot-change gearbox, sprung girder forks, plunger rear suspension.
£2,800–3,100 / €4,200–4,650
$5,200–5,800 ⊞ MW
The Benelli company launched its 250 Super Sport with plunger rear suspension at the Milan show in 1936. Giuseppe Benelli purchased a licence for this type of suspension from the German DKW factory, and was the first Italian manufacturer to use it.

▶ **1959 Benelli Sport,** 172cc, overhead-valve single, alloy head, cast-iron barrel, 4-speed gearbox, double-coil valve springs, wet-sump lubrication, 60 watt CEV dynamo, correct tinware, original, unrestored.
£900–1,000 / €1,350–1,500
$1,650–1,850 ⊞ NLM
A new 175 single appeared in 1959, with pushrod operated valves and over-square 62 x 57mm bore and stroke dimensions. The Sport put out 12bhp at 8,000rpm, giving a maximum speed of almost 70mph.

1978 Benelli 750 Sei, 747.7cc, overhead-camshaft across-the-frame six, 56 x 50.6mm bore and stroke, 3 Dell'Orto carburettors, 71bhp at 8,500rpm, electric start, 5-speed gearbox, 6-megaphone exhaust, top speed 120mph.
£3,150–3,500 / €4,700–5,200 / $5,800–6,500 ⊞ CotC

1979 Benelli 504 Sport, 498cc, overhead-camshaft across-the-frame four, 56 x 50.6mm bore and stroke, 52bhp at 8,900rpm, 5-speed gearbox, triple disc brakes, cast-alloy wheels, top speed 117mph, standard apart from engine crashbars.
£2,150–2,400 / €3,200–3,600 / $4,000–4,450 ⊕ BGB
The 504 Sport was identical to the smaller-capacity 354 Sport (345.5cc), but had a much superior power-to-weight ratio, giving considerably improved acceleration and a higher top speed.

1980 Benelli 654T, 654cc, across-the-frame four cylinder, 5-speed gearbox, electric start, triple Brembo disc brakes, cast-alloy wheels, fairing, grab rail and indicators, only 2,000 miles from new, original, excellent condition.
£1,500–1,700 / €2,250–2,550 / $2,800–3,150 ⊞ MW
The suffix 'T' stood for Turismo. There was also a Sport version with lower bars and a more racy specification.

Beta *(Italian 1948–)*

◄ **1972 Beta 50 Sport,** 49cc, 2-stroke single, piston-port induction, alloy head, cast-iron barrel, duplex cradle frame, racing-style tank, seat and clip-on handlebars, full-width hubs, exposed-spring front and rear suspension.
£450–500 / €680–750 / $830–920 ⊞ MW

Bianchi *(Italian 1897–1967)*

▶ **1954 Bianchi 150 2T,** 149cc, 2-stroke single, piston-port induction, unit construction, alloy head, cast-iron barrel, 4-speed gearbox, telescopic forks, swinging-arm rear suspension, rocking heel/toe gear lever, dualseat.
£800–900 / €1,200–1,350
$1,500–1,650 ⊞ NLM
The 150 was developed from the new 125 two-stroke which had been put on sale at the end of 1947.

Bimota *(Italian 1972–)*

The Bimota marque was born more by accident than design, although for sports bike enthusiasts, the accident was a singularly happy event. Massimo Tamburini owned a heating business in Rimini, an area of Italy that had long been a centre of motorcycle manufacture. As a hobby, Tamburini modified several local riders' machines to make them faster and lighter with sharper handling. Before long, his work on the MV Agusta 600 four had gained the admiration of the Italian motorcycling community.

But it was in 1972, at the Misano race circuit, where Tamburini, his friend Giuseppe Morri and racer Luigi Anelli were testing a specially-framed Honda CB750, that Bimota was born. A journalist who was present wrote about Tamburini's Honda, creating such interest that a company was established to meet the consequent influx of orders. It took its name from the three partners who set it up: Bianchi, Morri and Tamburini.

The new venture began trading on 1 January 1973. In addition to the Honda, Tamburini had just completed a pure racing machine powered by a Yamaha TR2 two-stroke engine. This too was an instant success, and in 1975 Johnny Cecotto won the 350cc World Championship on a Bimota-framed TZ Yamaha.

The first Bimota superbike was the Suzuki GS750-engined SB2 (the SB1 was a racer), which debuted at the Bologna show in January 1977. The next development in the evolution of the Bimota street bike came at the 1977 Milan show in the shape of the KB1, housing either a Kawasaki 903 or 1015cc double-overhead-camshaft, four-cylinder power unit.

The publicity and sales success led to more superbikes. Soon Honda, and later Yamaha, wanted a piece of the action. Bimota received support from the companies it worked with. During this period, Bimota introduced several innovative features for production roadsters, including variable steering geometry and the space frame.

During the late 1970s and early 1980s, Bimota boomed. Then came the crunch. At the 1983 Milan show the marque foolishly displayed a prototype of the futuristic Tesi, which wasn't ready for sale. The result was no sales and bankruptcy.

The company was only saved by government support, and the emergence of the first Bimota to feature a Ducati engine, the DB1 in 1985.

The success of the DB1 ensured a comeback that continued into the 1990s with Ducati and Yamaha engines. Then Bimota got into financial difficulties again, not helped by the high costs incurred by the largely unsuccessful 499cc V-Due, a high-tech V-twin two-stroke featuring (at least on paper) low pollution and high output thanks to its radical new lubrication system. Unveiled in 1997, the V-Due suffered more than its share of problems, and Bimota was forced to withdraw it from sale.

Late in 1998, Bimota was purchased by Francesco Tognon, who earlier in the decade had rescued Laverda from the scrap heap. However, Tognon was unable to do the same for Bimota, and as the 21st century dawned, Bimota was struggling once again.

◀ **1982 Bimota HB2,** 901.8cc, double-overhead-camshaft across-the-frame four, 64.5 x 69mm bore and stroke, 95bhp at 9,000rpm, chrome-moly steel frame, 40mm telescopic front forks, monoshock rear suspension, 16in wheels, top speed 150mph.
£5,000–5,500 / €7,500–8,300 / $9,200–10,200 ⊞ NLM

1993 Bimota DB2, 944cc, Ducati single-overhead-camshaft, 90-degree V-twin engine, 6-speed gearbox, Brembo 4-piston racing brake calipers and fully-floating discs at front, 3-spoke 17in wheels, concours condition.
**£6,000–7,200 / €9,000–10,800
$11,100–13,300 ⋏ BB(S)**
The DB (Ducati Bimota) series began in 1985, when Frederico Martini, Bimota's Technical Director, utilized a 750 Ducati F1 engine with a Bimota chassis. This design not only saved Bimota, but also had a profound influence on motorcycle styling for the rest of the 1980s (Honda CBR 600/1000, Ducati Paso). The DB2 followed, making its debut at the Cologne Show in late 1992. This 1993 fully-fired example is one of only 408 machines built, 285 of which had a full fairing, the other large 123 half fairings. The engine of this machine was modified with a 944cc big-bore kit.

1997 Bimota YB8, 1002cc, Yamaha liquid-cooled double-overhead-camshaft 4-cylinder engine, 20 valves, 149bhp at 10,000rpm, 12:1 compression ratio, 5-speed gearbox, top speed 175mph, concours condition, 12,000 miles from new.
£4,950–5,900 / €7,400–8,800 / $9,200–11,000 ⋏ COYS
The YB8 ran from the late 1980s until 1997, using the FZR Ex-Up 1000 engine, and thus this example is one of the very last built.

2003 Bimota DB4ie, 944cc, very low mileage, concours condition.
£6,700–7,500 / €10,000–11,200
$12,400–13,900 ⊞ NLM
This is one of the very rare EF1 fuel-injected Ducati 900SS engined DB4 (ie). Much revised compared to the original production DB4, with a fitted dualseat.

2003 Bimota V Due, 499cc, liquid-cooled, 90 degree V-twin engine, 135bhp, 72 x 61.25mm bore and stroke.
£9,500–10,500 / €14,200–15,700 / $17,600–19,400 ⊞ NLM
One of only 24 built, the previous models having EFI. This was the test bed for the Evoluzion model which Bimota did not produce. The production of this model is now left to others. It has 25bhp more than the original production model of 1997.

BMW *(German 1923–)*

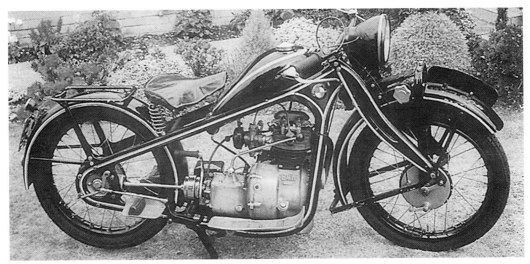

1931 BMW R2, 198cc, overhead-valve single, 63 x 64mm bore and stroke, 19mm Sum carburettor, 6bhp at 3,500rpm, wet sump, shaft final drive, leading-link front forks, top speed 58mph.
£3,800–4,550 / €5,700–6,800 / $7,000–8,400 ↗ B(Kn)
Although BMW's considerable reputation as a manufacturer of fine touring motorcycles had been founded on its superbly engineered flat-twins, the catastrophic economic downturn of the early 1930s brought with it the need for a simpler type of machine. The German government's measures to stimulate demand in the economy included the suspension of vehicle road tax, a move that encouraged the purchase of cheap, lightweight motorcycles as basic transport. BMW was well-placed to capitalize on this with its first single-cylinder model, the 198cc, overhead-valve R2. Launched in 1930 and equipped with the same pressed-steel frame and shaft drive as the larger models, the R2 would prove to be the best selling BMW to date.

◄ **1959 BMW R50,** 494cc, overhead-valve flat-twin, twin 24mm Bing carburettors, 26bhp at 5,800rpm, 4-speed gearbox, Noris magneto, 18in wheels, Earles forks, Denfeld dualseat, bar-end indicators, top speed 87mph.
£4,000–4,500 / €6,000–6,700
$7,600–8,400 ⊞ BLM
This example is finished in the rare optional white finish with black lining. It is believed to be the actual London show model. A total of 13,510 R50s were sold between 1955 and 1960.

BMW Model	ENGINE cc/cyl	DATES	CONDITION 1	2	3
R50 & R50/2	494/2	1955–69	£3,500	£2,100	£1,700
R69 & R69S	594/2	1955–69	£4,800+	£3,000	£2,000
R26/R27	247/1	1956–66	£2,000	£1,600	£1,000
R75/5	745/2	1969–73	£1,800	£1,500	£1,000
R905	898/2	1973–76	£3,000+	£2,300	£1,800
R100RS	980/2	1976–84	£2,000	£1,600	£1,100

1959 BMW R26, 247cc, overhead-valve vertical single, 4-speed foot-change gearbox, shaft final drive, Earles front forks, swinging-arm rear suspension, unrestored, paintwork, chrome and aluminium in excellent condition.
£2,100–2,500 / €3,150–3,750 / $3,900–4,600 ⚒ B(Kn)
The single-cylinder BMW first appeared in pre-war days. Indeed, BMWs first new post-war model was a single-cylinder design – the 250cc R24 – which arrived in 1948, looking pretty much like the pre-war R23, but producing an additional 2bhp. In mid-1950, the R24 was superseded by the R25, which featured plunger rear suspension. A revised R25/2 version was introduced in 1952, and a further-improved R25/3, featuring full-width alloy brake drums and hydraulically damped front forks, in October 1953. The next stage in the development of the luxury lightweight was the R26, introduced for 1956, which boasted a more powerful (15bhp) engine and larger fuel tank among numerous improvements.

▶ **1964 BMW R69S,** 594cc, overhead-valve flat-twin, 4-speed foot-change gearbox, Earles front forks, swinging-arm frame, full-width hubs, shaft final drive, standard apart from stainless steel exhaust system, bar-end mirrors, headlamp guard and chrome air cleaner cover.
£5,000–5,500 / €7,500–8,300 / $9,200–10,200 ⊞ CotC

1961 BMW R69S, 594cc, overhead valve flat-twin, 72 x 73mm bore and stroke, twin 26mm Bing carburettors, Bosch magneto, 18in wheels, twin-leading-shoe front brake, fully restored during 1990s, Schorsch Meier dualseat.
£4,100–4,900 / €6,100–7,300 / $7,600–9,100 ⚒ B(Ba)
A luxury tourer capable of over 100mph, the R69 cost as much as a small family car. The R50 and 69 were built until the arrival of the slightly more powerful 'S' versions for 1961. The larger of these, the R69S, produced 42bhp and was good for a top speed of around 110mph.

◀ **1967 BMW R50/2,** 494cc, overhead-valve flat-twin, 68 x 68mm bore and stroke, 30bhp at 5,800rpm, Earles forks, swinging-arm rear suspension.
£2,900–3,500 / €4,350–5,200 $5,400–6,500 ⚒ B(Kn)
This example was imported into the UK from Holland in 1979 and restored in 1998. A total of 19,036 R50/2s were built between 1960 and 1969.

▶ **1969 BMW R60 US,** overhead-valve flat-twin, Meier large-capacity fuel tank, crashbars.
£3,450–4,150 / €5,200–6,200 / $6,400–7,700 ⚒ B(Kn)
Dating from the final year of production this example has the American-market telescopic front fork fitted to the 'stroke 5' series frame, together with a single seat, braced handlebars and the touring R60-type rocker covers. The US-fork twin commands a lower price than its Earles-fork sibling.

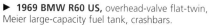

1973 BMW R60/5, 599cc, overhead-valve flat-twin, 73.5 x 70.6mm bore and stroke, 40bhp at 6,400rpm, 4-speed gearbox, shaft drive, top speed 100mph, carrier, pannier, windscreen, 1 owner from new, fewer than 10,000 miles recorded.
£1,700–2,050 / €2,550–3,050 / $3,150–3,800 ✗ B(Kn)
The long-awaited replacements for BMW's R50 and R60 long-running Earles-forked flat twins arrived in 1969. As well as a telescopic, leading-axle front fork, the newcomers featured a lightweight, fully welded duplex frame. The engine also came in for revision, employing a one-piece forged crankshaft, aluminium cylinder barrels and camshaft located below the crank. Coil ignition and 12 volt electrics were other new features. The new '5' models came in three capacities, the variation being achieved by different bore sizes in what were otherwise virtually identical machines. The R60/5 produced a claimed 46bhp, good enough to propel the 419lb machine to 103mph.

1975 BMW R75/6, 745cc, overhead-valve flat-twin, 82 x 70.6mm bore and stroke, 50bhp at 6,200rpm, twin 32mm Bing carburettors, 19in front/18in rear wheels, single 260mm front disc, 200mm drum rear brake, telescopic forks, swinging-arm rear suspension, fully restored, fitted R90S-type fairing, top speed 113mph.
£1,300–1,550 / €1,950–2,300 $2,400–2,850 ✗ B(Kn)
In October 1973, the launch of the BMW/6 series introduced the R60/6, R75/6 and the trend-setting 'superbike' R90S. Front disc brakes featured on all but the 600cc machine, new instrumentation with separate rev-counter and speedometer replaced the old motometer in the headlight shell and five-speed transmission was included. Redesigned exhausts and plastic side panels distinguish the '6' series from its predecessor.

◄ **1975 BMW R90S,** 898cc, overhead-valve flat-twin, 90 x 70.6mm bore and stroke, 67bhp at 7,000rpm, twin 38mm Dell'Orto carburettors, 5-speeds gearbox, shaft final drive, top speed 125mph, largely standard apart from black rocker covers, pannier frames and cast-alloy wheels.
£2,900–3,200 / €4,350–4,800 $5,300–5,900 ⊞ MW
The Daytona orange R90S with drilled disc brakes arrived in 1975. Both it and the smoke-grey version of 1973–74 became instant classics and are two of the most desirable post-1970 BMWs.

1977 BMW R75/7, 745cc overhead-valve flat-twin, 82 x 70.6mm bore and stroke, 50bhp at 6,200rpm, disc front/drum rear brakes, wire wheels, 5-speed gearbox, top speed 115mph, restored.
£1,600–1,800 / €2,400–2,700 $2,900–3,250 ⊞ BLM
The R75/7 was the last of BMW's 750 flat-twins.

1977 BMW R75/7, 745cc, overhead-valve flat-twin, twin Bing 32mm carburettors, 82 x 70.6mm bore and stroke, 50bhp at 6,200rpm, 5-speed foot-change gearbox, shaft final drive, twin disc front brake, drum rear brakes, concours condition.
£2,000–2,200 / €3,000–3,300 / $3,700–4,100 ⊘ T&DC
The R75/7 was built in 1976 and 1977. A total of 6,264 examples were sold.

1978 BMW R60/7, 599cc, flat-twin, 73.5 x 70.6mm bore and stroke, 32bhp at 6,400rpm, 9:2:1 compression ratio, 5-speed gearbox , single disc front brake, drum rear brake, top speed 98mph, Polaris fairing, stiffer front fork springs, panniers, cylinder protection bars, also equipped with stainless steel exhaust system, original cables and front indicators, 1 owner from new, fewer than 15,000 miles recorded.
£1,800–2,150 / €2,700–3,200 / $3,350–4,000 ⋗ B(Kn)

1979 BMW R45, 473cc, overhead-valve flat-twin, 70 x 61.5mm bore and stroke, 35bhp at 7,250rpm, twin 28mm Bing carburettors, 5-speed gearbox, 18in cast-alloy wheels, coil ignition, single front disc brake, drum rear brake.
£1,050–1,200 / €1,600–1,800 / $1,950–2,200 ⊞ MW
The middleweight R45 and R65 machines were essentially the same except for engine displacement. This example is in pristine condition, with BMW panniers and rear carrier. A total of 28,158 R45s were built; a large percentage was sold on the home market in 27bhp guise; the export market got the higher 35bhp output.

1980 BMW R80/7, 797cc, overhead-valve flat-twin,84.8 x 70.6mm bore and stroke, 55bhp at 7,000rpm, twin 32mm Bing carburettors, twin 260mm front disc brakes, drum rear brake, fork gaiters, top speed 110mph, original.
£1,600–1,800 / €2,400–2,650 / $3,000–3,300 ⊞ BLM
The R80/7 is seen by many as the best BMW touring bike of the late 1970s and early 1980s, giving a good combination of performance, smoothness and reliability.

► **1983 BMW R65LS,** 649cc, overhead-valve flat-twin, 82 x 61.5mm bore and stroke, 50bhp at 7,250rpm, 5-speed gearbox, cast-alloy wheels, top speed 119mph.
£1,500–1,700 / €2,250–2,550 / $2,800–3,150 ⊞ MW
The R65LS appeared for the 1981 model year, with revised styling compared to the standard R65, including a headlamp fairing, different seat tail, black exhaust system and a twin-disc front brake.

Bown *(British 1950–58)*

◄ **1953 Bown 98,** Villiers IF single-cylinder 2-stroke engine, 47 x 57mm bore and stroke, 2.8bhp at 4,000rpm, 2-speed gearbox, rigid frame with duplex downtubes, tubular front forks on girder links, top speed 40mph, restored, excellent condition.
**£900–1,000 / €1,350–1,500
$1,650–1,850 ⊞ CotC**
The Bown company, whose trademark was 'Aberdale', was based in Tonypandy, South Wales. It built mopeds, autocycles and lightweights powered by bought-in engines, notably Villiers. The marque lasted from 1950 until 1958.

BSA (British 1906–71, late 1970s–)

BSA (Birmingham Small Arms) began life in 1854 as an association of 14 gunsmiths formed to supply weapons to the British forces in the Crimean War, hence the company badge of a trio of stacked rifles.

A year after its formation, BSA moved into the Small Heath factory that was to be home for the next 120 years. By the 1880s, it was making bicycle components, before building its first powered two-wheeler, using an imported Belgian Minerva engine, in 1905. The first all BSA model, a 499cc side-valve single, arrived in 1910.

During 1914 BSA built its first sidecars, and returned to mass production of munitions following the outbreak of WWI. By the end of the war in 1918, BSA had five factories employing a total of 13,000 workers.

In 1919, the Model E 770cc V-twin was announced, with the 986cc Model G V-twin debuting in 1922. Then, in 1923, the model range was expanded with the introduction of the Model L (350cc) and Model S (Sport) five hundred. The following year, the hugely popular Model B 'Round Tank' was put into mass production, while Harry Perry ascended Mount Snowdon on his BSA three-fifty overhead-vale single.

In 1926, BSA won the coveted Maudes Trophy for the first time, while the Birmingham marque was able to claim that 'one in four motorcycles was a BSA,' figures helped at that time by such excellent sellers as the Round Tank and the new 'Sloper'. Bert Perrigo won the inaugural British Experts Trial, a trend where BSA was to enjoy huge success in off-road motorcycle sport.

During the Depression in 1931, BSA was still able to launch a new range of wet-sump-lubricated, upright-cylinder models.

In 1935, to commemorate King George V's Silver Jubilee, BSA announced its Empire Star models. Wal Handley won a Brooklands Gold Star in 1937 on a dope-tuned M23 Empire Star; a production version, the alloy-engined M24 Gold Star was launched later that year.

During WWII, BSA again played a major role in providing the military with equipment, including no fewer than 126,000 M20 motorcycles. In 1944, Ariel was acquired, while the following year civilian model production resumed, headed by the new B31 three-fifty. This was followed by the brand-new A7 (500cc) and A10 (650) twins. In 1948, the first of 500,000 Bantam two-strokes was built; its engine was based on the German DKW RT125. After acquiring Sunbeam and New Hudson, BSA bought Triumph in 1951.

BSA's most famous motorcycle for many years was the Gold Star. Few machines can be everything to everyone, but the famous 'Goldie' came closer than most as a Clubmans TT winner, scrambler, trials mount and, of course, the ultimate sports roadster of its era. Production finally ceased in 1962.

BSA built a truly vast array of models during the 1950s and 1960s, the best-known being new versions of the Bantam with 150 and 175cc engine sizes, C-series unit-construction singles, A-series twins in pre-unit and unit guises, and finally the 750cc Rocket 3 triple.

Then it all went wrong, and the entire BSA group foundered as the 1970s dawned, bringing the demise of this once great company.

1921 BSA Model L 2¾hp, 349cc, side-valve vertical single, 72 x 85.5mm bore and stroke, forward-mounted magneto, primary and final drive chaincases, all-chain drive, caliper brakes.
£2,050–2,450 / €3,050–3,650 / $3,800–4,550 ⚙ CGC
Writing in 1920, 'Ixion' the venerated sage of *The Motor Cycle* described BSA's 557cc model as follows; 'I did not know that a single-cylinder could develop so much power. I never unearthed a gradient that could bring her down to first, using that gear only for starting off. And talk about substantial! The BSA is built like a tank, and is fundamentally incapable of fracturing anything, whilst she creates the pleasant impression that nothing will ever wear out.'

A known continuous history can add value to and enhance the enjoyment of a motorcycle.

1929 BSA S29-13 Sloper, 493cc, overhead-valve single, twin-port head, 80 x 98 bore and stroke, 25bhp at 4,800rpm, hand-change gearbox, girder forks, rigid frame, top speed 72mph.
£3,150–3,500 / €4,700–5,200 / $5,800–6,400 ⚙ EWC

1934 BSA W34-10 Blue Star, 499cc, overhead-valve single, 85 x 88mm bore and stroke, 4-speed foot-change gearbox, twin-port cylinder head with high-level exhausts, restored 1998–99.
£6,900–8,300 / €10,400–12,500 / $12,800–15,400 ✗ BB(L)
The Depression of the early 1930s forced a cut-back in the number of BSA models, just 10 being offered for 1932. Among these were three new 500s, one a side-valve and two with overhead-valves, all of which shared a bottom end and the 85 x 88mm bore/stroke dimensions that would characterize all BSA's 500cc singles, including the legendary Gold Star, right up to the beginning of the unit-construction era in the 1960s. The two overhead-valve 500s were typed W32–7, the sports version being given the name 'Blue Star'. Both featured engines with vertical cylinders and magneto ignition, carried in conventional cycle parts with rigid frames and girder front forks. The Blue Star came with a high-compression piston and 'hotter' cams, twin-port cylinder head and a four-speed foot-change gearbox.

1939 BSA M24 Gold Star, 496cc, overhead-valve single, 82 x 94mm bore and stroke, 4-speed foot-change gearbox, girder forks, rigid frame.
£4,300–5,100 / €6,400–7,600 / $8,000–9,400 ✗ B(Ba)
On 30 June 1937, a specially prepared Empire Star 500, ridden by the great Wal Handley, achieved a 100mph lap of the Brooklands circuit on its way to a debut race victory and award of the gold star that would give BSA's new supersports model its evocative name. The M24 Gold Star was announced as part of the BSA range for 1938. Itr differed from its Empire Star progenitor in several respects, most obviously by its alloy cylinder barrel and head, cast-in pushrod tunnel, Amal TT carburettor and Elektron gearbox casing. The frame was subtly different too, being made of lighter tubing and devoid of sidecar lugs. All Gold Star engines were guaranteed to produce at least 28bhp. The M24 did not re-emerge post–WWII, and today is the rarest of all Goldies.

1947 BSA B31, 348cc, overhead-valve single, 71 x 88mm bore and stroke, 17bhp at 5,500rpm, iron head and barrel, 4-speed foot-change gearbox, telescopic forks, 19in wheels, rigid frame, tank-mounted speedo, top speed 75mph.
£1,650–1,950 / €2,500–3,000 / $3,050–3,650 ✗ CGC

1935 BSA J35, 499c, overhead-valve V-twin, 63 x 80mm bore and stroke, dry-sump lubrication, foot-change gearbox, front-mounted magdyno, all-chain drive, girder forks, rigid frame, original specification, good condition.
£10,000–11,000 / €15,000–16,500 / $18,500–20,400 ⊞ VER
Originally designed for military service, but then modified for civilian use, the J-series of overhead-valve 500 V-twins arrived for 1934. In this first year, the valves were exposed, but from then on they were fully enclosed. Production ended during 1936.

1939 BSA C10, 249cc, side-valve single, 63 x 80mm bore and stroke, 8bhp at 5,000rpm, 3-speed foot-change gearbox, girder forks, rigid frame, top speed 60mph.
£1,350–1600 / €2,000–2,400 / $2,500–2,950 ✗ CGC
The C10 was first offered in 1938 and was the first of BSA's C-series of two-fifty models, which became popular in the immediate post-WWII period. The last C10, the 'L' version went out of production in 1957.

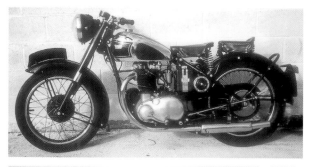

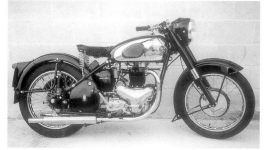

◀ **1948 BSA A7,** 495cc, overhead-valve vertical twin, 62 x 82mm bore and stroke, 26bhp at 6,000rpm, magneto ignition, duplex primary chain, 19in wheels, top speed 90mph.
£3,500–3,900 / €5,200–5,800
$6,500–7,200 ⊞ BLM
The rigid-framed A7 was BSA's first vertical twin. The original engine, used until 1950 had different bore and stroke dimension to the later unit. these early engines are most easily recognised by their screw-in rocker box caps.

1951 BSA A10, 646cc, overhead-valve vertical twin, telescopic forks, rigid frame, single seat, pillion pad, engine recently rebuilt, new magneto, in need of cosmetic restoration.
£1,950–2,350 / €2,950–3,500 / $3,600–4,300 ⚒ PS
The rigid-frame A10 is worth considerably less than the plunger and swinging-arm versions.

1953 BSA A10, 646cc, overhead-valve vertical twin, dry-sump lubrication, magneto and dynamo, single Amal carburettor, 4-speed foot-change gearbox, plunger frame with bolt-up gearbox, duplex primary chain, headlamp nacelle, single sprung saddle, fully restored, concours condition.
£3,150–3,500 / €4,700–5,200 / $5,800–6,500 ⊞ BLM

▶ **1954 BSA BM33,** 499cc, overhead-valve single, 85 x 88mm bore and stroke, iron head and barrel, headlamp nacelle, plunger frame, oil-damped telescopic front forks, original specification, very good condition.
£3,150–3,500
€4,700–5,200
$5,800–6,500 ⊞ BLM
The BM33 was basically the B33 with a plunger frame.

Restored values

The cost of a professional restoration will have an influence on, but no direct relation to, a motorcycle's market value. A restored motorcycle can have a market value lower than the cost of its restoration.

◀ **1955 BSA Bantam D3,** 148cc, single-cylinder 2-stroke, piston-port induction, 5.3bhp at 5,000rpm, 3-speed gearbox, plunger frame, 19in wheels, top speed 50mph, restored at a cost of almost £8,500 / €12,700 / $15,700, concours condition.
£1,600–1,800 / €2,450–2,700 / $3,000–3,300 ⚒ CGC

BSA Model	ENGINE cc/cyl	DATES	CONDITION 1	2	3
Bantam D1	123/1	1948–63	£1,000+	£600	£400
C15	247/1	1958–67	£1,100	£800	£400
B33	499/1	1947–60	£2,600	£1,800	£1,200
B40	343/1	1960–65	£1,200	£900	£500
A10 Golden Flash	646/2	1950–61	£3,000	£2,000	£1,500
A50	499/2	1962–65	£2,900	£1,900	£1,300
Rocket 3	740/3	1968–73	£3,200	£2,200	£1,800

Miller's
Motorcycle Milestones

BSA Bantam 123–172cc (1948–71)
Price Range £500–1,800 /€750–2,700 / $920–3,350
The BSA Bantam was the machine with which
many novice riders of the post-war era cut their
motorcycling teeth, and it was also one of the top
selling British bikes from the late 1940s until its
demise in the early 1970s.
But this most British of all bikes wasn't actually
British at all, having its roots in a German design
that had originated during the 1930s – to be
precise, the DKW RT125. This advanced
lightweight had been designed by the engineer
Hermann Weber towards the end of the 1930s,
and had entered production on the eve WWII
in the summer of 1939.
The basis of both the DKW design and the
Bantam was its engine, a single -cylinder two-stroke
with piston-port induction and bore and stroke
dimensions of 52 x 58mm. This was built in unit
with a three-speed, foot-change gearbox.
The 'new' 123cc BSA was launched in June 1948
as the D1, but it soon became known as the
Bantam. Like the majority of British production at
that time, it was listed for export only.
The power unit was mounted in an all-welded,
rigid frame, with a single main tube running
under the crankcases, and rear loops to the

wheel. The front forks were simple telescopics
with internal springs but no damping, while the
legs slid on grease-lubricated, sintered-bronze
bushes fitted into the fixed outer tubes.
For 1950, a competition model was added to the
Bantam range, and buyers could opt for a
plunger chassis rather than the original rigid
frame. Then in 1954, a big-fin head and barrel,
heavier front forks and a flat silencer were
introduced for the competition bike, while a
larger-engined D3, with a displacement of 148cc
was introduced to complement the D1.
At the end of 1957, the D3 was discontinued, and
for 1958, the 172cc D5 appeared. However this
only lasted 12 months before the improved D7
arrived to replace it. By this time, all models, except
the D1, sported swinging-arm rear suspensions.
The D7 continued in production until 1966, the
long-running D1 having finally been axed in 1963.
Next, for the 1966 season, came the D10 and D10-
4 Sports, the '4' denoting an extra gear ratio.
Another D10 was the Bushman, best described as
an early example of a trail bike, a concept that
was to be marketed so successfully by the Japanese
in the 1970s.
The final Bantam models were the D14/4 and D175,
the last examples of which were built in 1971.

1955 BSA Bantam Major D3, 148cc, single-cylinder 2-stroke,
57 x 58mm bore and stroke, 6:4:1 compression ratio, Amal
523/1 carburettor, 5.2bhp at 5,000rpm, 3-speed gearbox,
plunger frame, top speed 50mph, average condition.
£670–750 / €1,000–1,100 / $1,250–1,400 ⊞ NLM
The D3 was introduced in October 1953. Its running
gear featured a heavier front fork than the previous
version, taken from the D1 competition model.

1955 BSA B31, 348cc, overhead-valve single, 4-speed
gearbox, alloy primary chaincase, telescopic forks,
swinging-arm frame, 8in single-sided front brake (as fitted
to Gold Star), restored to original specification.
£2,500–2,800 / €3,750–4,200 / $4,600–5,200 ⊞ BLM
The B31 employed the same cycle parts as bigger B33
five-hundred and thus suffered in the performance
stakes. However, it made up for this in being both
smoother and exceptionally reliable.

1955 BSA C11G, 249cc, overhead-valve single, 63 x 80mm
bore and stroke, 6:5:1 compression ratio, 11bhp at
5,400rpm, 4-speed gearbox, 19in wheels, top speed 60mph.
£1,200–1,450 / €1,800–2,150 / $2,200–2,650 ↗ CGC
Introduced in 1939, the C11 was a tough, good looking,
no frills machine. Equipped with an overhead-valve
version of the C10's 249cc (63 x 80mm) single-cylinder
engine, it was capable of 70mph. It evolved into the
C11G in late 1953, gaining better brakes. It was
available as either a three-speeder with rigid frame or
four-speeder with plunger rear.

1956 BSA Shooting Star, 497cc, overhead-valve pre-unit
vertical twin, magdyno, alloy head, iron barrel, single
carburettor, 4-speed foot-change gearbox, Ariel full-width
alloy hubs, original specification.
£5,400–6,000 / €8,100–9,000 / $10,000–11,100 ⊶ WCMC
The Shooting Star was BSA's answer to Triumph's
Tiger 100, but it lacked the latter's glamour and did
not sell as well.

◀ **1957 BSA A7,** 497cc, overhead-valve pre-unit twin, 66 x 72mm bore and stroke, iron head and barrel, 6:6:1 compression ratio, 28bhp at 5,800rpm, Amal 376 Monobloc carburettor, Ariel brakes, top speed 88mph.
**£3,500–3,900 / €5,200–5,800
$6,500–7,200 ⊞ BLM**
The swinging-arm A7 was built between 1954 and 1962.

Miller's
Motorcycle Milestones

BSA Gold Star 499cc (1938–62)
Price Range £3,000–9,000 / €4,500–13,500 / $5,500–16,600

Few motorcycles can be everything to everyone, but the Gold Star – known to its countless fans worldwide simply as the 'Goldie' – came closer than most. Its cv included a 100mph lap at Brooklands, Clubmans TT victories, and scrambling, trials and street bike versions; the versatile Goldie could cope with virtually anything asked of it.

The origins for this classic machine go back to 1937, when, on the final day of June, legendary TT rider, Wal Handley, won a Brooklands Gold Star for lapping the Surrey circuit at over 100mph on a 499cc, iron-engined BSA Empire Star, specially fettled by ace tuners Jack Arnott and Len Crisp to run on dope. This outstanding performance resulted in the Empire Star title being ditched in favour of Gold Star for 1938.

Three versions were offered: standard, competition and pure racing. Light alloy was employed for the

cylinder barrel and head, with screw-in valve seats, while the pushrod tower was an integral part of the castings. An Amal TT carburettor was standardized and, most surprising of all, the gearbox shell was cast in magnesium alloy. For the following year, the shell reverted to aluminium, but there was the advantage of an optional close-ratio cluster. The 1939 Gold Star was the last for nine years, WWII causing BSA to concentrate on production of side-valve M20 military machines. After the conflict, the factory began building the touring B31 and B33 models, which were fitted with telescopic forks. A competition model – the 350 B32 – with an iron engine was offered for trials. The post-war Gold Star story really began in 1948 with the arrival of high-performance variants of the B31/B33 series. These were known as the B32 and B34. The series sequence was Z and B (small-fin) and C, D and DBD (big-fin); but the last mentioned being only produced in 500 form. Production of the Gold Star came to an end during 1962.

▶ **1957 BSA DBD34 Gold Star,** 499cc, overhead-valve single, 85 x 88mm bore and stroke, 42bhp, RRT2 close-ratio 4-speed gearbox, alloy head and barrel, top speed 112mph, full Clubman's specification including exhaust, optional 190mm full-width front brake, clip-ons, rearsets, rev-counter, optional alloy rims, chrome tank and guards.
£7,600–8,500 / €11,400–12,700 $14,000–15,700 ⊞ VER
To a generation of motorcyclists in the 1950s and early 1960s the 'Goldie' was an icon.

1959 BSA A10 Gold Flash, 646cc, overhead-vertical twin, 70 x 84mm bore and stroke, iron head and barrel, single carburettor, full-width hubs, all correct tinware, unrestored.
£2,700–3,000 €4,000–4,500 $5,000–5,500 ⊶ EWC

1959 BSA A10 Super Rocket, 646cc, overhead-valve vertical twin, 43bhp at 6,250rpm, separate Lucas headlamp, twin gauges, alloy head, iron barrel, Amal Monobloc carburettor, top speed 108mph, concours condition.
£3,800–4,200 / €5,700–6,300 / $7,000–7,800 ⊞ BLM
For 1958 the sports 650 A10 was known as the Super Rocket (previously the Road Rocket) and gained a revised cylinder head with Amal Monobloc carburettor.

1960 BSA Bantam DI, 123cc, single -cylinder 2-stroke, 52 x 58mm bore and stroke, alloy head, cast-iron barrel, 3-speed gearbox, plunger frame, un-damped telescopic front forks.
£1,350–1,500 / €2,000–2,200 / $2,500–2,800 ⌀ **WCMC**
During the 1950s and early 1960s, the humble but hugely successful Bantam became one of the most ubiquitous of all British bikes, used by commuters, postmen, policemen and even Australian sheep farmers. It also proved successful in trials, scrambles and road racing.

1961 BSA A10 Golden Flash, 646cc, overhead-valve vertical, separate gearbox and clutch, fully restored, small amount of non-original chroming to rear mudguard stays, rear brake pedal, etc.
£2,900–3,200 / €4,350–4,800
$5,400–6,000 ⊞ **BLM**
Designed by Bert Hopwood, the A10 was prompted by the combination of extra cubes for the export market and the need for BSA to provide sidecar enthusiasts with more power and torque.

1961 BSA B40, 343cc, overhead-valve unit single, 79 x 70mm bore and stroke, 7:1 compression ratio, alloy head, cast-iron barrel, 21bhp at 7,000rpm, 4-speed foot-change gearbox, 18in wheels, top speed 85mph.
£1,500–1,700 / €2,250–2,550 / $2,800–3,150 ⊞ **CotC**

1961 BSA A10 Super Rocket, 646cc, overhead-valve twin, 70 x 84mm bore and stroke, alloy head, iron barrel, single Amal Monobloc carburettor, full-width hubs, telescopic forks, swinging-arm rear suspension.
£2,700–3,000 / €4,000–4,500 / $5,000–5,500 ⌀ **WCMC**
The Super Rocket (which replaced the Road Rocket) was essentially a high-performance version of the A10 Golden Flash.

1962 BSA A10 Golden Flash, 646cc, overhead-valve twin, 70 x 84mm bore and stroke, single Amal Monobloc carburettor, iron head and barrel, 4-speed foot-change gearbox, rebuilt engine, good condition.
£3,000–3,300 / €4,500–4,950 / $5,500–6,100 ⌀ **T&DC**

1964 BSA A50 Star, 499cc, overhead-valve unit-construction vertical twin, 65.5 x 74mm bore and stroke, 360-degree crankshaft, alloy head, iron barrel, 28.5bhp at 6,000rpm, 4-speed gearbox, wet clutch, top speed 98mph, fully restored, concours condition.
£2,350–2,600 / €3,500–3,900
$4,350–4,800 ⊞ MW
The unit-construction A50 (500) and A65 (650) twin-cylinder models were introduced for 1962 to replace the A7 and A10 series.

▶ **1966 BSA Spitfire Mark 2**, 654cc, overhead-valve unit twin, 75 x 74mm bore and stroke, original specification.
£3,600–4,000 / €5,400–6,000
$6,700–7,400 ⊞ MW
The top machine in BSA's twin-cylinder range in the mid-1960s had a supersports specification. It was in the style of the 1965 Lightning Clubman, but with the compression ratio raised to 10.5:1, and fitted with racing camshafts and twin Amal GP carburettors.

1965 BSA A65 Lightning Clubman, 654cc, overhead-valve unit twin, twin Amal Monobloc carburettors, chrome headlamp, fork gaiters, single racing seat, matching speedo/rev-counter, siamesed exhaust, 8in front brake.
£3,400–3,800 / €5,100–5,700
$6,300–7,000 ⊞ MW

1968 BSA Bantam Sports D14/4S, 172cc, piston-port 2-stroke, 61.5 x 58mm bore and stroke, 12bhp at 5,750rpm, 5.5in brakes front and rear, 18in wheels, oil-damped telescopic forks, top speed 68mph, unrestored.
£550–660 / €830–990 / $1,000–1,200 ⚡ PS
The Bantam Sports D14/4S featured a four-speed gearbox. It was also equipped with a larger diameter exhaust pipe and a raised compression ratio compared to previous models.

1969 BSA B44 Shooting Star, 441cc, overhead-valve unit single, 79 x 90mm bore and stroke, 28bhp at 6,500rpm, Amal Concentric MkI carburettor, 4-speed gearbox, duplex primary chain, top speed 90mph.
£1,500–1,700 / €2,250–2,550 / $2,800–3,150 ⊞ BLM
With its twin-leading-shoe front brake and high-level stubby exhaust system, this is the roadster version of the world-famous Victor scrambler.

1970 BSA A65 Firebird Scrambler, 654cc, overhead-valve unit twin, alloy head, cast-iron barrel, twin Amal Concentric carburettors, 4-speed foot-change gearbox, USA export model with later Starfire-styled fuel tank, small headlamp, wide handlebars and twin high-level exhaust, non-standard alloy wheel rims, concours condition.
£3,600–4,000 / €5,400–6,000 / $6,700–7,400 ⊞ BLM

1971 BSA Starfire, 247cc, overhead-valve single, 67 x 70mm bore and stroke, 4-speed gearbox, twin-leading-shoe front brake, fork gaiters, original.
£1,125–1,250 / €1,700–1,900 / $2,100–2,300 ⊞ CotC
One of the last Starfires to be sold.

Cagiva *(Italian 1978–)*

◄ **1986 Cagiva Elefant 650,** 649cc, overhead-camshaft Ducati V-twin engine, 82 x 61.5mm bore and stroke, 66bhp at 9,000rpm, top speed 103mph.
£1,350–1,500 / €2,000–2,200 $2,450–2,750 ⊞ NLM
The Elefant was one of the first designs to appear following the Cagiva take-over of Ducati in May 1985. It was built using a Ducati-made engine at Cagiva's Varese plant, not Ducati's Bologna works.

Calthorpe *(British 1909–47)*

► **1923 Calthorpe 2-stroke,** 349cc, single-cylinder, side-mounted carburettor, hand-change gearbox, sprung forks, rigid frame.
£2,500–2,750 €3,700–4,100 $4,600–5,100 ⊞ VER
Built by the Minstrel & Rea Cycle Co of Birmingham, the Calthorpe marque was already well-known for its cars when it made its motorcycle debut at the Stanley show in late 1909.

Cemec *(French 1945–55)*

1955 Cemec L7, 750cc, side-valve flat-twin, alloy cylinder heads, cast-iron cylinder barrels, 4-speed foot-change gearbox, telescopic front forks, plunger rear suspension, single sprung saddle, rear carrier.
£2,700–3,000 / €4,000–4,500 / $5,000–5,500 ⊞ MW
This motorcycle was based on a pre-war BMW design.

Condor *(Swiss 1901–80s)*

1949 Condor, 750cc, side-valve flat-twin, 4-speed foot-change gearbox, shaft final drive, telescopic front forks, rigid frame, concours condition.
£5,000–5,500 / €7,500–8,300 / $9,200–10,200 ⊞ MW
Condor was a major player in the Swiss motorcycle industry for most of the 20th century.

Cossack *(Russian 1974–77)*

◄ **1976 Cossack Voskhod 2,** 175cc, single-cylinder engine, twin-port head, 4-speed foot-change gearbox, telescopic front forks, swinging arm rear suspension, needing cosmetic restoration.
£90–105 / €135–160 / $165–195 ⤳ PS
Russian motorcycles under the Cossack brand name were imported into Britain by Satra Belarus. Legshields and carriers were standard equipment.

Coventry Eagle *(British 1901–40)*

1928 Coventry Eagle C1351, 300cc, JAP side-valve engine, forward-mounted magneto, 70 x 78mm bore and stroke, drum brakes, all-chain drive.
£3,150–3,500 / €4,700–5,200 / $5,800–6,400 ⚙ EWC

CZ (Czechoslovakian 1932–)

◀ **1978 CZ 250 Sport,** 246cc, twin-cylinder 2-stroke, piston-port induction, alloy heads, iron barrel, 4-speed gearbox, twin-leading-shoe front brake, complete with all correct tinware, needing attention.
£90–110 / €135–160 / $170–200 ⚲ PS
This machine was built during the days of close co-operation between CZ and Jawa under the Communist regime. The engine was a smaller version of that used in the Jawa 634 three-fifty twin.

Derbi (Spanish 1950–)

▶ **1980 Derbi Sport Coppa,** 49cc, single-cylinder 2-stroke, piston-port induction, 5-speed gearbox, only 116 miles from new.
£500–600 / €750–900 / $920–1,100 ⚲ BB(L)
The name Derbi first appeared in the early 1950s on a motorcycle built by Nacional Motor SA, of Barcelona, Spain. The latter company was an offshoot of Bicicletas Rabasa, one of Spain's largest cycle manufacturers that had been founded by Simeon Rabasa Singla in the early 1920s. Its first powered two-wheelers were marketed as SRS (the founder's initials), but soon took the name Derbi (from the phrase 'derivados de bicicletas'). Derbi remained little known outside Spain until Angel Nieto took the World 50cc Championship in 1969, a feat he repeated for the Spanish marque in 1970 and '72 in addition to taking the 125cc title for them in 1971 and '72.

DKW (German 1919–81)

1978 DKW W2000 Rotary, 294cc, single-chamber rotary engine, 6-speed foot-change gearbox, disc front/drum rear brakes, USA specification, unregistered, 1 mile recorded.
£3,400–4,100 / €5,100–6,100 / $6,300–7,500 ⚲ B(Kn)
Three major motorcycle manufacturers released models using rotary engines: Suzuki, Norton and DKW. Introduced to the UK market in 1973, DKW's offering was the W2000 (marketed as the Hercules W2000 elsewhere), which was powered by a single-rotor Sachs engine displacing 294cc. This fan-cooled unit drove via a six-speed transmission and was suspended from a tubular spine frame, while the rest of the cycle parts were entirely conventional for the time. It goes without saying that this rotary engine was vibrationless, but the little Deek possessed other virtues: excellent build quality, superb handling and BMW-like rider comfort. Top speed was around 95mph.

Douglas *(British 1906–57)*

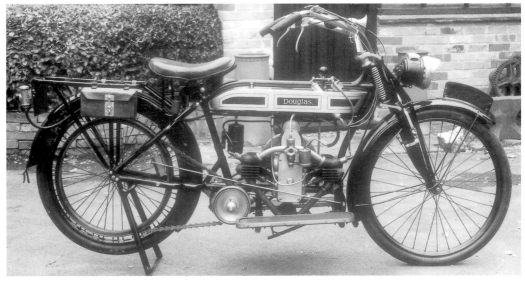

1913 Douglas Model R, 348cc, side-valve fore-and-aft flat-twin, 60.8 x 60mm bore and stroke, belt final drive, lighting equipment.
£7,000–7,700 / €10,500–11,600 / $13,000–14,300 ⊞ **VER**
The Bristol based Douglas Foundry took up motorcycle production in 1907 with a machine powered by a horizontally-opposed twin, and the company would keep faith with this engine layout until it ceased motorcycle production in 1957. Fore-and-aft installation made for a slim machine with a low centre of gravity, and the design's virtues were soon demonstrated in competition, Douglas machines taking first, second, and fourth places in the 1912 Junior TT in the Isle of Man. Douglas was quick to realize the advantages of the countershaft gearbox, its three-speed entries gaining the Team Prize in the 1914 Six Days Trial, a conspicuous success that resulted in the firm obtaining a contract for the supply of machines for military use.

1921 Douglas 4hp, 495cc, side-valve fore-and-aft flat-twin, 74.5 x 68mm bore and stroke, 3-speed gearbox, fuel tank repainted, remaining cycle parts needing refurbishment.
£3,800–4,550 / €5,700–6,800 / $7,000–8,400 ⋋ **B(Kn)**

◀ **1915 Douglas Model V,** 348cc, side-valve fore-and-aft flat-twin, 2-speed gearbox, no clutch, chain-cum-belt drive, older restoration.
£4,500–5,000 / €6,700–7,500 / $8,300–9,200 ⋌⋋ **VMCC**

1931 Douglas A31, 348cc, side-valve flat-twin, 60.8 x 60mm bore and stroke, single carburettor, magneto ignition, wet-sump lubrication with submerged oil pump, dynamo and electric lighting.
£2,200–2,650 / €3,300–3,900 / $4,100–4,900 ⋋ **B(Kn)**
Winner of the Isle of Man Sidecar TT in 1923, when he rode the legendary Douglas 'banking' sidecar outfit, ace rider/engineer Freddie Dixon took up a technical post with the company in 1925. One of his first commissions was the design of the S5 and S6 models. Launched in 1929, the 'Dixon Douglases' set new standards of quietness and refinement for the motorcycle industry. The duo featured side-valve engines with detachable cylinder heads, fully enclosed valve gear, dry-sump lubrication, cast-in inlet manifolding for better cold starting and a gear-driven 'pancake' dynamo. Although he left Douglas early in 1930, Dixon's hand was clearly behind its 1931 range. The new A31 carried on the themes of usability and refinement established by the S5/S6. It sold for £41 / €60 / $76 complete with full electric lighting equipment.

◀ **1924 Douglas SW 2¾hp,** 348cc, good unrestored condition.
£2,700–3,000 / €4,000–4,500 / $5,000–5,500 ⋌⋋ **LDM**

1937 Douglas Aero, 596cc, side-valve fore-and-aft flat-twin, 68 x 82mm bore and stroke, hand-change 4-speed gearbox, single carburettor, outside flywheel, chain final drive, fully restored, concours condition.
£3,500–3,900 / €5,200–5,800 / $6,500–7,200 ⊞ MW
The Aero series ran from the beginning of 1936 until the end of 1937, being built in 245, 348, 494 and 596cc engine sizes, all of which featured side-valve operation.

◄ **1955 Douglas Dragonfly,** 348cc, flat-twin, 60.8 x 68mm bore and stroke, 17bhp at 6,000 rpm, 4-speed foot-change gearbox, chain final drive, Earles-type front forks, top speed 72mph.
£2,500–2,800 / €3,750–4,200 $4,600–5,200 ⮰ LDM
The Dragonfly – known in prototype form as the Dart – was the Douglas marque's last motorcycle design.

► **1956 Douglas Dragonfly,** 348cc, overhead-valve flat-twin, 60.8 x 60mm, 4-speed gearbox, chain final drive.
£1,800–2,000 / €2,700–3,000 / $3,350–3,700 ⮰ LDM
The Dragonfly was an attempt to update the Douglas flat-twin, by way of giving it more modern suspension, including a new duplex frame, swinging-arm rear suspension, twin-shock rear end and a pair of Earles-type front forks.

D-Rad (*German 1921–33*)

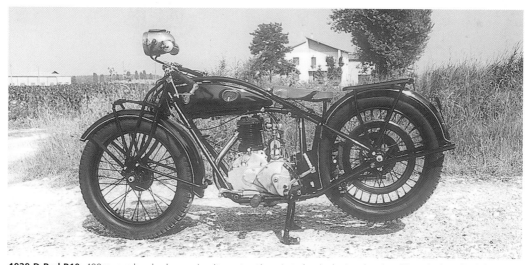

1929 D-Rad R10, 499cc, overhead-valve semi-unit construction, 4-stroke single, iron head and barrel, chain final drive, drum front/caliper rear brakes, fully restored, very rare.
£5,400–6,000 / €8,100–9,000 / $10,000–11,100 ⊞ MAY
Deutsche Industriewerk AG (D-Rad) began life in WWI as an armaments factory. In 1923, it entered the motorcycle industry with a 393cc side-valve flat-twin. This was followed in 1926 by a side-valve five hundred single. Then in 1929 came an overhead-valve version. During the Depression of the early 1930s, D-Rad was absorbed by NSU.

Ducati *(Italian 1946–)*

Ducati's position today as the leading Italian marque, and its string of high-profile race victories of the last 15 years are miles apart from its 1930s beginnings as a radio manufacturer. During WWII, Ducati's production concentrated on the manufacture of radio transmitters and components for military purposes.

After the conflict, Ducati's plant lay idle – and suffering from the effects of bomb damage. So its workforce, totalling several thousand, was laid off. This, in turn, led to a reformed organization headed by a partnership between the Italian government and the Vatican! One of the first moves was to take an existing design for an auxiliary 48cc four-stroke engine with pull-rod operated valves. Thus, in 1946, the Cucciolo (Puppy) entered production at Ducati's Bologna factory, thousands being sold during the early post-war years.

The first complete Ducati motorcycle, powered by a 60cc engine that was based on the Cucciolo unit, made its debut in 1950. But the great days of Ducati as a motorcycle manufacturer really began in 1954, when the company signed up engineer Fabio Taglioni. Known as the 'Doctor', Taglioni was not only a talented designer, but also a racing enthusiast. The following year saw his first design make its debut, the 100 Gran Sport (the 'Marianna'), a machine that was the first of a lineage of overhead-cam singles, culminating with the 450 model in 1969.

Next came a 125cc single in both valve-spring and Desmo form. The latter won the first race it contested, the 1956 Swedish Grand Prix.

By 1958, Ducati not only had a new range of sports roadsters, headed by the 175 Sport and 200 Elite, but also finished the year runner-up in the World Championship, after a season-long battle with MV Agusta. In 1959, Mike Hailwood won his first ever grand prix on a Ducati (the 125cc Ulster).

The 1960s saw the introduction of the legendary 250 Mach 1. However, the company was in trouble, and the Italian government had bought out the Vatican's remaining shares by the end of the decade.

The 1970s saw the arrival of the superbike V-twin family, the first being the 750GT in 1971. Victory in the Imola 200 (1972) brought considerable prestige, as did Mike Hailwood's triumphant return to the Isle of Man TT in 1978. During the early 1980s the factory won no fewer than four world Formula 2 titles, the rider on each occasion being Englishman Tony Rutter.

A significant business partnership began in 1983, when Ducati began supplying engines to Cagiva. Two years later Cagiva acquired the Ducati business. Then in 1997, Cagiva sold half the shares to an American banking group. A few months later, the same company acquired the remaining shares, and in 1999 the Ducati marque was floated on the stock exchange.

1959 Ducati 175TS, 174cc, 4-stroke single, bevel-driven overhead camshaft, 62 x 57.8mm bore and stroke, 14bhp, unit construction, alloy head and barrel, 4-speed foot-change gearbox, wet clutch, top speed 70mph, fully restored, concours condition.
£3,150–3,500
€4,700–5,200
$5,800–6,400 ⊞ MW
'TS' stood for Turismo Sport.

◄ **1955 Ducati 98TL,** 98cc, overhead-valve unit construction single, 4-speed gearbox, pressed-steel open 'backbone' frame, single-sided front drum brake, Silentium silencer, dualseat, fully restored.
£2,000–2,200 / €3,000–3,300 / $3,700–4,100 ⊙ₒ IMOC

1961 Ducati Diana Mk 3, 248cc, overhead-camshaft single, 74 x 57.8mm bore and stroke, concours condition.
£2,900–3,200 / €4,350–4,800 / $5,300–5,900 ⊞ MW
Ducati's first 250 single was a racer, based on the 175 Formula III. This appeared during 1960, at the request of the American importer, the Berliner Corporation. After this prototype achieved considerable success, Ducati went on to build a production version in early 1961. This was followed by a roadster, the Diana, known in the States as the Diana Mk 3, and in the UK as the Daytona. From then until the last models were built in late 1974, a two-fifty was always a part of Ducati's range – first in 'narrowcase' (engine mountings the same front and rear) and, from the late 1960s, in 'widecase', meaning the rear engine mountings were three times wider than those of the front.

Miller's
Motorcycle Milestones

Ducati 750 Super Sport (1974–77)
Price Range 1974 £10,000–20,000 /€ 15,000–30,000 /
$18,500–37,000
1975–77 £3,000–5,000 /€ 4,500–7,500 / $5,500–9,200
The famous Ducati designer Fabio Taglioni first created the L-shape 90-degree V-twin for the Bologna marque with the prototype 750GT in the summer of 1970; production began the following year. The L-shape configuration of the cylinders meant that Taglioni needed to place the front cylinder between the frame tubes. Otherwise Otherwise the machine would have had and overlong wheelbase and poor handling. He also incorporated the engine as a stressed member of the frame. This combined with the smoothness provided by the 90-degree layout, excellent cooling and a low centre of gravity, resulted in a design that handled exceptionally well, and, although intended as a sports/tourer, quickly became a sportster and racer *par excellence*.

It was at Imola on 23 April 1972, when Paul Smart and Bruno Spaggiari piloted specially prepared Desmo versions of the Ducati 750 V-twin to bring the design alive. Against the leading superbikes of the day, from manufacturers such as Honda, Kawasaki, Suzuki, Moto Guzzi, BMW, Triumph, BSA and MV Agusta, Taglioni's design scored a

dramatic 1-2 victory.
Ducati subsequently cashed in by offering replicas of the Imola machines, known as the 750SS (Super Sport). Eventually some 450 examples were to be constructed.

The engines of these machines had the same 747.95cc (80 x 74.4mm bore and stroke) displacement as the GT version (which had conventional coil valve springs and one rocker per valve instead of the desmo system).

The 750SS embodied a number of features to improve performance besides its valve gear. The compression ratio was increased, and there were special double-webbed connecting rods for added strength, special camshafts and 40mm (instead of 32mm) carburettors.

In SS guise, the unit-construction, wet-sump engine would rev to 8,800rpm and drove through a five-speed gearbox. Primary drive was by the usual helical gears. For riders wanting even more performance, there was a kit to transform the bike into a full-blown F750 racer.

In 1975 the new 900SS, together with a matching square-case-engine 750SS was offered. These, however, were built in larger quantities and remained in production much longer. Thus the values for these later machines are considerably lower.

1961 Ducati 200 Elite, 204cc, overhead-camshaft single, 67 x 57.8mm bore and stroke, alloy head and barrel, full-width alloy hubs, 31.5mm front forks, swinging-arm rear with Marzocchi shock absorbers, fully restored with optional factory rev-counter kit, Borrani alloy rims and non-standard performance silencer, concours condition.
£3,800–4,200 / € 5,700–6,300 / $7,000–7,800 ⊞ MW

1964 Ducati Mach 1, 248cc, overhead-camshaft all-alloy engine, unit construction, wet-sump lubrication, battery/coil ignition, 29mm Dell'Orto SS129D carburettor, 5-speed gearbox, full-width drum brakes, original specification apart from Veglia rev-counter, concours condition.
£4,000–4,400 / € 6,000–6,600 / $7,400–8,200 ⊞ MW
The Mach 1 was the first production roadster to be capable of reaching 100mph.

▶ **1971 Ducati 350 Desmo,** 340cc, overhead-camshaft single, desmodromic valve gear, head, 76 x 75mm bore and stroke, 9:5:1 compression ratio, 29mm Dell'Orto VHB square-slide carburettor, 'as new' condition.
£2,900–3,200 / € 4,350–4,800 / $5,400–6,000 ⊞ MW
The new widecase series of Ducati overhead-camshaft engines arrived in 1968, having much wider rear engine mountings than the earlier motors. The widecase was also offered in desmo form, as the top-of-the-range model in 250, 350 and 450cc engine sizes.

◀ **1971 Ducati 250 Scrambler,** 248cc, overhead-camshaft single, valve-spring head, 5-speed gearbox, 19in front/18in rear wheels, fork gaiters, 35mm Marzocchi heavyweight front forks, toolbag and dualseat, correct apart from painted (rather than chromed) fuel-tank sides and aftermarket rear shock absorbers.
£1,700–1,900 / €2,550–2,850 / $3,150–3,500 ⊞ NLM

1974 Ducati 250 Mk 3, 248cc, overhead-camshaft single, valve-spring head, electronic ignition, 29mm Dell'Orto, VHB carburettor, 5-speed gearbox, non-standard paint job, aftermarket silencer and conventional handlebars, otherwise very original.
£1,700–1,900 / €2,550–2,850 / $3,150–3,500 ⊞ BLM

1974 Ducati 350 Scrambler, 340cc, overhead-camshaft single, 76 x 75mm bore and stroke, valve lifter, wet-sump lubrication, 70 watt generator, stainless steel mudguards, all-chrome tank, non-standard rear shock absorbers.
£1,700–1,900 / €2,550–2,800 / $3,150–3,500 ⊞ MW
The final version of the Scrambler (SCR) series had 35mm Marzocchi front forks and double-sided drum front brakes as fitted to the Mk 3 and desmo versions, but retained a smaller tank, chunky dualseat and high handlebars.

1981 Ducati Mike Hailwood Replica, 864cc, overhead-camshaft V-twin, desmodromic valve gear, 86 x 74.4mm bore and stroke, 2-valves-per-cylinder, 18in cast-alloy wheels, full fairing, unrestored.
£3,600–4,000 / €5,400–6,000 / $6,700–7,400 ⊞ VER
Mike Hailwood's 1978 Isle of Man TT comeback ride is the stuff of legend. Out of top-flight bike racing for seven years, he beat the might of the Honda works team to win the Formula 1 TT at record speed. His mount was a Sports Motorcycles-entered V-twin Ducati, and the Italian factory lost little time in capitalizing on this success by launching a road-going replica. Like the race bike, the MHR was based on the production 900SS, but had much more in common with the latter than the former. Most obvious difference was the full fairing finished in red, green and white, and complemented by a glassfibre tank and racing seat. In fact, the 'tank' hid a steel fuel reservoir, glassfibre being illegal in the UK for tanks, and the seat's clever two-piece design enabled it to accommodate a pillion passenger. Mechanical changes were confined to lighter wheels and improved Brembo brakes, and the MHR's performance was pretty much the same as that of the 900SS: around 135mph flat-out. The 1979 bikes were hand-built and came with a certificate to prove it.

1976 Ducati 860GT, 864cc, bevel-driven overhead-camshaft 90-degree V-twin, 2-valves-per-cylinder, unit construction, 32mm Dell'Orto PHF carburettors with accelerator pumps, non-standard paintwork, silencers, shock absorbers, chrome headlamp, mirrors, front brake master cylinder and SS-type kickstart lever, 5-speed gearbox, wet clutch, excellent condition.
£1,800–2,000 / €2,700–3,000 / $3,350–3,700 ⊞ NLM
This is one of the last 860GTs made before production switched to the 860GTS with round tank.

DUCATI Model	ENGINE cc/cyl	DATES	CONDITION 1	2	3
Elite	204/1	1959–65	£2,900+	£2,200	£1,800
Mach 1	248/1	1964–66	£3,000+	£2,200	£1,800
350 Mk 3	340/1	1968–74	£2,400	£1,500	£900
450 Desmo	436/1	1969–74	£3,000	£2,000	£1,500
750 Sport	748/2	1972–74	£5,500+	£3,500	£2,800
900MHR	864/2	1979–84	£4.500	£3,500	£2,800
			(1st year of production +20%)		
600SL Pantah	583/2	1981–83	£2,200	£1,800	£1,500

1982 Ducati Pantah 600SL, 583cc, desmodromic 90-degree V-twin, 2 valves per cylinder, wet clutch, 35mm front forks, 5-speed gearbox, trellis frame, alloy wheels.
£1,500–1,800 / 2,250–2,700 / $2,800–3,350 ➹ B(Kn)
The first of Ducati's 'new generation' desmodromic V-twins, the 500 Pantah appeared in 1978. Designed by Fabio Taglioni, the Pantah engine abandoned the company's traditional shaft-and-bevel gears camshaft drive in favour of toothed rubber belts. With 46bhp available at the back wheel, the Pantah was capable of close to 120mph. A straight-tube trellis frame and triple Brembo disc brakes ensured that the Pantah handled and stopped as well as it went in a straight line. New for 1982, the 600cc version incorporated a number of improvements in addition to a 6mm wider bore, including a stronger gearbox, hydraulic clutch, Bosch ignition and Japanese switchgear and instruments.

1983 Ducati Pantah 500SL, 499cc, belt-driven overhead-camshaft 90-degree V-twin, desmodromic valve gear, 52bhp at 9,000rpm, unit construction, 5-speed gearbox, cast-alloy wheels, 35mm forks.
£2,000–2,250 / €3,000–3,300 / $3,700–4,100 ⊞ NLM
This is the 500SL Pantah Mk 2, identified by the 'lip' on the bottom of the fairing and front mudguard (both from the 600SL). The later bike also had a stronger gearbox than the Mk 1.

1983 Ducati 350XL, 349cc, 90-degree V-twin, overhead-camshaft, 40bhp at 9,600rpm, 66 x 51mm bore and stroke, electric start, 5-speed gearbox, electronic ignition, triple disc brakes, cast-alloy 18in wheels, top speed 100mph.
£1,050–1,200 / €1,600–1,800 / $2,000–2,200 ⊞ MAY
The XL350 (and its larger brother the TL600) was built from 1982 to 1983, but did not sell well. Essentially, both machines were restyled and cheaper versions of the SL Pantah series.

1985 Ducati MHR Mille, 973cc, bevel-driven overhead-camshaft 90-degree V-twin, desmodromic valve gear, 88 x 80mm bore and stroke, 9:5:1 compression ratio, 83bhp at 7,500rpm, concours condition.
£4,500–5,000 / €6,800–7,500 / $8,300–9,200 ⊞ MW
For its final year of production the long-running Ducati bevel V-twin engine was redesigned, with revised lubrication system, plain-bearing big-ends and an increase in capacity of some 110cc.

▶ **1990 Ducati 906 Paso,** 904cc, liquid-cooled overhead-camshaft V-twin desmodromic valve gear, 92 x 68mm bore and stroke, 6-speed gearbox, anti-dive forks, monoshock rear suspension, fully enclosed bodywork, original specification.
£2,000–2,200 / €3,000–3,300 / $3,700–4,100 ⊞ NLM
Introduced for the 1989 model year, the 906 Paso was much as the 750 Paso, apart from its engine and gearbox.

Dunelt *(British 1919–35, 1957)*

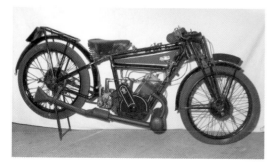

◀ **1928 Dunelt Model K,** 249cc, single-cylinder 2-stroke with inclined cylinder, all-chain drive, drum brakes, flat tank.
£2,100–2,500 / €3,150–3,750 / $3,900–4,600 ➹ B(Kn)
'Dunelt' is an amalgamation of Dunford and Elliott, the Sheffield steel company that fathered the motorcycle factory. Its special feature was a two-stroke engine that used a double-diameter piston in a double-diameter cylinder. The final and longest-lasting development of this was the light and low Model K, noted for increased performance, often better than that of comparable four-strokes, from the 'supercharged' engine. The Model K was last catalogued in 1930.

EMC *(British 1947–54)*

1950 EMC 350, 348cc, split-single 2-stroke, 2 x 50 x 88mm bore and stroke, rear-facing exhaust, magneto ignition, Dowty telescopic front forks, duplex cradle frame, concours condition.
£2,700–3,000 / €4,000–4,500 / $5,000–5,500 ⊞ MW
The Erlich Motor Company was owned by Dr Joe Erlich, who was also the chief designer. Based in Park Royal, London, the company built around 1,500 three-fifty split-singles between 1947 and 1953.

Excelsior *(British 1896–1964)*

◄ **c1924 Excelsior,** 600cc, side-valve single, rear-mounted magneto, total-loss lubrication, all-chain drive, sprung girder forks, rigid frame.
£9,000–10,000 / €13,500–15,000 $16,600–18,500 ⊞ AtMC

Francis-Barnett *(British 1919–64)*

1932 Francis-Barnett Condor Model 26, 172cc, Villiers Brooklands single-cylinder 2-stroke engine, 57.15 x 67mm bore and stroke, radial-fin alloy cylinder head, central spark plug, hand-change gearbox.
£2,700–3,000 / €4,050–4,500 / $5,000–5,500 ⚲ FBC
The Condor was only built in 1932 and is extremely rare.

1932 Francis-Barnett Kestrel 24, 147cc, Villiers single-cylinder 2-stroke engine, 55 x 62mm bore and stroke, flywheel magneto ignition, forward-facing carburettor, hand-change gearbox, fitted with period accessories.
£900–1,000 / €1,350–1,500 / $1,700–1,900 ⚡ FBC

◄ **1938 Francis-Barnett Cruiser,** 249cc, Villiers single-cylinder 2-stroke engine, 63 x 80mm bore and stroke, coil ignition, 4-speed gearbox, restored, unused last 8 years.
£800–960 / €1,200–1,400 $1,500–1,800 ⚡ PS
'Built like a Bridge' was the Francis-Barnett advertising slogan of the 1930s. The Cruiser was launched in early 1933, and featured engine enclosure and comprehensive mudguarding. Designed by Bill King, it was a considerable sales success and was one of the very few fully-enclosed bikes ever to succeed.

1939 Francis-Barnett Seagull H43, 249cc, Villiers single-cylinder 2-stroke engine, 63 x 80mm bore and stroke, side-mounted carburettor, flywheel magneto ignition, twin-port exhaust, kickstart, original, unrestored.
£810–900 / €1,200–1,350 / $1,500–1,650 ⚡ FBC

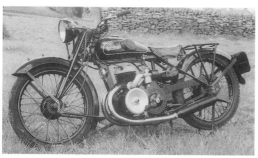

1939 Francis-Barnett Seagull J43, 249cc, Villiers twin-port single-cylinder 2-stroke engine, 4-speed, I-beam frame foot-change gearbox, nice original example in good working order.
£1,350–1,600 / €2,000–2,400 / $2,500–3,000 ⚡ CGC
The Francis-Barnett concern were founded in 1919 by Gordon Francis (son of Graham, co-founder of the Lea-Francis marque) and his father-in-law, Arthur Barnett. During the 1920s and 1930s Francis-Barnett enjoyed considerable success, building both two and four-stroke models ranging from 98–249cc.

1954 Francis-Barnett Falcon 67, 197cc, Villiers 8E single-cylinder 2-stroke engine, 59 x 72mm bore and stroke, 3-speed foot-change gearbox, undamped telescopic front forks, swinging-arm frame, immaculate condition.
£1,150–1,300 / €1,700–1,900 / $2,150–2,400 ⚡ BLM
The original Francis-Barnett factory was destroyed in the blitz that Coventry suffered during November 1940, in the same raid that flattened nearby Triumph. It was not until 1945 that the Lower Ford Street works was re-opened for motorcycle manufacture. In mid-1947, the concern was taken over by AMC. The Falcon 67 was introduced as a new model at the end of 1953.

Gilera *(Italian 1909–)*

◄ **1951 Gilera Saturno Sport,** 499cc, overhead-valve vertical single, 84 x 90mm bore and stroke, 22bhp at 5,000rpm, 4-speed foot-change gearbox, full-width front hub, telescopic front forks, top speed 81mph.
£5,200–6,200 / €7,800–9,300 / $9,600–11,500 ⚒ B(Kn)

► **1952 Gilera Nettuno 250 Sport,** 247cc, overhead-valve single, 68 x 68mm bore and stroke, 14bhp at 6,000rpm, Marelli magneto ignition, Dell'Orto RCF25 carburettor, 19in wheels, full-width front hub, top speed 78mph, original, unrestored, chromework in poor condition.
£2,250–2,500 / €3,400–3,750 / $4,150–4,600 ⊞ NLM
The Nettuno Sport is a rare sight, even in Italy.

1989 Gilera RC600R, 558cc, liquid-cooled double-overhead-camshaft 4-valve single, 54.5bhp at 7,500rpm, twin exhaust ports, twin carburettors, 5-speed gearbox, 46mm front fork, monoshock rear suspension, top speed 100mph, original, excellent condition.
£1,800–2,000 / €2,700–3,000 / $3,350–3,700 ⊞ NLM
Works-prepared RC600s had considerable success in events such as the prestigious Paris-Dakar Rally in the early 1990s.

1991 Gilera CX125, 124cc, liquid-cooled, single-cylinder 2-stroke, 6-speed foot-change gearbox, single-sided front and rear suspension, disc front brake, fairing.
£1,700–2,000 / €2,550–3,000 / $3,100–3,700 ⚒ B(Kn)
The CX125 was based on the Crono race replica, using a similar twin-spar steel frame and identical water-cooled, single-cylinder two-stroke engine producing 30bhp. Less conventional, it featured hub-centre steering. The suspension comprised a single-sided swinging arm at the rear with a similar-sized alloy arm at the front, connected to the 'bottom yoke' by a series of articulated alloy rods. The wheels were 17in diameter aluminium discs. First seen at the Milan show in 1989, the CX125 entered production in December 1990.

Gnome-Rhône *(French 1919–59)*

◄ **1942 Gnome Rhône R1,** 100cc, single-cylinder twin-port, 2-stroke, all-chain drive, girder forks, rigid frame, hand-change gearbox, concours condition.
£1,050–1,200 / €1,550–1,800 $1,900–2,200 ⊞ MW
Gnome-Rhône, well known as an aircraft engine manufacturer, began motorcycle construction with the British Bradshaw-designed ABC flat-twin made under licence in 1919. By 1923, it had begun to make its own range of machines, from 300 to 500cc. From 1931, it manufactured BMW-like flat-twins, including later in the 1930s an 800cc side-valve model for the French Army. Thereafter came a range of two-strokes from 100cc to 250cc. Production ceased in 1959.

Greeves *(British 1952–78)*

◀ **1960 Greeves Sports Twin,**
249cc, Villiers 2T twin-cylinder
2-stroke engine, piston-port induction,
50 x 63.5mm bore and stroke,
15bhp at 5,500rpm, Villiers carburettor,
leading-link front forks,
top speed 70mph.
**£1,450–1,600 / €2,200–2,450
$2,700–3,000** ⚙ CMT

Harley-Davidson *(American 1903–)*

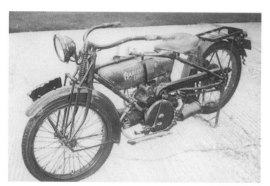

1922 Harley-Davidson Model WJ Sport Twin, 584cc,
fore-and-aft flat-twin, external flywheel, 80mph, Corbin
speedometer, lighting set.
**£8,600–10,300 / €12,900–15,500
$15,900–19,000** ⚲ B(Kn)

Restored values

The cost of a professional restoration will have
an influence on, but no direct relation to,
a motorcycle's market value. A restored
motorcycle can have a market value lower
than the cost of its restoration.

c1923 Harley-Davidson Model J 74 cubic inch,
1200cc, unrestored.
£4,200–5,000 / €6,300–7,500 / $7,800–9,200 ⚲ B(Kn)
Harley-Davidson's first V-twin appeared in 1909,
although it was not until the adoption of mechanically
operated inlet valves in 1911 (replacing the 'atmospheric'
type inherited from the single) that production really
took off. This inlet-over-exhaust engine – built in 61 and
74 cubic inch capacities – would remain in production
for the next 20 years. The need to make better use of
the engine's power characteristics, particularly for
sidecar pulling, prompted the introduction of a two-
speed rear hub for 1917, by which time chain drive
and a proper clutch had been adopted. Later that year,
a conventional three-speed sliding-gear transmission
was introduced on the top-of-the-range version of the
twin, which from now on was listed as the Model J.

◀ **1927 Harley-Davidson Model FD,**
1200cc, inlet-over-exhaust, 45 degree
V-twin, single carburettor, all-chain
drive, kickstarter, footboards,
fully restored.
**£10,800–12,000 / €16,200–18,000
$20,000–22,200** ⊞ NLM

1936 Harley-Davidson Model EL, 1000cc, overhead valve 45-degree V-twin, 45bhp, 4-speed hand-change gearbox, top speed 100mph, restored to concours condition.
£15,900–19,100
€23,900–28,600
$29,400–35,000
⚒ BB(L)

1937 Harley-Davidson Model EL, 1000cc, overhead-valve V-twin, iron heads and barrels, 4-speed foot-change gearbox, springer forks, rigid frame, 18in wheels, original specification, very good condition.
£11,700–14,000 / 17,500–21,000 / $21,600–26,000 ⚒ BB(L)
The E/EL series was the ancestor of all Harley's later engines, and besides all the other major changes introduced on this model, the biggest technical leap concerned the oil system. Whereas previous Harleys had used the old-fashioned total-loss system, the Model E/EL featured a double oil pump and separate tank (dry sump).

1938 Harley-Davidson Model EL, overhead-valve 45-degree V-twin, 4-speed hand-change gearbox, sprung forks, fully restored to concours condition.
£15,900–19,100 / €23,800–28,600 / $29,400–35,000 ⚒ BB(L)
In one studies the engine of the late 1930s Model E or EL it becomes obvious why it became known as the 'knucklehead'. The camshaft was behind the cover, the pushrods were inside their angled tubes, while the chromed object to the right of the front pushrods was the ignition distributor. The generator, driven by the same gear train that worked the camshaft and distributor, was bolted to the timing case at the front of the crankcase.

1939 Harley-Davidson Model EL, 1000cc, overhead valve, 45-degree V-twin, sprung forks, 16in wheels, single saddle, front crashbar, restored regardless of cost.
£27,600–33,000 / €41,000–49,000 / $51,000–61,000 ✈ BJ

c1939 Harley-Davidson G/WL, 742cc, G-series overhead-valve V-twin engine, WL frame, Duo Glide/Electra Glide wheels, forks and other running gear, unused for several years, in need of recommissioning.
£3,400–4,100 / €5,100–6,100 / $6,300–7,500 ✈ BB(L)

1941 Harley-Davidson Model FL, 1200cc, overhead-valve 45-degree V-twin, sprung forks and seat, saddlebags, footboards, crashbars, extra chrome, excellent condition.
£12,400–14,900 / €18,600–22,400 / $23,000–27,600 ✈ BB(L)
The FL (there were also F and FS models) arrived in 1941. Like the E series, it used the famous 'knucklehead' engine, but with the displacement increased to 74 cubic inches (1200cc).

1941 Harley-Davidson Model WLA, 750cc, side-valve V-twin, customized with additional headlamps, whitewall tyres, side bags, crashbars and masses of chrome.
£5,300–6,400 / €8,000–9,600 / $9,800–11,800 ✈ B(Kn)

1946 Harley-Davidson Model UL, 1200cc, side-valve engine, hydraulic trappets, iron heads and barrels, 16in wheels.
£4,650–5,600 / €7,000–8,400 / $8,600–10,300 ✈ BB(L)
The UL side-valve engine was the dependable workhorse of the Harley-Davidson line. With 5:1 compression ratio, 32hp at 5,000rpm, and no external valve gear to adjust, these machines would run thousands of miles with virtually no maintenance.

◄ **1957 Harley-Davidson Model FL,** 1200cc, overhead-valve V-twin, 55bhp, alloy hollow tappets, enlarged oil pump and internal oil passages, fully restored, top speed 102mph.
£19,800–23,800 / €30,000–36,000
$37,000–44,000 ✈ BJ
The 'panhead' series, comprising the EL, FL and FL11 ran from 1948 until 1965. The 'panhead' engine replaced the 'knucklehead'. The main problems of the latter had been oil levels and oil consumption, the bottom half essentially being sound. So on the 'panhead' only the top end was new.

◀ **1994 Harley-Davidson ELH Electra Glide,** 1340cc, overhead-valve V-twin 'Evolution' engine, foot-change gearbox, front and rear disc brakes, cast alloy wheels, panniers, crashbars and additional lights.
£7,600–9,100 / €11,400–13,600 / $14,100–16,800 ✦ BB(L)
The Electra Glide made its debut in 1965 and was the first big twin produced by Harley-Davidson with an electric starter. By 1966 the Shovelhead engine, so named because of the shape of its individual-style rocker boxes, became standard equipment in the FLH, and would endure for 18 years. In 1984, after a seven-year development, the V2 Evolution engine was announced. This was Harley's first all-new engine in 50 years, and would replace the mighty Shovelhead. This 1992 Electra Glide, with the Evolution engine, has adjustable forks and dual disc brakes.

1996 Harley-Davidson FLHCU Ultra Classic Electra Glide, 1350cc.
£7,500–9,000 / €11,300–13,500 / $14,000–16,600 ✦ BB(L)
These machines utilize an 88ci engine with electronic fuel injection. Showing 792 miles on the odometer, the bike is fitted with stage 1 performance kit, which includes special camshafts and Supertrap exhaust. Additionally the bike has chrome brake discs, chrome floor board inserts, saddlebags with light kit, safety rails, backrest, luggage rack, chrome transmission and oil pumps covers, fender skirts, highway pegs, light visors, tourpack lights and accent covers.

Hesketh *(British 1981–)*

> A known continuous history can add value to and enhance the enjoyment of a motorcycle.

◀ **1983 Hesketh V1000,** 992cc, double-overhead-camshaft 90-degree V-twin, 86bhp at 6,500rpm, 5-speed gearbox, Marzocchi forks, triple disc brakes, top speed 130mph, low mileage, excellent condition.
£4,000–4,800 / €6,000–7,200
$7,400–8,900 ✦ H&H

▶ **c1988 Hesketh V1000,** 992cc, double-overhead-camshaft V-twin, nickel-plated frame, Marzocchi 38mm front forks, twin-shock rear suspension, electronic ignition, concours condition.
£9,000–10,000 / €13,500–15,000
$16,600–18,500 ⊞ MW
The original Hesketh operation was set up in 1981, and in the depth of worldwide recession soon ran into trouble, caused by three problems: lack of development, lack of finance and generally poor motorcycle sales. A skeleton organization has continued under Mick Broom to service existing machines and build small numbers of new machines (around ten per year) ever since. This example is unusual in having wire wheels.

Colour Review

1959 AJS Model 31 de luxe, 646cc, overhead-valve
vertical twin, 40bhp, 72 x 79.3mm bore and stroke,
top speed 101mph, concours condition, only 20 miles
since full restoration.
£4,000–4,800 / €6,000–7,200 / $7,400–8,900 ⚡ CGC
Evolving from the 500cc Model 20, and then the 600cc
Model 30, the Model 31 six-fifty arrived for the 1959
model year. The larger engine had a longer cylinder
barrel with an extra fin.

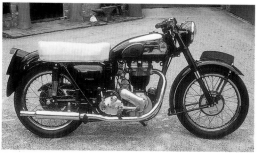

1955 Ariel VH Red Hunter, 497cc, overhead-valve single,
alloy head, cast-iron barrel, duplex cradle all-steel frame,
telescopic forks, swinging-arm rear, original specification.
£2,700–3,000 / €4,000–4,500 / $5,000–5,500 ⊞ VER

1957 Ariel Square Four 4G Mk II, 997cc, overhead-valve
four, 65 x 75mm bore and stroke, single-downtube frame,
plunger rear suspension, 7in full-width drum front, 8in single-
sided rear brake, basically all correct apart from recovered
seat in black rather than original specification sand colour.
£4,300–4,800 / €6,500–7,200 / $8,000–8,900 ⊞ VER

1961 Ariel Golden Arrow, 247cc, 2-stroke twin, alloy
heads, cast-iron barrels, inclined forward by 45 degrees,
10:1 compression ratio, Amal 376 Monobloc carburettor,
restored, concours condition.
£2,250–2,500 / €3,400–3,750 / $4,150–4,600 ⊞ CotC
The Arrow Super Sport (more commonly known as
the Golden Arrow) was launched in January 1961.
Besides a higher compression ratio, it had a larger
1¼in carburettor, larger main jet and attention to the
inlet passages, plus a gold and white paint job and
extra chrome.

◀ **1968 Benelli Wards Riverside,** 350cc, overhead-valve,
unit-construction single, alloy head and barrel, chrome
petrol tank, alloy rims, full-width alloy hubs, lever-action
filler cap, concours condition.
£2,000–2,200 / €3,000–3,300 / $3,700–4,100 ⊞ MW
This American model was sold under the Wards Riverside
name, and was distributed in the USA by Cosmopolitan.

1976 Benelli 500 Quattro, 498cc, across-the-frame
4-cylinder engine, single overhead camshaft, 4-pipe
exhaust, 56 x 50.6mm bore and stroke, 5-speed
gearbox, top speed 105mph, 0–60mph in 5.8 seconds,
standard apart from fork gaiters and chrome mirrors.
£2,250–2,500 / €3,400–3,750 / $4,150–4,600 ⊞ CotC

◀ **1981 Benelli 900 Sei,** 906cc, overhead camshaft six,
60 x 53.4mm bore and stroke, 80bhp at 8,400rpm,
5-speed gearbox, duplex final drive chain, electric start,
top speed 133mph, concours condition.
£3,000–3,300 / €4,500–4,950 / $5,500–6,100 ⊞ MW

1991 Benelli 900 Sei, 905.9cc, six cylinders, 1 of last 80 produced.
£3,800–4,250 / €5,700–6,400 / $7,000–7,800 ⊞ NLM

1982 Bimota B2, 901.8cc, Honda CB900, 4-cylinder, double-overhead- camshaft engine, Maxton swinging arm, concours condition.
£5,000–5,500 / €7,500–8,300 / $9,200–10,200 ⊞ MW

1986 Bimota DB1, 748cc, Ducati single-overhead-camshaft, 90-degree V-twin engine, 70bhp at 8,000rpm, 88 x 61.5mm bore and stroke, top speed 135mph, original concours condition, apart from after-market carbon fibre silencers.
£5,000–5,500 / €7,500–8,300 / $9,200–10,200 ⊞ MW

2000 Bimota V Duo, 499cc, liquid-cooled, 2-stroke, 90-degree V-twin, 5-speed cassette gearbox.
£7,200–8,000 / €10,800–12,000 / $13,300–14,800 ⊞ MW
Direct fuel injection was a first on a two-stroke engine. Styling by Sergio Robbiano.

1951 BMW R51/2, overhead-valve flat-twin, 24bhp at 5,800rpm, 68 x 68mm bore and stroke, single Bing carburettor, 4-speeds, shaft final drive, 19in wheels, top speed 85mph, superb original condition.
£4,300–4,800 / €6,400–7,100 / $8,000–8,900 ⊞ MW

1922 BSA Model E, 771cc side-valve V-twin, 76 x 85mm bore and stroke, 3-speed hand-change gearbox, single carburettor, all-chain drive, aluminium footboards, immaculate condition with many original features.
£5,900–6,500 / €8,800–9,700 / $10,900–12,000 ⊞ VER
The 1919 London Olympia show was the launch pad for the first of a notable range of BSA side-valve V-twins, aimed mainly at sidecar work. This Model E is in solo guise. The last Model E was built in 1931. A development of the design, the Model G survived until WWII.

1930 BSA Sloper, 500cc, overhead-valves inclined cylinder, iron head and barrel, hand-change gearbox, drum brakes.
£3,000–3,300 / €4,500–5,000 / $5,500–6,100 ⊞ CotC

1937 BSA Empire Star, 349cc, overhead-valve single, iron head and barrel, 4-speed foot-change gearbox, chrome tank, very original.
£2,900–3,200 / €4,350–4,800 / $5,400–6,000 ⊞ CotC

1951 BSA A10 Plunger, 646cc, overhead-valve pre-unit twin, 70 x 84mm bore and stroke, iron head and barrel, plunger frame, dualseat, original specification, fitted screen and topbox, 3 owners from new.
£3,150–3,500 / €4,700–5,200 $5,800–6,400 ⊞ MW
The A10 was built with rigid (1950–51), plunger (1950–58) and swinging- arm (1954 onwards) suspension.

1954 BSA Bantam D1, 123cc, single-cylinder 2-stroke, piston-port induction, plunger frame, undamped telescopic front forks.
£1,050–1,200 / €1,600–1,800 / $1,950–2,250 ⚹ VMCC

► 1955 BSA A7 Shooting Star, 497cc, overhead-valve vertical twin, 32bhp at 6,250rpm, 66 x 72.6mm bore and stroke, alloy head, iron barrel, single Amal 376 Monobloc carburettor, 19in wheels, top speed 93mph, excellent mechanical and cosmetic condition.
£4,000–4,500 / €6,000–6,700 $7,400–8,300 ⊞ VER

1967 BSA A65 Firebird, 654cc, overhead-valve unit twin, twin Amal carburettors, 55bhp, high-level separate exhausts, 2-gallon tank, centre stand, 190mm front brake, matching instruments.
£4,300–4,800 / €6,500–7,200 / $8000–8,900 ⊞ BLM
This is a very early example of an A65 Firebird, which was built mainly for the American market.

1968 BSA Starfire, 247cc, overhead-valve unit single, points in timing cover, twin-leading shoe front brake, fork gaiters, 7in Lucas headlamp, non-standard Dunstall silencer.
£1,150–1,300 / €1,700–1,950 / $2,100–2,400 ⊞ CotC

► 1959 Ducati 175 Silverstone Super, 174cc, single overhead bevel-driven camshaft, alloy head and barrel, unit construction, wet clutch, 4-speed gearbox, wet-sump lubrication, full-width alloy hubs, Dell'Orto SS125A carburettor, restored, concours condition.
£5,000–5,500 / €7,500–8,300 $9,200–10,200 ⊞ MW
The Silverstone Super was the most highly tuned and fastest of the 175 Ducati overhead-camshaft bevel singles to be offered for road use; with a roadgoing silencer, it could achieve a maximum speed of 92mph. This made it as quick as many bikes with over three times more engine capacity. It is now highly sought-after, both by collectors and those wishing to take part in the annual Moto Giro event, which has made a successful return to Italy.

1964 Ducati Mach 1, 248cc, overhead-camshaft single, 5-speed gearbox, 29mm carburettor, 31.5mm front forks, 3-way adjustable rear shock absorbers.
£3,800–4,200 / €5,700–6,300 / $7,000–7,700 ⊞ MW
The Mach 1 was designed as a fast roadster or clubman's racer, and was the work of Fabio Taglioni.

1974 Ducati 350 Desmo, 340cc, overhead-camshaft single, desmo cylinder head, Marzocchi forks, Grimeca double-sided drum brakes, alloy rims, rearsets, racing seat, concours condition.
£4,000–4,500 / €6,000–6,700 / $7,400–8,200 ⊞ MW
Only seven of this model were officially imported into the UK during the 1970s. All others are Italian imports since that date.

1988 Gilera Nuovo Saturno, 492cc, liquid-cooled 4-valve single, 45bhp, 92 x 74mm bore and stroke, twin exhaust ports, 5-speed gearbox, hydraulic clutch, 40mm front forks, monoshock, top speed 111mph, concours condition.
£2,350–2,600 / €3,500–3,900 / $4,350–4,800 ⊞ MW
The Nuovo Saturno made its debut at the 1987 Milan show.

1973 Ducati 250 Mk3, 248cc., earlier rear light, aftermarket rear shock absorbers, rearset footrests, very good condition.
£2,000–2,300 / €3,000–3,450 / $3,700–4,250 ⊞ NLM

1928 Dunelt Model K, 249cc, single-cylinder 2-stroke, hand-change 2-speed gearbox, girder front forks, rigid frame, restored with correct paintwork.
£2,450–2,700 / €3,700–4,100 / $4,500–5,000 ⊞ CotC
The Dunelt marque was owned by Dunford & Elliott, a Sheffield steel producer, but was based in Birmingham.

1949 Gilera Nettuno, 247cc, overhead-valve single, 68 x 68mm bore and stroke, 4-speed foot-change gearbox, girder forks, Gilera pivoted rear suspension, original and unrestored.
£2,000–2,200 / €3,000–3,300 / $3,700–4,100 ⊞ MAY

1991 Gilera CX125, 124cc, liquid-cooled, single-cylinder 2-stroke-, reed-valve induction, 17in disc-type wheels, top speed 100mph.
£1,700–1,900 / €2,550–2,800 / $3,150–3,500 ⊞ NLM
The futuristic CX went on sale in Italy during early 1991.

◀ **1930 Harley-Davidson Model 30D,** 747cc, side-valve, 45-degree V-twin, single carburettor, iron heads and barrels, footboards, leather pannier bags.
£6,100–6,800 / €9,200–10,200 / $11,400–12,600 ⊞ VER

◀ **1962 Honda CB92**, 124cc, single-overhead-camshaft twin, 15bhp at 10,500rpm, 44 x 41mm bore and stroke, leading-link forks, full-width hubs, twin-leading shoe front brake, top speed 76mph, restored to concours condition.
£2,800–3,100 / €4,200–4,650 $5,200–5,800 ⊞ MW
The CB92, launched in 1959, is seen as one of the true classics of the early Japanese motorcycle industry.

1965 Honda CB450, 444.9cc, double-overhead-camshaft twin, torsion-bar valve springs, steel cradle frame, full-width alloy hubs, electric start, 4-speed gearbox, concours condition.
£2,250–2,500 / €3,400–3,750 / $4,150–4,600 ⊞ MW

1971 Honda CL350, 349cc, overhead-valve twin, high-level exhaust, twin-leading shoe front brake, speedo/rev-counter, very original, restored.
£1,550–1,700 / €2,300–2,550 / $2,850–3,150 ⊞ CotC

1972 Honda CB250 K4, overhead-camshaft twin, 62 x 41.4mm bore and stroke, 5-speed gearbox, electric start, centre and side stands, dualseat, matching instruments, excellent unrestored condition.
£1,100–1,250 / €1,700–1,900 / $2,000–2,300 ⊞ OxCH

1973 Honda SL125, 122cc, overhead-camshaft single, 12hp, 56 x 49.5 bore and stroke, 5-speed gearbox, top speed 60 mph, concours condition, only 350 miles recorded.
£1,550–1,750 / €2,350–2,600 / $2,950–3,250 ⊞ OxCH
The SL125 was one of Honda's earliest trail bikes.

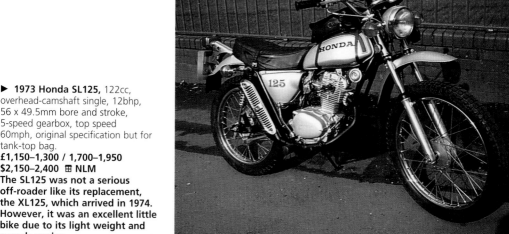

▶ **1973 Honda SL125**, 122cc, overhead-camshaft single, 12bhp, 56 x 49.5mm bore and stroke, 5-speed gearbox, top speed 60mph, original specification but for tank-top bag.
£1,150–1,300 / 1,700–1,950 $2,150–2,400 ⊞ NLM
The SL125 was not a serious off-roader like its replacement, the XL125, which arrived in 1974. However, it was an excellent little bike due to its light weight and superb engine.

1975 Honda 400 Four, 408cc, overhead-camshaft across-the-frame four, 37bhp at 8,500rpm, 51 x 50mm bore and stroke, single disc front brake, exposed-stanchion, telescopic forks, exposed-spring twin-shock rear suspension, top speed 104mph, concours condition.
£1,600–1,800 / €2,450–2,700 / $3,000–3,300 ⊞ MW
An instant favourite on its launch in the UK in 1975, the 400 four was the first truly European-market Honda. Although the engine was based on the smaller CB350/4, the rest of the machine bore little relationship. Particularly interesting features were its six-speed gearbox, quartet of exhaust header pipes running into a single silencer on the offside and its compact build.

1977 Honda ST70, 71.8cc, overhead-camshaft horizontal single.
£550–660 / €830–990 / $1,000–1,200 ⋏ PS
The ST70 was a grown-up monkey bike with a larger engine, but it was built to the same basic formula. It was a popular 'leisure vehicle' during the 1970s. It has retained its charm to the present day as a holiday runabout, paddock bike – even general transport.

1916 Indian Powerplus, 997.6cc, side-valve 42-degree V-twin, magneto, chain drive, foot-change gearbox, accessory lighting set, totally restored 15 years ago.
£12,500–15,000 / €18,700–22,500
$23,100–27,800 ⋏ BB(S)

1979 Laverda Alpino 500, 496.7cc, double-overhead-camshaft twin with cylinders inclined 20 degrees from vertical, 4-valves-per-cylinder, 72 x 61mm bore and stroke, 6-speed gearbox, Eaton-type oil pump, wet sump lubrication, triple Brembo disc brakes, 18in 5-spoke cast-alloy wheels, non-standard silencers, top speed 105mph.
£1,750–1,950 / €2,600–2,900 / $3,250–3,600 ⊞ NLM

1950 Moto Guzzi Falcone, 498.4cc, 88 x 82mm bore and stroke, 23bhp at 4,500rpm, top speed 90mph.
£5,500–6,600 / €8,000–9,600 / $10,200–12,200 ⋏ BB(L)

1949 Moto Guzzi Motoleggera 65, 64cc, disc-valve single-cylinder 2-stroke, 42 x 46mm bore and stroke, 3-speed hand-change gearbox, gear primary and chain final drive, blade girder forks, fully restored, concours condition.
£1,550–1,700 / €2,300–2,550 / $2,850–3,150 ⊞ MW
Until the arrival of the Motoleggera 65 in 1946, Moto Guzzi had no experience with two-stroke engines.

▶ **1982 Moto Guzzi SP1000NT,** 948cc, overhead-valve 90-degree V-twin, 9:2:1 compression ratio, wet sump, electric start, 5-speed gearbox, 18in cast alloy wheels.
£2,150–2,400 / €3,250–3,600 / $4,000–4,400 ⊞ NLM
For 1982, the SP1000NT was offered in a striking red and white paint job, otherwise it was largely unchanged.

◄ **1976 Moto Morini 3½ Sport,** 344cc, 72-degree V-twin with offset cylinders, Heron heads, electronic ignition, 6 volt alternator, helical primary drive gears, dry multi-plate clutch, drum brakes, duplex frame.
£3,150–3,500 / €4,700–5,200 $5,800–6,500 ⊞ NLM
The Sport engine featured 11:1 pistons and a higher state of tune, developing 39bhp at 8,500rpm. Maximum speed was 108mph, compared to 99mph for the Strada.

1982 Moto Morini 3½ Strada, 344cc, overhead-valve 72-degree V-twin, 6-speed gearbox, cast-alloy wheels, matching speedometer and rev-counter, Italian import, unrestored.
£1,700–1,900 / €2,550–2,850 / $3,150–3,500 ⊞ NLM
By the early 1980s, the 3½ Strada had been updated cosmetically with new side panels, rear seat fairing and square headlamp. The chainguard was now plastic instead of stainless steel.

1989 Moto Morini Kanguro X3, 344cc, overhead-valve 72-degree V-twin, 6-speed gearbox, square-tube frame, monoshock rear suspension, high-level exhaust, sump guard, excellent condition.
£1,750–1,950 / €2,600–2,900 / $3,250–3,600 ⊞ NLM

1990 Moto Morini Dart 350, 344cc, overhead-valve 72-degree V-twin, 6-speed gearbox, monoshock rear suspension, fully enclosed bodywork, 3-spoke cast-alloy wheels, original specification.
£1,700–1,900 / €2,550–2,850 / $3,150–3,500 ⊞ NLM
The Dart was built in both 350 and 400 versions; the latter largely for the Japanese market.

1991 Moto Morini Kanguro X3, 344cc, overhead-valve 72-degree V-twin, 6-speed gearbox, square-tube frame, monoshock rear suspension.
£1,700–1,900 / €2,550–2,850 / $3,150–3,500 ⊞ NLM
The X3 was the final version of the long-running Kanguro model.

► **1974 MV Agusta 750S,** 743cc, double-overhead-camshaft across-the-frame four, 69bhp at 8,500rpm, 5-speed gearbox, shaft final drive, concours condition.
£14,500–16,000 €21,700–24,000 $26,800–29,600 ⊞ MW
The 1974 model year saw the introduction of several improvements on the 750S, notably Scarab dual front disc brakes.

1980 MZ TS250/1, 247cc, single-cylinder 2-stroke, piston-port induction, 5-speed gearbox, fully enclosed final drive chain, alloy wheel rims.
£315–350 / €470–520 / $580–650 ⊞ NLM

1947 Norton Model 30 International, 490cc, overhead-camshaft single, 79 x 100mm bore and stroke, 4-speed foot-change gearbox, telescopic forks, plunger rear suspension, enclosed clutch mechanism, single saddle, very original.
£5,800–6,500 / €8,700–9,700 / $10,700–12,000 ⊞ CotC
The Model 30 was the first of the post-war International models.

◄ **1962 Norton ES2,** 490cc, overhead-valve single, 79 x 100mm bore and stroke, alloy head, iron barrel, Amal Monobloc carburettor, AMC 4-speed gearbox, original and unrestored.
£3,600–4,000 / €5,400–6,000 / $6,700–7,400 ⊞ BLM
Late versions of the ES2, with wideline Featherbed frame, full-width hubs and Roadholder forks, are now quite hard to find. Many were broken up to build Tritons during the 1960s and 1970s.

1965 Norton Atlas, 745cc, overhead-valve vertical twin, 49bhp at 6,800rpm, 73 x 89mm bore and stroke, 7:6:1 compression ratio, magneto ignition, single Amal Monobloc carburettor, excellent fully restored condition.
£4,300–4,800 / €6,500–7,200 / $8,000–8,800 ⊞ BLM
The Atlas arrived in 1962 and differed from the 650SS by having only a single caburettor.

▶ **1975 Norton Commando Interstate Mk3,** 828cc, overhead-valve vertical twin, alloy head, iron barrel, electric start, front and rear disc brakes, mirrors, rear grab rail, excellent condition.
£4,000–4,500
€6,000–6,700
$7,400–8,300 ⊞ CotC

Honda *(Japanese 1946–)*

Soichiro Honda was born in 1906, the eldest son of a village blacksmith in Komyo, long since swallowed up by the urban sprawl of modern-day Hamamatsu. He left school in 1922, taking up an apprenticeship in Tokyo as a car mechanic. Later he returned to his home in Hamamatsu, opened his own garage business and with his new-found source of income went motor racing. This came to an abrupt end after a serious accident in July 1936.

Following his unfortunate incident Honda sold his garage and set up a business to manufacture piston rings. Then came the war, which saw the Honda organization making aircraft propellers.

In 1946, Honda set up the Honda Technical Research Institute. In contrast to its grand title, this venture was actually located in a small wooden hut, little more than a garden shed, on a levelled bomb site on the fringe of Hamamatsu. For once, luck was on his side, and after uncovering a cache of 500 war-surplus petrol engines, he launched himself on the road to being a motorcycle manufacturer.

The rapid sale of those first bikes encouraged Honda to move into motorcycle design. Shortly after the incorporation of the Honda Motor Company in 1948, it produced over 3,500 98cc Model D two-strokes, and by 1953 had built and sold 32,000 Model E four-strokes.

But the design that really put Honda on the map appeared in October 1958, in the form of the 50cc C100 Cub. This sold in vast numbers straight away, and in 1959 production of this single model reached an incredible 755,589 units. The Cub was the brainchild of Honda's partner and managing director, Takeo Fujisawa. Until this time, the world's motorcycle manufacturers had largely catered for the enthusiast market, which had kept sales down, but the new Honda enabled the company to open up a vast new market for the man (and woman) in the street.

Honda and Fujisawa saw that, despite increasing production numbers, to really become successful, the company needed to export bikes on a grand scale. To achieve this, they used a combination of clever advertising, efficient reliable production models at affordable prices and Grand Prix winning racing machines, which simply blew the European models away, at least in the smaller classes.

This recipe worked like magic, and by the mid-1960s Honda's production levels had reached 130,000 bikes a month. The top selling 'real' motorcycle of this first generation of Japanese exports was the CB77, a 305cc, overhead-camshaft parallel twin with electric start and a maximum speed approaching 100mph.

Other well-known Hondas of the classic period include the CB92, CB72, CB450 and the legendary CB750 four – which broke the big-bike mould when it arrived during the late 1960s, and almost single-handedly drove the final nail into the once-great British motorcycle industry's coffin.

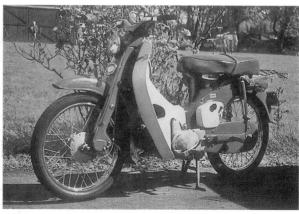

◀ **1962 Honda CB92,** 124cc, chain-driven overhead-camshaft vertical twin, 15bhp at 10,500rpm, 44 x 41mm bore and stroke, top speed 76mph, concours condition.
£2,700–3,000 / €4,000–4,500 / $5,000–5,500 ⊞ MW
In 1959, Honda introduced the C95 touring model and its sporting brother, the CB92. The specification and finish were excellent putting many European lightweights to shame.

1962 Honda C100 Super Cub, 49cc, horizontal single-cylinder 4-stroke engine, leading-link front forks, swinging-arm rear suspension, 4-speed foot-change gearbox.
£470–560 / €700–840 / $880–1,050 ⚡ BB(L)
When the Honda Super Cub was introduced in the late 1950s, no one expected the impact it would have on the small company. The 50cc four-stroke overhead-valve engine would push the needle to just two-strokes could not attain at that time. The appeal of the Super Cub was completely utilitarian. It was a quick, easy and inexpensive form of transportation, the automatic centrifugal clutch allowing entry-level riders to engage gears without fussing with a hand clutch. The Super Cub was virtually indestructable, and still is today. That is one reason it became the world's best-selling vehicle, with over 30 million sold.

1963 Honda CL250, 247cc, chain-driven overhead-camshaft twin, 4-speed gearbox, high-level exhaust, twin-leading-shoe front brake, braced handlebars, dualseat, concours condition.
£2,000–2,200 / €3,000–3,300 / $3,700–4,100 ⊞ MW
This model was developed for the lucrative American 'street scrambler' market, basically from the CB72 model.

1965 Honda CB450, 444.9cc, double-overhead-camshaft twin, torsion-bar, valve springs, unit construction, 4-speed gearbox, restored.
£2,250–2,500 / €3,400–3,750 / $4,150–4,600 ⊞ MW
Honda's British advertising campaign, showing an ageing BSA Star Twin and a Vincent V-twin as rivals caused many enthusiasts to get hot under the collar when the CB450 was launched.

1966 Honda CB72, 247cc, overhead-twin, electric start, rev-counter, twin-leading-shoe front brake, 12 volt electrics, telescopic forks, swinging-arm frame, dualseat, good condition.
£2,000–2,200 / €3,000–3,300 / $3,700–4,100 ⊞ OxCH

▶ **1966 Honda CB160,** 161cc, chain-driven overhead-camshaft twin, 50 x 41mm bore and stroke, 360-degree crankshaft, electric start, restored to 'as new' condition.
£1,700–1,900 / €2,500–2,800 / $3,150–3,500 ⊞ MW
Because of its unusual engine size, the CB160 is often overlooked. However, it is one of the very best of the 1960s Japanese models, from any manufacturer.

1966 Honda S90, 89.5c, overhead-camshaft horizontal single, 50 x 45.6mm bore and stroke, pressed-steel frame, telescopic front forks, swinging-arm twin-shock rear suspension, full-width alloy brake hubs.
£1,600–1,800 / €2,450–2,700 / $3,000–3,300 ⊞ MW

1967 Honda CD175A, 174cc, overhead-camshaft twin, 17bhp, pressed-steel open frame, telescopic forks, swinging-arm rear suspension, dualseat, top speed 75mph.
£700–800 / €1,050–1,200 / $1,300–1,450 ⊞ OxCH

HONDA Model	ENGINE cc/cyl	DATES	CONDITION		
			1	2	3
CB92	124/2	1960–65	£2,500+	£1,700	£1,200
SuperCub	49/1	1958–69	£800	£400	£200
CB72	247/2	1961–66	£2,000	£1,600	£1,200
CD175 1st Series	174/2	1967–69	£800	£600	£300
CB750 SOHC	736/4	1969–75	£3,000	£2,200	£1,600
400F	408/4	1975–77	£1,800	£1,400	£1,000

◄ **1969 Honda CB450,** 444cc, double-overhead-camshaft twin, electric start, 5-speed gearbox, matching speedo/rev-counter, twin-leading-shoe front brake, 12 volt electrics, indicators.
£1,800–2,000
€ 2,700–3,000
$3,350–3,700 ⚲ EWC

► **1970 Honda CB750,** 736cc, overhead-camshaft across-the-frame four, 61 x 63mm bore and stroke, 67bhp at 8,000rpm, dry-sump lubrication, 4-pipe exhaust, 5-speed gearbox, single disc front/drum rear brakes, matching speedo/rev-counter, top speed 124mph.
£2,900–3,200 / € 4,350–4,800
$5,300–5,900 ⊞ MW
The arrival of the CB750 four marked the birth of the modern superbike. It offered a level of sophistication that was unmatched at the time. It proved a massive sales success, particularly in the lucrative American market.

1974 Honda CB175K6, 174cc, overhead-camshaft twin, 52 x 41mm bore and stroke, 20bhp, 5-speed gearbox, twin Keihin carburettors, twin-leading-shoe front brake, battery/coil ignition, 18in wheels, top speed 80mph.
£800–900 / € 1,200–1,350 / $1,500–1,650 ⊞ OxCH

1974 Honda CB500/4, 498cc, overhead-camshaft four, 5-speed gearbox, electric start, disc front/drum rear brakes, unrestored, original 4-pipe exhaust.
£2,250–2,500 / € 3,350–3,750 / $4,150–4,600 ⚲ WCMC

Cross Reference
See Colour Review (pages 53–54)

1974 Honda XL250, 248cc, overhead-camshaft single, 4-valve head, 74 x 57.8mm bore and stroke, 20bhp at 8,000rpm, 5-speed gearbox, conical front hub, 19in front/18in rear wheels, top speed 80mph, concours condition.
£1,250–1,400 / € 1,900–2,100 / $2,350–2,600 ⊞ MW
In 1972, both Honda and Yamaha launched new four-valve engines in the USA, and months later both turned up in Europe. The Honda had by far the most success, the XL250 being a top seller (in various guises) over the years.

1977 Honda CB400F2, 408cc, overhead-camshaft across-the-frame four, 6-speed gearbox, 4-into-1 exhaust.
£1,700–1,900 / € 2,550–2,850 / $3,150–3,500 ⚲ BLM
This CB400 four is the final F2 version, distinguished by revised paintwork and new graphics. This particular example has higher handlebars and engine protection bars.

1977 Honda CB750F2, 736cc, overhead-camshaft four, 4 Keihin carburettors, matching speedo and rev-counter, direction indicators, standard apart from rear carrier and topbox.
£1,500–1,700 / €2,250–2,500 / $2,800–3,100 ⊞ MW
The last of the single-overhead-camshaft fours.

1977 Honda ST70, 71.8cc, overhead-camshaft horizontal single, high-level exhaust, fold-down handlebars, 10in wheels, restored in original white finish with 'flowered' seat.
£690–830 / €1,050–1,250
$1,300–1,550 ⚒ B(Kn)
The ST70 was a 'grown-up' monkey bike with a larger-displacement engine, but built to the same formula.
It proved popular in the 1970s, having a good performance.

◄ **1978 Honda CB500T**, 499cc, double-overhead-camshaft twin, 70 x 67.8mm bore and stroke, 44bhp at 8,500rpm, 5-speed gearbox, battery/coil ignition, disc front brake, drum rear brake, top speed 106mph, unrestored, chromework poor.
£500–600 / €750–900 / $920–1,100 ⚒ PS
A decade after the CB450 appeared, Honda resurrected the medium-sized vertical twin with the 500T in 1975.

1980 Honda CB250N Super Dream, 249cc, overhead-camshaft vertical twin, 3-valve heads, 62 x 41.4mm bore and stroke, 27bhp at 10,000rpm, electric start, 6-speed gearbox, rivetted Comstar wheels, top speed 90mph.
£360–400 / €540–600 / $670–740 ⊞ MW
Thousands of Honda CB250N Super Dreams were sold around the world, but very few survive today. This was for a variety of reasons. Most were owned by novice riders who did little in way of maintenance, and there were one or two major weaknesses, particularly a failure of the ignition, which was very expensive to replace.

1980 Honda CBX, 1047cc, double-overhead-camshaft across-the-frame six, 64.5 x 83.4mm bore and stroke, 108bhp at 9,000rpm, 5-speed gearbox, electronic ignition, twin-shock rear suspension, Comstar wheels, oil cooler, top speed 135mph.
£2,900–3,200 / €4,350–4,800 / $5,300–5,900 ⊞ MW
The CBX was in many ways the ultimate Japanese motorcycle of its era, offering six cylinders, double overhead camshaft, 24 valves, 0–100mph in 7 seconds and much more. The CBX was designed by Soichiro Irimajari.

1981 Honda XL500S, 499cc, overhead-camshaft single, 5-speed gearbox, long travel telescopic forks, twin-shock rear suspension, very good original condition.
£630–700 / €950–1,050 / $1,150–1,300 ⊞ MW
The XL500S was essentially a trail bike in the same mould as Yamaha's XT500.

◀ **1984 Honda CBX750F,** 750cc, double-overhead-camshaft across-the-frame four, triple disc brakes with 4-piston calipers, monoshock rear suspension, Comstar wheels, original, very good condition.
£1,700–1,900 / € 2,550–2,800
$3,150–3,500 ⊞ MW
Honda had decided to axe its across-the-frame fours following the arrival of the V4 VF750 in 1982, but a catalogue of problems with its new model caused a major rethink. The result was a stay of execution which saw the introduction of a new across-the-frame four, the CBX750F.

1984 Honda XBR500, 499cc, overhead-camshaft 4-valve single, twin-port head, Comstar wheels, dualseat, telescopic forks, twin-shock rear suspension, electric start.
£1,350–1,500 / € 2,000–2,200 / $2,500–2,800 ⊞ MW

1984 Honda 650 Nighthawk, 649cc, double-overhead-camshaft across-the-frame four, cast-alloy wheels, dual-disc front brake, leading-axle front forks, twin-shock rear suspension.
£1,150–1,300 / € 1,700–1,900 / $2,150–2,400 ⊞ MW
This Nighthawk is an American import.

HRD *(Italian 1978–86)*

◀ **1986 HRD WH125 Red Horse,** 124cc, liquid-cooled single-cylinder 2-stroke engine, 20bhp, 6-speed gearbox, cast-alloy wheels, expansion chamber exhaust, full fairing, top speed 90mph.
£630–700 / € 950–1,050 / $1,150–1,300 ⊞ NLM
The Italian HRD concern was based in Milan and produced a series of high-performance 125s.

Humber *(British 1900–30)*

▶ **1913 Humber,** 500cc, side-valve single, iron head and barrel, caliper rear brake, belt drive, footboards, Druid forks, acetylene lighting equipment, excellent condition, full running order.
£6,700–7,500 / € 10,000–11,100
$12,400–13,800 ⊞ VER
Founded by Thomas Humber to produce bicycles, Humber began building motorcycles in 1902, offering two models, both of which were a success. This led to a profitable business that had expanded into cars by 1905, so until 1909, bikes took a back seat. The company enjoyed considerable racing success, winning the 1911 Junior TT with a V-twin. After 1930, Humber switched its production exclusively to four wheels.

Indian *(American 1901–53)*

Indian is probably the most charismatic name in American motorcycling history, Harley-Davidson included. The company was founded in 1901 by two former racing cyclists, George M. Hendee and Carl Oscar Hedstram.

Indian's first production roadster (it also built some amazingly successful racing machines in those pioneering days) was a four-stroke single with a vertical cylinder. With this design and the famous V-twin, which appeared in 1907, Indian soon developed a reputation for sophisticated design and excellent quality, which was to stand for many decades.

One of the twins, a 600cc model, was despatched to Great Britain and competed in the 1907 ACU Thousand Mile Trial.

To further encourage exports across the Atlantic, Indian entered no fewer than four works riders in the 1911 Isle of Man Senior TT, scoring an impressive 1-2-3 with the help of its newly created 2 speed gearboxes. Indian's reputation in Europe was cemented, and in the following year, over 20,000 machines were exported. By 1915, Indian was the biggest motorcycle manufacturer in the world, building a record 31,950 bikes.

The Scout 600cc v-twin appeared in late 1919 and proved an instant hit, generating large sales for the company. Designed by Charles B. Franklin, the Scout was renowned for its staying power, witnessed by the factory's famous advertising slogan: 'You can't wear out an Indian Scout'. This was no idle boast, because a Scout set a new 24-hour road record in 1920, covering 1,114 miles (1,792km) over a closed course in Australia.

The Scout was followed by the 1000cc Chief (1922) and the 1200cc Big Chief. But the introduction of

the mass-produced car in the USA, combined with import tariffs in Great Britain and much of Europe by the mid-1920s, followed by the Wall Street stock market crash in October 1929, conspired to hit Indian sales hard. The acquisition of the Ace Company in 1927, and the arrival of a new four-cylinder Indian in 1928 also didn't help matters. This caused a financial black hole, and the company was taken over in 1930 by E. P. Du Pont.

For the remainder of the 1930s, Indian soldiered on, but with profits proving elusive. Then came WWII. This resulted in an order for 5,000 Chiefs from France, complete with sidecars. Not all of these had been delivered by the time the country was overrun by the Germans in 1940. So the bulk of Indian's wartime production was supplied to the American and British forces. These totalled to over 42,000, while some 9,000 machines were supplied to the Soviet Union.

Peacetime did not bring happy days for Indian, cash-rich former American GIs opted for imported bikes and Harley-Davidsons.

In 1949, a cash injection was made by British entrepreneur John Brockhouse, who assumed control of Indian, but this failed to halt the financial slide, and production was terminated in 1953. However, Indian was also the importer of several British marques in the 1950's: AJS, Matchless, Norton, Vincent and Royal Enfield; the last were sold under the Indian name in the States until 1959.

After this, several people attempted to relaunch the brand, but largely without success, until 1998, when a new firm, The Indian Motorcycle Company, with its headquarters in Gilroy, California, began to offer 1440cc V-twins.

1916 Indian Powerplus, 997.6cc, side-valve 42-degree V-twin, 18bhp, total-loss lubrication, magneto ignition, 3-speed hand-change gearbox, top speed 60mph, recently restored.
£21,900–26,300 / €33,000–39,000 $41,000–49,000 ⚘ B(Kn)

▶ **1930 Indian Four**, 1265cc, side-valve engine, 69.9 x 82.6mm bore and stroke, 3-speed hand-change gearbox, chain final drive.
£20,200–24,200 / €30,000–36,000 $37,000–44,000 ⚘ CGC

◀ **1936 Indian Scout**, 745cc, side-valve 42-degree V-twin, 73 x 88.9mm bore and stroke, 21bhp, 3-speed hand-change gearbox, chain drive, leaf-spring front forks, rigid frame, top speed 75mph.
£8,900–10,700 / €13,300–16,000 $16,500–19,800 ⚒ B(Kn)
The Scout was introduced in 1921 with a 596cc engine; the 745cc machine (with bigger bore and stroke) was introduced in 1928.

▶ **c1939 Indian Four Special 'Fluid Four'**, 1265cc, side-valve inline four, 841 Indian V-twin frame, plunger rear suspension, telescopic front forks.
£5,500–6,600 / €8,200–9,800 / $10,200–12,200 ⚒ BB(L)
This machine has been the subject of considerable redesign and development by noted Indian specialist Wilson Plank. The Indian telescopic front fork has been adapted to take a Honda disc brake. Fitted to an Indian 841 frame, the engine has had the original gearbox replaced by a Chevrolet Corvair torque converter and housing, with BMW shaft final drive.

1941 Indian Scout 'Bobber', 935cc, side-valve V-twin, alloy heads, iron barrels, rigid frame, girder forks.
£5,100–6,100 / €7,600–9,100 / $9,400–11,300 ⚒ BB(L)

1941 Indian Sport Scout, 745cc, side-valve V-twin, 73 x 88.9mm bore and stroke, plunger frame.
£8,700–10,400 / €13,000–15,600 $16,100–19,200 ⚒ BB(S)
A smaller V-twin model, the 600cc Scout, joined the existing 1000cc Powerplus in 1920, to be followed by a 750cc variant in 1927. Introduced in April 1928, the 101 Scout featured a revised 750cc side-valve engine in a new frame, and this sporting machine would prove an immense success, so much so that its replacement in 1931 by a heavier Chief-framed model was greeted with dismay. Introduced in 1934, the Sport Scout went some way towards retrieving the Scout's reputation, featuring a lighter frame and European-style girder forks.

1942 Indian 741B, 499cc, side-valve V-twin, girder forks, plunger frame, leather panniers, handlebar-mounted auxiliary lights.
£5,800–7,000 / €8,700–10,500 / $10,800–13,000 ⚒ B(Kn)

1946 Indian Chief, 1200cc, side-valve V-twin, alloy heads, iron cylinders, hand-change gearbox, tank-mounted instruments, leaf-spring front suspension, leather side bags.
£9,000–10,000 / €13,500–15,000 $16,600–18,500 ⚙ IMC

1948 Indian Roadmaster Chief, 1206cc, side-valve V-twin engine, 3-speed hand-change gearbox, screen, crashbars, leather saddle bags, completely restored by Glen Shaffer, concours condition.
£20,500–24,600 / €31,000–37,000 / $38,000–45,000 ⚒ BJ

James *(British 1902–66)*

1952 James J8 Captain, 197cc, Villiers 6E single-cylinder 2-stroke engine, 59 x 72mm bore and stroke, 3-speed foot-change gearbox, 5in brakes, plunger frame, undamped telescopic front forks, concours condition.
£1,050–1,200 / 1,600–1,800 / $1,950–2,200 ⚙ **WCMC**

Restored values

The cost of a professional restoration will have an influence on, but no direct relation to, a motorcycle's market value. A restored motorcycle can have a market value lower than the cost of its restoration.

1954 James J5 Cadet, 122cc, Villiers 7E 2-stroke single-cylinder engine, piston-port induction, alloy head, cast-iron barrel, 50 x 62mm bore and stroke, 5bhp, top speed 45mph.
£500–600 / €750–900 / $920–1,100 ⚙ **PS**
The James marque was founded by the manager of a Birmingham engineering works, Harry James, when he was already well advanced in age and approaching retirement. However, this did not stop the James Cycle Company from being a success, and in 1902 it emulated many of its contemporaries by fitting engines into its bicycles. At first, the motorcycle operation had bought in Belgian FN and Minerva engines, but in 1908 came a motorcycle of their own, using a 523cc single-cylinder power unit. The driving force behind the James motorcycle empire was Fred Kimberley, who had joined in 1902 and was still running the operation some 50 years later. The J5 Cadet was built in 1953 and 1954.

1959 James Captain, 197cc, Villiers 10E single-cylinder 2-stroke engine, 4-speed foot-change gearbox, alloy head, iron barrel, cradle frame, swinging-arm rear suspension, telescopic front forks, full-width hubs, dualseat, original specification, very good condition.
£900–1,000/ €1,350–1,500 / $1,650–1,850 ⚙ **EWC**

Jawa *(Czechoslovakian/Czech Republic 1929 –)*

1958 Jawa, 488cc, overhead-camshaft twin, 28bhp at 5,500rpm, 65 x 73.6mm bore and stroke, 4-speed foot-change gearbox, top speed 91mph, concours condition.
£2,000–2,200 / €3,000–3,300 / $3,700–4,100 ⊞ **MW**
If Jawa's 250/350 two-strokes earned the Prague marque its basic income, its four-stroke five-hundred twin created the prestige in the early post-war era.

JES *(British 1910–24)*

► **1914 JES,** 116cc, overhead-valve single, front-mounted magneto, cycle-type frame and forks, pedalling gear, original, extremely rare.
£3,800–4,250 / €5,700–6,400
$7,000–7,800 ⊞ VER
JES was based in Birmingham. Prior to WWI, this firm produced 116 and 189cc overhead-valve singles. After the conflict, it built 169 and 247cc two-strokes, and Blackburne 250, 350 and 500cc side-valve and overhead - valve powered machines. Ultimately, the company was taken over by Connaught.

Jonghi *(French 1931–56)*

◄ **1955 Jonghi H54 4C,** 250cc, twin-port 2-stroke single, alloy head and barrel, telescopic forks, unit construction, plunger rear suspension, Gurner carburettor, full-width alloy hubs, original, very good condition.
£2,200–2,600 / €3,300–3,900
$4,000–4,800 ⊞ MW
This marque was built in France by two Italians, Giuseppe Remondi and Tito Jonghi. The latter was very successful in road racing, winning several French championships.

Kawasaki *(Japanese 1962–)*

► **1973 Kawasaki Z1,** 903cc, double-overhead-camshaft across-the-frame four, 66 x 66mm bore and stroke, 82bhp at 8,500rpm, 5-speed foot-change gearbox, top speed 130mph, concours condition.
£2,900–3,200 / €4,350–4,800 / $5,300–5,900 ⊞ MW
The Z1 was the fastest and most powerful superbike of its era; only its handling left something to be desired.

1975 Kawasaki HIF, 499cc, across-the-frame triple, 60 x 58.8mm bore and stroke, piston-port induction, 5-speed gearbox, disc front/drum rear brakes, excellent original condition.
£1,450–1,600 / €2,200–2,450 / $2,700–3,000 ⋊ CotC
The 1975 HIF was very similar to the larger H2C seven-fifty. It was replaced by the KH500 for 1976.

1979 Kawasaki KH250, 249.5cc, across-the-frame 3-cylinder 2-stroke, 32bhp at 8,000rpm, alloy heads and barrels, 3 carburettors, pump lubrication, 5-speed gearbox, disc front/drum rear brakes, top speed 100mph.
£2,250–2,500 / €3,350–3,750 / $4,150–4,600 ⊕⁄⊘ WMC

1979 Kawasaki Z650B, 652cc, double-overhead-camshaft across-the-frame four, 62 x 54mm bore and stroke, 2-valves-per-cylinder, duplex steel frame, double-disc front brake, twin-shock rear suspension.
£1,600–1,800 / €2,450–2,700 / $3,000–3,300 ⊞ NLM
The Z650B arrived in 1979 (the first Z650 had been launched in late 1976 and apart from having seven-spoke-cast alloy wheels instead of the original wires was little changed. Production ended in 1983.

1982 Kawasaki Z440 LTD Custom, 443cc, overhead-camshaft twin, duplex steel frame, twin-shock absorbers, disc front/drum rear brakes, 'king and queen' seat, 7-spoke alloy wheels.
£300–360 / €450–540 / $550–660 ⚲ PS

▶ **1994 Kawasaki GPZ500S,** 498cc, liquid-cooled double-overhead-camshaft vertical twin, 65bhp at 10,000rpm, 4-valves-per-cylinder, 6-speed gearbox, monoshock rear suspension, square-tube steel frame and swinging arm, top speed 120mph.
£1,500–1,700 / €2,250–2,500 / $2,800–3,100 ⊞ NLM
Introduced in the late 1980s, the GPZ500S has filled a niche by providing a relatively small sports/touring mount.

Kerry *(British 1902–early 1960s)*

◀ **1904 Kerry 3½hp,** inlet-over-exhaust vertical single, total-loss lubrication, chain and belt drive, certificate.
£9,200–11,000 / €13,800–16,500 $17,000–20,300 ⚲ B(Kn)
Only seven veteran Kerrys are known to survive.

Laverda *(Italian 1949–)*

▶ **1970 Laverda SFO,** 743.92cc, single-overhead-camshaft twin, 60bhp, 80 x 74mm bore and stroke, twin-leading-shoe front brake, 5-speed gearbox, triplex primary chain, 12-volt electrical system, electric start, stainless steel mudguards, top speed 115mph.
£2,500–2,800 €3,750–4,200 $4,650–5,200 ⊞ NLM
The SF was introduced in 1970; 'SF' stood for Super Freno (Super Brake). This version is now extremely rare.

1978 Laverda Jarama, 981cc, double-overhead-camshaft triple, alloy heads and barrels, 3 Dell'Orto carburettors, right-hand gearchange, triple Brembo disc brakes, dualseat with tail section, 5-spoke FAMM cast-alloy wheels. **£2,700–3,000 / €4,000–4,500 / $5,00–5,500** ⚙ ILO
The Jarama was produced with the original 3C/3CL frame with its vertically-mounted rear shocks (seen here) and also the 1200 type with canted shocks.

1980 Laverda Mirage, 1115.8cc, double-overhead-camshaft across-the-frame triple, 80 x 74mm bore and stroke, 88bhp at 7,300rpm, 3 Dell'Orto 32mm carburettors, 5-speed gearbox, triplex primary chain, top speed 130mph. **£2,700–3,000 / €4,000–4,500 / $5,000–5,500** ⊞ CotC
The Mirage was essentially a 1200T with Jota camshafts and exhausts. Additionally, (as with this bike) Mirages came with Marzocchi, instead of Ceriani, front forks.

1981 Laverda Jota, 980.7cc, double-overhead-camshaft triple, 5-speed gearbox, Marzocchi 38mm front forks, twin-rear suspension, triple Brembo disc brakes with 2-piston calipers, cast-alloy wheels, ND instruments. **£3,400–3,800 / €5,100–5,700 / $6,300–7,000** ⊞ NLM
The 1981 Jota was the last year of the 180-degree crankshaft version. It was followed by the smoother-running 120-degree engine.

1982 Laverda Jota 120, 981cc, double-overhead-camshaft triple, 8.8:1 compression ratio, rubber engine mounts, left-hand gearchange, 5-speed gearbox, duplex frame, Marzocchi forks, 3-into-2 exhaust, Brembo disc brakes with 2-piston calipers, 5-spoke cast-alloy wheels, half fairing, grab rail. **£3,600–4,000 / €5,400–6,000 / $6,600–7,400** ⚙ ILO
Apart from the crankshaft, connecting rods and camshafts, there were very few changes to the engine of the 120 from that of the 180.

Miller's
Motorcycle Milestones

Laverda Jota 981cc (1976–82)
Price range £2,800–3,800 /€4,200–5,700 / $6,300–7,000
Enthusiasts have Roger Slater, the British Laverda importer of the 1970s, to thank for the Jota, the fastest-series production road bike of its era (timed at 140mph in 1976).
The first Jota arrived at Slater's headquarters in Bromyard, Herefordshire, in January, 1976. These were factory-built bikes, intended at first for the UK only, which should not be confused with the 3C (E) that had begun life as a UK special in 1975, with 10:l pistons, a higher-lift camshaft, beefier fork yokes and less-restrictive exhausts.
The Jota had the engine spec of the 3C (E), but also featured a change in the layshaft gear ratio, which closed up the previous gaps between the gears. Bottom was some 18 per cent higher than that of the 3C (E).
Another new feature was the seat, which opened sideways and was also lockable. Another was the handlebars, the being multi-adjustable – using a socket key. The footrests could be rotated, giving almost 3 inches (7.5cm) of adjustment. The Jota changed very little between 1976 and 1978. The rear-wheel cush-drive bearings were enlarged and harder rubber inserts specified in 1977, while in early 1978 the colour scheme

changed from silver to metallic gold. At the end of 1978, the Bosch CD1 box was superseded by Bosch's coil and battery-assisted BTZ system.
In 1979, the Jota underwent several changes, some of which caused a bout of mechanical glitches that year. There were Marzocchi instead of Ceriani front forks rather than chrome a black exhaust system. Another change was a new livery of silver frame with orange bodywork. The 1980 model essentially incorporated improvements aimed at curing the previous year's mechanical problems. Later in 1980, a hydraulic clutch was introduced, which was a considerable improvement over the old mechanical type.
Nineteen-eighty-one was the final year before the 120 model. A new fairing and colour-coded front mudguard were tell-tale changes. Also, the ignition was moved to the primary chaincase, so the nearside now sported a large circular bulge. Except for the crankshaft, connecting rods and camshafts, there were very few changes to the engine of the new 120 Jota, which debuted for 1982.
The original Jota sported a 180-degree crank, but the 120 motor dispensed with the old two-up, one-down crankshaft operation. Instead Laverda introduced a one-down, one-up and one-half-way-up sequence. The main advantage of the change was less vibration.

Levis *(British 1911–40)*

Formed in 1911 in Birmingham and run by the Butterfield brothers, Levis began building single-cylinder two-stroke machines. For years, the company produced its own engines, but these were less efficient – and more expensive – than those supplied to rival concerns by Villiers. However, despite the slightly old-fashioned product, Levis was well regarded for its engineering integrity and enjoyed a good reputation in motorcycle competition. Among a clutch of European victories, Levis also won the 1922 Lightweight TT, with a 'slimline' Geoff Davidson in the saddle; later, in the 1930s, its Levis Cup Trial – held in the West Midlands – was an integral part of the Reliability Trial scene.

'Titch' Allen himself recalls riding in a snowbound Levis Cup, after which every competitor was treated to a hot meal at the factory. He also remembers a small test track on the factory roof, with access by means of an incredibly steep ramp. Levis duly entered the ranks of four-stroke producers in 1927, effectively triggering a new lease of life, in as much as within five years the range stretched from 250 to 600cc, including an attractive overhead-camshaft quarter-litre model. Sales slowed in the period approaching WWII and certainly were not helped by the introduction of a side - valve three-fifty in 1938. Like several other manufacturers, Levis did not survive the war.

◄ **1928 Levis Model Z,** 247cc, vertical 2-stroke single, 67 x 70mm bore and stroke, rear-mounted magneto, original, unrestored.
£1,500–1,800 / €2,250–2,700 / $2,800–3,350 ⚹ CGC
Levis were famous for its fine two-stroke engines, even supplying the German Zündapp marque during the 1920s. This original and unrestored Levis was first registered in Norwich on 18th September, 1928.

Maserati *(Italian 1953–61)*

1959 Maserati 4T, 158cc, overhead-valve single, 10bhp, unit construction, 4-speed foot-change gearbox, wet clutch, duplex frame, heel-and-toe gear lever, top speed 65mph.
£2,050–2,300 / €3,050–3,450 / $3,800–4,250 ⊞ MW
Of the six Maserati brothers, from Voghera near Milan, five became engineers: Alfrieri, Bindo, Carlo, Ernesto and Ettore. Carlo, the eldest, also raced cars and motorcycles and won several events in 1899 and 1900 on a Carcano machine, which he had designed and built himself. He worked as an engineer for Bianchi, Fiat and Junior. He died in 1911. Alfieri worked as a test driver for Isotta-Fraschini and raced for the marque. Bindo also worked for Isotta. From 1910 to 1913, Alfieri and Ettore spent time in Isotta's Argentina works. Having returned to Italy, Alfieri, with Bindo and Ettore set up Officine Alfieri Maserati SpA in Bologna in 1914. During WWI, Maserati overhauled aero engines and manufactured spark plugs. In 1919, youngest brother Ernesto joined the firm. From then until the late 1940s, Maserati concentrated on sports and racing cars. After WWII came a move to Modena, more Grands Prix and a new venture: motorcycles. Until 1961, the company turned out a number of different models, from a 49cc two-stroke to an impressive 246cc overhead-valve model with a disc front brake. After 1961, Maserati concentrated on expensive supercars.

Matchless
(British 1901–69, 1987–)

Henry Collier and his sons, Harry and Charlie, were true pioneers of the British motorcycle industry. They began manufacturing bikes at Plumstead, southeast London works during 1901, using de Dion and MMC engines, having built an experimental machine in 1899. Not only did the Collier family build the bikes but they also rode them with great success. Harry Collier won the 1903 ACU Thousand Mile Reliability Trial, while brother Charlie won the Single Cylinder class of the first Isle of Man TT in 1907, at a record average speed of 40mph. The following year, the two brothers finished first and second in the TT – a feat never to be equalled.

During WWI production switched to aircraft parts and bayonets. However, post-war the company returned to two wheels – plus sidecars — and even the Model K car (1923). In 1928, the firm officially became Matchless Motor Cycles Ltd.

Then in 1930, the famous Silver Arrow narrow-angle side-valve V-twin was produced, with an engine size of 400cc. This was followed by the even more exciting and glamorous Silver Hawk, with an overhead-camshaft V4 power unit in 1931. The same year, Matchless took over AJS. More expansion followed in 1937, with the acquisition of the Sunbeam marque, and the 'group' was re-registered under the Associated Motor Cycles (AMC) banner.

Throughout the 1930s Matchless produced a comprehensive range of side-valve and overhead-valve singles in 250, 350 and 500cc engine sizes, plus its 1000cc V-twin. The Silver Arrow and Silver Hawk models had not achieved their expected sales – mainly due to the effects of the Depression of the early 1930s.

During WWII, AMC was a major supplier of military motorcycles to the British armed forces, the G3/L (Lightweight) three-fifty proving a popular machine with despatch riders. This model used AMC's Teledraulic front forks, a development of a type pioneered by the German BMW company. It was while testing a machine with these forks that the youngest Collier brother, Bertie, met his death in 1941.

In the immediate post-war period, the bulk of AMC's production was exported, including the new five-hundred vertical twin, the Matchless G9 (AJS Model 20). Then in 1951, the famous AMC - made 'jampot' rear shock absorbers were introduced.

Matchless (and AJS) sold well during the 1950s, helped by the company's participation in major racing, scrambles and trials events. More expansion had taken place during that period with the purchase of Francis-Barnett, James and Norton.

However, when the last of the Colliers, Charlie, died in mid-1954, the rot set in. First there was a decision to pull out of Grand Prix racing and a general lack of investment in new models. Then came a disastrous decision to cease purchasing Villiers engines for James and Francis Barnett, and instead produce AMC's own engines.

Finally, in the 1960s came increased badge-engineering, which did not go down well with potential buyers. Thus, in 1966, AMC collapsed.

Although the Matchless name was revived for an Austrian Rotax-powered 500cc four-stroke single in 1987, the truly great days of the famous 'Matchbox' were over.

1928 Matchless T3, 497cc, side-valve single, 82.5 x 93mm bore and stroke, drum brakes, hand-change gearbox, all-chain drive, saddle tank.
£3,600–4,000 / €5,400–6,000
$6,700–7,400 ⊶ **EWC**

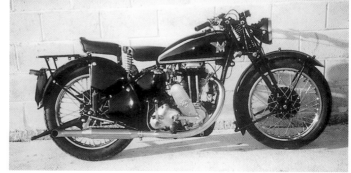

▶ **1940 Matchless G3,** 348cc, overhead-valve single, 69 x 93mm bore and stroke, iron head and barrel, fully enclosed valve gear, rear-mounted magneto, 4-speed foot-change gearbox, rigid frame, girder forks, fully restored.
£2,800–3,100 / €4,200–4,650
$5,200–5,800 ⊞ **BLM**

◀ **1953 Matchless G3LS,** 348cc, overhead-valve single, 69 x 93mm bore and stroke, hairpin valve springs, front-mounted magneto, alloy head, iron barrel, 4-speed Burman gearbox, separate speedometer and headlamp, 'jampot' rear shocks, very good original specification.
**£2,500–2,800 / €3,750–4,200
$4,600–5,200 ⊞ BLM**
This was the final year of the half-width front and rear brakes.

▶ **1955 Matchless G3LS,** 348cc, overhead-valve single, auto advance, Amal Monobloc carburettor, Burman 4-speed foot-change gearbox, full-width alloy hubs, dualseat, good condition.
**£2,500–2,800 / €3,800–4,200
$4,650–5,200 ⊞ BLM**
The G3LS was one of the best heavyweight British three-fifty singles of the 1950s, offering an excellent blend of reliability, smoothness and comfort, combined with safe handling and good brakes.

1958 Matchless G80, 497cc, overhead-valve vertical single, 82.5 x 93mm bore and stroke, coil ignition, 4-speed gearbox, swinging-arm frame, Teledraulic front forks, alloy full-width hubs, unrestored.
£1,800–2,000 / €2,700–3,000 / $3,350–3,700 ⮬ EWC
This is the coil-ignition engine with the large timing cover of the magneto version. It also has a polished two-piece aluminium primary chaincase assembly.

◀ **1959 Matchless G9 de luxe,** 498cc, overhead-valve twin, 66 x 72.8mm bore and stroke, 30.5bhp at 6,800rpm, Amal Monobloc carburettor, AMC 4-speed gearbox, full-width alloy hubs, Girling rear shock absorbers, chrome tank panels, top speed 95mph, standard specification.
£2,050–2,300 / €3,100–3,450 / $3,800–4,250 ⊞ BLM
The G9 was one of AMC's first post-war twins (the other was the AJS Model 20). The heart of the bike was the engine, which followed the basic British vertical twin formula, with two pistons moving together dictated by the magneto, then considered mandatory. However, in many other respects, the G9 was different: it had a third, central main bearing between the crank throws. It also had separate heads and barrels, and gear-driven camshafts fore and aft.

▶ **1959 Matchless G12CS,** 646cc, overhead-valve vertical twin, alloy heads and barrels, single Amal Monobloc carburettor, AMC 4-speed gearbox, alloy mudguards, excellent condition.
**£4,000–4,500 / €6,100–6,800
$7,400–8,300 ⊞ VER**
This CS (scrambler) has the optional lighting kit and siamesed exhaust with single silencer.

Minerva *(Belgian 1895–1909)*

◀ **1907 Minerva 4½hp,** 577cc, 45-degree V-twin, belt drive, braced forks, rigid frame, restored to concours condition.
£10,900–13,100 / €16,300–19,600
$20,200–24,200 ✗ B(Kn)
Minerva was founded by Sylvain de Jong to produce bicycles, and from early on was involved with de Dion-Bouton. In 1900, de Jong purchased a Zürcher & Lüthi engine, subsequently acquiring a licence to manufacture this 211cc power unit. By the following year, Minerva had its own motorcycle. Soon the marque was building a range of singles plus racing and roadster V-twins.

Mi-Val *(Italian 1950–67)*

▶ **1954 Mi-Val Sport 125,** 124cc, single-cylinder 2-stroke, piston-port induction, alloy head, cast-iron barrel, unit construction, telescopic front forks, swinging-arm twin-shock rear suspension, flywheel magneto electrics.
£1,050–1,200 / €1,600–1,800 / $1,950–2,200 ⊞ NLM
Metalimeccanica Italiana Valtrompia SpA of Gardone Val Trompia, Brescia, was an established machine-tool manufacturer that produced motorcycles during the 1950s and 1960s.

MM *(Italian 1924–57)*

◀ **1951 MM 250 Model 51AS,** 247.7cc, overhead-camshaft vertical single, 64 x 77mm bore and stroke, unit construction, 4-speed foot-change gearbox, telescopic front forks, plunger rear suspension, fully restored to 'as new' condition.
£3,150–3,500 / €4,700–5,200 / $5,800–6,500 ⊞ NLM
The Bologna based MM marque (the initials stood for the co-founders Mario Mazzetti and Alfonso Morini of Moto Morini fame) began trading in 1924 with the launch of a neat little 125cc two-stroke racing model. After 1930, it became increasingly well known for a range of four-stroke machines.

Monet-Goyon *(French 1917–57)*

1930s Monet-Goyon LS4, 350cc, overhead-valve twin-port single, iron head and barrel, sprung girder forks, rigid frame.
£2,150–2,400
€3,250–3,600
$4,000–4,400 ⊞ MW

The French Monet Goyon marque ran for over four decades, employing a mixture of bought-in engines (including British Villiers) and units of their own design. By the 1930s, the company was offering a comprehensive range from 147cc two-strokes to 500cc four-strokes, the latter with side- or overhead-valve engines.

Motobécane *(French 1923–)*

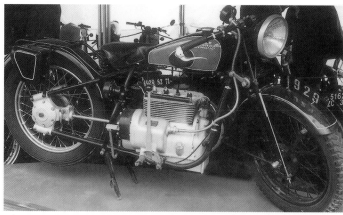

◀ **1929 Motobécane B5,** 498cc, 4-cylinder inline engine, hand gearchange straight off box by lever action, shaft final drive, gearbox-driven speedometer.
£12,500–14,000 / €18,700–21,000
$23,100–25,900 ⊞ MW

1938 Motobécane, 500cc, overhead-valve single, twin-port alloy head, foot-change gearbox, Novi magdyno, girder forks, plunger rear suspension, full cradle frame, fully restored to concours condition.
£5,000–5,500 / €7,500–8,300 / $9,200–10,200 ⊞ MW

Founded by Abel Bardin and Charles Benoît, Motobécane's first prototype was built in 1922 and went into production two years later. This first motorcycle featured a 175cc two-stroke engine with a chain-driven magneto. By 1929 the company had sold no less than 150,000 of this model, placing it at the very top of the French motorcycle industry sales charts. In the 1930s, the firm expanded its range to include 350 and 500cc side- and overhead-valve singles, and even a 750cc overhead-camshaft inline four (listed as a Motoconfort). However, it was the range of four-stroke singles that really cemented Motobécane's reputation, with such technical innovations as four-valve cylinder heads and unit construction.

▶ **1950 Motobécane R46C,** 350cc, overhead-valve single-cylinder engine, alloy head, cast-iron barrel, 4-speed foot-change gearbox, telescopic front forks, plunger rear suspension.
£2,800–3,200 / €4,200–4,800 / $5,200–6,000 ⊞ MW

The R46C was essentially a development of the 1930s overhead-valve, single-cylinder, unit-construction engine. Thus it still had a modern appearance in the 1950s, helped by the introduction of telescopic forks in place of the original girders.

1958 Motobécane Special, 175cc, overhead-valve single, alloy head and barrel, unit construction, 4-speed foot-change gearbox, telescopic forks, swinging-arm frame, concours condition.
£2,400–2,700 / €3,600–4,100 / $4,450–5,000 ⊞ MW
This machine was originally a 125cc Special, but has been fitted with a 175cc engine.

1975 Motobécane 125LT, 124cc, inclined twin-cylinder 2-stroke, alloy heads, cast-iron barrels, 5-speed foot-change gearbox, unit construction, full-width alloy hubs, 12 volt electrics, direction indicators, unrestored.
£700–800 / €1,050–1,200 / $1,350–1,500 ⊞ MW

Motobi *(Italian 1949–76)*

1960 Motobi Catria, 172cc, overhead-valve unit-construction horizontal single, alloy head, cast-iron barrel, 67 x 57mm bore and stroke, fully restored.
£1,900–2,100 / €2,850–3,150 / $3,500–3,900 ⊞ MW
The Catria was a considerable sales success, being built in a number of guises for touring and clubmans racing. The spur-driven camshaft was located under the base of the cylinder barrel, while the pushrods ran on each side of the cylinder. The camshaft also drove the gear-type oil pump, which operated in conjunction with a wet-sump lubrication system.

▶ **1978 Motobi 250 2C,** 231cc, twin-cylinder 2-stroke, piston-port induction, 56 x 47mm bore and stroke, alloy heads and barrels, 5-speed gearbox, electronic ignition, disc front brake, standard apart fromt alloy wheel rims.
£720–800 / €1,100–1,250 / $1,350–1,500 ⊶ BGB
This design was sold by both Benelli and Motobi. In revised form it was also marketed as the Moto Guzzi 250TS. At the time, all three brand names were owned by De Tomaso.

Motoconfort *(French 1922–84)*

◀ **1938 Motoconfort,** 100cc side-valve single, hand-change gearbox, rigid frame, girder front forks, aluminium silencer, fully restored.
£2,500–2,800 / €3,750–4,200 / $4,600–5,100 ⊞ MW
Motoconfort was a brand of the Motobécane firm, which often sold its mopeds under the Mobylette tag.

Moto Guzzi *(Italian 1921–)*

> **Cross Reference**
> See Colour Review (page 54)

▶ **1935 Moto Guzzi Tipo S,** 498.4cc, inlet-over-exhaust horizontal single, 13.2bhp at 4,000rpm, iron head and barrel, girder forks, rigid frame, 19in wheels, magneto ignition, 4-speed hand-change gearbox, top speed 67mph.
£5,000–5,500 / €7,500–8,300
$9,200–10,200 ⊞ NLM
The Tipo S ran from 1934 until the Italians entered WWII in June 1940.

1949 Moto Guzzi Airone, 247cc, overhead-valve horizontal single, 70 x 64mm bore and stroke, 9.5bhp at 4,800rpm, 19in wheels, top speed 72mph, restored.
£2,850–3,400 / €4,300–5,100 / $5,300–6,300 ⚡ CGC

1952 Moto Guzzi Falcone, 498.4cc, horizontal single, 88x 82mm bore and stroke, 23bhp at 4,500rpm, 4-speed foot-change gearbox, telescopic front forks, Lafranconi 'fishtail' silencer.
£7,100–8,500 / €10,600–12,700 / $13,100–15,700 ⚡ CGC
Together with the similar two-fifty Airone, the five-hundred Falcone was one of Moto Guzzi's most popular models of the early 1950s.

1950 Moto Guzzi Superalce, 498.4cc, overhead-valve horizontal single, 4-speed foot-change gearbox, girder front forks, centre and prop stand.
£2,700–3,000 / €4,000–4,500 / $5,000–5,500 ⊞ NLM
The Superalce was a post-war development of the Alce which saw widespread use in WWII. The main difference was that the later machine had overhead-valve rather than inlet-over-exhaust arrangement.

1963 Moto Guzzi Lodola 235GT, 235cc, overhead-valve single, 68 x 64mm bore and stroke, 7.5:1 compression ratio, 11bhp at 6,000rpm, 4-speed foot-change gearbox, telescopic front forks, swinging-arm frame, top speed 70mph, restored, good condition.
£1,250–1,400 / €1,900–2,100 / $2,350–2,600 ⊞ NLM

◄ **1964 Moto Guzzi Galletto 92 Elettrico,** 192cc, overhead-valve single, leading-link forks, swinging-arm frame, 4-speed gearbox, 17in wheels, very good condition.
£1,600–1,800 / €2,450–2,700 / $3,000–3,300 ⊞ NLM
The Galletto first appeared in 1950 as a 150cc machine, then from later that year to 1952, it had a 160cc engine; from 1952 to 1953, it had a 175cc motor, and finally from 1954, a 192cc power unit.

▶ **1972 Moto Guzzi Nuovo Falcone 500 Civilian,** 498.4cc overhead valve single, 30bhp at 5,000 rpm, unit construction, Grimeca brakes, 5-speed gearbox, 2 silencers, 12 volt electrics, square-slide Dell'Orto VHB29 carburettor, electric start, top speed 82mph, original, very good condition.
£2,250–2,500
€3,400–3,750
$4,150–4,600 ⊞ NLM
This is the 'pukka' civilian Falcone Nuovo which is much rarer than military or police bikes. A very nice, original example.

◄ **1978 Moto Guzzi Le Mans Mk1,** 844cc, overhead-valve transverse V-twin, 83 x 78mm bore and stroke, 70bhp at 6,200rpm, Lafranconi performance silencers, top speed 125mph.
£3,400–3,800 / €5,100–5,700 $6,300–7,000 ⊞ CotC
The Le Mans was developed from the V7 Sport (1971) and its successors, the 750s (1974) and S3 (1975). It appeared in 1976 and was a competitor to BMW's R90S and Ducati's 900SS. Many consider the Mk1 to be the best of the Le Mans series, successive versions taking on ever more angular lines.

▶ **1978 Moto Guzzi V35 Series 1,** 346cc, overhead-valve V-twin, 5-speed gearbox, linked Brembo disc brakes, cast-alloy 18in wheels, electric start, SP-type fairing, rear carrier and crashbars.
£1,000–1,100 / €1,500–1,650 / $1,850–2,050 ⊞ NLM
The V35 Series I was offered between 1977 and 1979. It had electronic ignition, which proved something of a weak point. Series 2 bikes reverted to contact-breaker points to cure mid-range glitches.

1979 Moto Guzzi V50 Series 2, 490cc, overhead-valve 90-degree V-twin, 74 x 57mm bore and stroke, tubular steel frame, aluminium swinging arm, Moto Guzzi front forks, pristine condition, only 827 miles recorded, excellent condition.
£1,500–1,800 / €2,250–2,700 / $2,800–3,350 ⋊ B(Kn)
The V50 Series 2 was made between early 1979 and late 1980.

1982 Moto Guzzi 850 Le Mans Series 3, 844cc, overhead-valve 90-degree V-twin, minus original handlebar fairing, hence relatively low price.
£1,500–1,800 / €2,250–2,700 / $2,800–3,350 ⋊ B(Kn)

◄ **1982 Moto Guzzi Monza,** 490cc, 90-degree V-twin, 5-speed gearbox, shaft final drive, low handlebars, hydraulic steering damper, handlebar fairing, cast-alloy wheels, triple Brembo disc brakes, original specification, unrestored.
£1,700–1,900 / €2,550–2,800 / $3,150–3,500 ⊞ NLM
The original V50 Monza ran from 1980 until 1983. Compared to the standard V50 Series 3, upon which it was based, it had a more sporty appearance and improved suspension. The gearing was also raised allowing the Monza to turn 1,000rpm less in top gear at 70mph.

MOTO GUZZI Model	ENGINE cc/cyl	DATES	CONDITION 1	2	3
Airone	247/1	1939–51	£2,800	£2,000	£1,200
Falcone	498/1	1950–67	£5,500+	£4,000	£2,000
Motoleggera 65	64/1	1946–54	£1,200	£750	£400
Falcone Nuovo	498/1	1970–76	£2,100	£1,500	£900
V7 700	703/2	1967–76	£2,800	£1,800	£1,200
850T3	844/2	1975–82	£2,100	£1,500	£1,000
850 Le Mans I	844/2	1976–78	£3,000+	£2,200	£1,800
V50 Series 1/2	490/2	1977–80	£1,200	£800	£600

1982 Moto Guzzi V50C, 490cc, overhead-valve V-twin, 40bhp at 7,500rpm, electric start, 18in front/16in rear cast-alloy wheels, triple disc brakes.
£1,350–1,500 / €2,000–2,200 / $2,500–2,800 ⊞ NLM
The 'C' (Custom) was built in response to a craze that swept Italy during the early 1980s for US-style custom cruisers.

1987 Moto Guzzi Le Mans 1000, 948.8cc, 88 x 78mm bore and stroke, twin Dell'Orto PHM 40mm carburettors, electric start, triple disc brakes.
£2,250–2,500 / €3,400–3,750 / $4,150–4,600 ⊞ NLM
When the new Le Mans 1000 was launched in 1985, its 16 in front wheel was found to cause problems with the bike's handling. This example has the 18 in front wheel conversion kit, which was later incorporated into production.

1991 Moto Guzzi 1000SE, 948.8cc, semi-floating twin front disc brakes, stainless steel mudguards, clip-ons, Le Mans-type fairing, 5-spoke cast-alloy wheels, non-standard paint job and black silencers.
£3,150–3,500 / €4,700–5,200
$5,800–6,500 ⊞ NLM
The 1000S (and SE) was very much a modern take on the V7 Sport 750S/S3 of the early 1970s, and ran from 1989 until 1991.

1982 Moto Guzzi V50III, 490cc, overhead-valve V-twin, 5-speed gearbox, shaft final drive, duplex steel frame, cast-aluminium swinging arm with twin shock absorbers, standard specification.
£1,600–1,800 / €2,400–2,700 / $3,000–3,300 ⊞ NLM
It is generally agreed that the V50III was a much improved bike over the earlier Series I and II machines. It was more reliable, and its coil ignition provided smoother running

◄ **1982 Moto Guzzi V65,** 643.4cc, overhead-valve 90-degree V-twin, 52bhp at 7,000, 10:1 compression ratio, battery/coil ignition, shaft final drive, very good condition.
£1,700–1,900 / €2,500–2,800 / $3,150–3,500 ⊞ NLM
The V65 was developed from the V35/50 series and benefited from a variety of improvements.

◄ **1989 Moto Guzzi SP1000 Series 3,** 948.8cc, overhead-valve 90-degree V-twin, semi-floating front brake discs, tall screen, lifting handle, complete touring package.
£2,150–2,400 / €3,250–3,600 / $4,000–4,400 ⊞ NLM
Between 1984 and 1987, Moto Guzzi offered the largely unloved SP Series 2. Initially, this had a 16 in front wheel – later changed to 18 in, but it still did not prove popular. So for 1988 came the new SP Series 3. Besides having 18 in wheels front and rear, the newcomer featured new bodywork, including a totally new four-piece fairing. There were also new large-capacity Givi panniers, which Guzzi even claimed were waterproof! Another innovation, a first on the big Guzzi twins, was electronic ignition.

Moto Morini *(Italian 1937–)*

A native of Bologna, Alfonso Morini was born in 1892. His first manufacturing experiences came in partnership with Mario Mazzetti in 1924, but he left in 1937 to start a business under his own name.

Moto Morini's first product was not a motorcycle but a three-wheel truck. With the outbreak of war, production was switched to military equipment. Late in 1943, the Morini plant was partly destroyed by bombing, for although Italy had surrendered, Bologna was still controlled by the Germans.

In 1945, with the conflict over, Alfonso Morini could at last begin rebuilding his badly damaged factory. This was a task he did well, as his firm was one of the first Italian marques to resume production. Launched in 1946, the first new Morini was clearly influenced by the pre-war German DKW RT125 two-stroke design. Like the German machine, the newcomer featured a single-cylinder, unit-construction engine with three speeds. A racing version was also built.

By the early 1950s Morini had switched, at least for racing, to an overhead-camshaft design for his 125. On the production front, a brand-new 175cc overhead-valve single debuted at the Milan show at the end of 1952.

By the mid 1950s, there was a full range of 175s, including the Briscola, Tressette and Settebello. Of these, the last was the sports (and racing) model.

There was also a 175 overhead-camshaft single, the Rebello, and a 250 version, which made its debut at the Italian GP at Monza 1957. This was later developed into what is generally

acknowledged as the fastest ever single-cylinder two-fifty, which was ridden by the likes of Tarqunio Provini, Angelo Bergamonti and the young Giacomo Agostini to Grand Prix and Italian championship successes.

On the series-production front, 1959 had seen the introduction of the Corsaro. Derived from the 98cc Sbarazzino, which had been successful over the previous three years, the Corsaro featured a 123cc-overhead-valve engine and was capable of 63mph. The Corsaro remained in production until the 1970s and was also built in 150 and 160cc engine sizes.

Alfonso Morini died in 1969, the factory was run by his daughter, Gabriella, until it was taken over by the Cagiva Group in the late 1980s.

The early 1970s was a particularly busy time for Morini. Not only did it garner success with specially prepared Corsaro 125 and 160cc models in the International Six Days Trial, but also it launched what was to become the marque's most well-known model, the famous 3½ V-twin. The latter entered production in early 1973. The basis of the 3½ was a 344cc, 72-degree V-twin with Heron combustion chambers and belt-driven camshaft. From the original 3½ Strada came the higher-performance Sport. This was followed by 500 and 250 V-twins, plus 125 and 250cc singles.

Besides conventional roadsters, from the early 1980s Moto Morini offered on/off-road versions: Camel (500cc) and Kanguro (350cc). There was also the Dart, which appeared in 1988, combining a Cagiva 125 Freccia chassis with a Morini 350 engine.

◄ **1952 Moto Morini 125 Turismo,** 123.1cc, 2-stroke single, 52 x 58mm bore and stroke, alloy head, cast-iron barrel, unit construction, 4-speed gearbox, telescopic forks, swinging-arm frame, top speed 50mph.
£800–900 / €1,200–1,350 $1,500–1,650 ⊞ NLM
One of Morini's earliest designs, the 124cc two-stroke single entered production in 1946, originally with blade girder forks, plunger rear suspension and three speeds.

1956 Moto Morini Sbarazzino, 98.1cc, overhead-valve single, 50 x 50mm bore and stroke, cylinder inclined 15 degrees from vertical, 4-speed foot-change gearbox, telescopic front forks, swinging-arm frame, dualseat, original, unrestored.
£1,000–1,100 / €1,500–1,650 / $1,850–2,050 ⊞ NLM
During the mid-1950s, the Sbarazzino was Morini's best-selling model.

1974 Moto Morini 3½ Strada, 344cc, overhead-valve 72-degree V-twin, 68 x 57mm bore and stroke, offset cylinders, 10:1 compression ratio, coil valve springs, plain-bearing big-ends, 6-speed gearbox, drum brakes, original, unrestored.
£1,600–1,800 / €2,450–2,700 / $3,000–3,300 ⊞ MW

1975 Moto Morini 3½ Strada, 344cc, overhead-valve 72-degree V-twin, 6-speed gearbox, electronic ignition, Marzocchi suspension, seat recovered, non-standard (Japanese) front mudguard.
£920–1,100 / €1,400–1,650 / $1,700–2,000 ✈ B(Kn)
Although quite similar in basic details (frame, engine, suspension), the 3½ Strada and Sport models today command very different prices, the latter being considerably higher.

1977 Moto Morini 3½ Sport, 344cc, overhead-valve 72-degree V-twin, 6-speed gearbox, gear primary drive, dry clutch, duplex frame, single seat, 6 volt electrics, stainless steel mudguards and chainguard, unrestored, good condition.
£2,000–2,200 / €3,000–3,300 / $3,700–4,100 ⊞ NLM
From 1976 onwards, Morini offered a revised 3½ Sport with Grimeca front disc, Grimeca cast-alloy wheels and revised styling.

1979 Moto Morini 125H, 122.96cc, overhead-valve single, 13.75bhp at 9,000rpm, unit construction, 59 x 45mm bore and stroke, 6-speed gearbox, disc front/drum rear brakes, cast-alloy wheels, top speed 73mph, non-standard fork gaiters, average condition for year.
£900–1,000 / €1,350–1,500 / $1,650–1,850 ⊞ NLM

1980 Moto Morini 2C, 239.4cc, overhead-valve 72-degree V-twin, 26.8bhp at 9,000rpm, 59 x 43.8mm bore and stroke, 6 volt electrics, Grimeca cast-alloy wheels, disc front/drum rear brakes, top speed 87mph, unrestored.
£1,150–1,300 / €1,700–1,900 / $2,150–2,400 ⊞ NLM
Built from 1980 until 1984, the 2C suffered from a high price and cost-cutting, hence 31.5mm Paioli front forks and black exhaust system (for example).

1981 Moto Morini 500/6 Tour, 498cc, overhead-valve 72-degree V-twin, 6-speed gearbox, electric starter, Marzocchi front forks and rear shock absorbers, triple Grimeca disc brakes, colour-coded top and bottom fairings, hydraulic steering damper.
£2,600–2,900 / €3,900–4,350 / $4,800–5,300 ⊞ NLM
Much rarer than the three-fifty, the five-hundred V-twin Morini is often overlooked, but is an excellent machine.

1984 Moto Morini Kanguro X1, 344cc, 72-degree V-twin, offset cylinders, twin carburettors, 6-speed gearbox, monoshock rear suspension, disc front/drum rear brakes, full cradle duplex frame, square-section swinging arm, shorter front mudguard, rear carrier.
£1,050–1,200 / €1,600–1,800 / $1,950–2,200 ⊞ NLM
During the early 1980s the 350 Kanguro was Moto Morini's best-selling model.

◄ **1985 Moto Morini 500 Model Special**, 478.6cc, overhead-valve V-twin, 6-speed gearbox, electric start, Marzocchi forks, Grimeca 7-spoke cast-alloy wheels, triple disc brakes, original, very good condition.
£2,600–2,900 / €3,900–4,300 / $4,850–5,400 ⊞ NLM
The 500 roadster was updated in line with the new 350K2 at the end of 1983. The alterations were mainly cosmetic, but there were a few technical changes, most notably to the electrics, with a more powerful 24 amp/hour battery and stronger 160 watt alternator.

1985 Moto Morini 501 Camel, 507cc, overhead-valve 72-degree V-twin, 6-speed gearbox, monoshock rear suspension, long-travel Marzocchi front forks, braced handlebars, square-tube frame, disc front brake, unrestored.
£1,600–1,800 / €2,450–2,700 / $3,000–3,300 ⊞ NLM
In 1985, Morini introduced the 501 Camel. Its actual displacement was 507cc, which was achieved by increasing the cylinder bore to 71mm. The cylinders themselves were Nikasil-coated.

▶ **1990 Moto Morini Coguaro 350,** 344cc, overhead-valve 72-degree V-twin engine, 6-speed foot-change gearbox, dry multi-plate clutch, square-tube frame, monoshock rear suspension, disc front brake, sump bash plate, standard specification, unrestored.
£1,250–1,500 / €2,000–2,200 / $2,500–2,800 ⊞ NLM
The Coguaro trail bike made its appearance at the Milan show in November 1987, after the Cagiva take-over.

1990 Moto Morini Dart 350, 344cc, overhead-valve 72-degree V-twin engine, 6-speed gearbox, monoshock frame, fully-floating single front disc, enclosed bodywork, concours condition.
£1,800–2,000 / €2,700–3,000 / $3,350–3,700 ⊞ NLM
Cagiva took over Moto Morini in the spring of 1987. The first fruit of the new ownership was the 350 Dart, which made its debut at the Milan show later that year. The Dart was essentially one of the old 344cc V-twin engines slotted into the chassis of a 125cc Cagiva Freccia.

1993 Moto Morini Excalibur 501, 507cc, V-twin, 6-speed gearbox, chrome headlamp, matching speedometer and rev-counter, carrier/grab rail, standard, unrestored, good condition.
£1,500–1,650 / €2,250–2,500 / $2,800–3,100 ⊞ NLM

1985 Moto Morini Kanguro X2, 344cc, overhead-valve 72-degree V-twin, 6-speed gearbox, electronic ignition, high-level exhaust, fork gaiters, monoshock rear suspension, built-in rear carrier.
£1,250–1,400 / €1,900–2,100 / $2,350–2,600 ⊞ NLM
The Kanguro X2 can be distinguished from the X1 not only by its bodywork, but also by its square-section tubing main frame.

MV Agusta
(Italian 1945–78, 1998–)

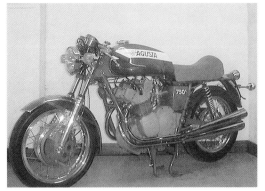

◄ **1972 MV Agusta 750S,** 743cc, restored, concours condition.
**£15,500–18,600 / €23,200–27,900
$28,700–34,000** ⚲ B(Kn)
Developed from MV Agusta's long line of successful multi-cylinder racers, the first road going four – a twin-carburettor, 600cc tourer – appeared in 1965. But the public demanded something more exciting, and MV duly obliged in 1969, upping capacity to 743cc and further boosting maximum power (to 69bhp) by fitting a quartet of Dell'Orto carburettors to the revised 750GT. Also in the line-up was the more sporting 750S, which continued in production after the GT's demise in 1973, bowing out in 1975 to make way for the 750S America. This machine was previously owned by multiple World Champion John Surtees and was restored by UK specialist Meccanica Verghera.

1973 MV Agusta 750S, 743cc, double-overhead-camshaft across-the-frame-four, 5-speed gearbox, shaft final drive, wire wheels, drum brakes, factory optional fairing, 6,500 miles from new.
**£18,000–21,600 / €27,000–32,000
$34,000–40,000** ⚲ B(Kn)
MV Agusta first displayed a four-cylinder machine in 1950. However, it was not until 1966 that a production model was released. Unfortunately, the company chose to produce a portly 600cc touring machine that could not have been farther from the device craved by the enthusiasts. Finally, in 1969 at the Milan show, the motorcycling world first saw what it had waited so long for. This was a sporty four-cylinder MV of 743cc, designed and built in the true sporting traditions of the famous Italian factory. It is thought that the 750cc capacity was chosen to allow the machine to compete in the production derived Formula 750 Series, and indeed two machines did race in 1972 at the Imola 200, although both failed to finish. In spite of this setback, on the road there is no doubt that few machines could compete in terms of performance.

1973 MV Agusta 350S Elettronica, 349cc, overhead-valve vertical twin, 63 x 56mm bore and stroke, unit construction, twin carburettors, 5-speed gearbox, drum brakes, original, good condition.
£2,000–2,250 / €3,000–3,300 / $3,700–4100 ⚲ NLM
The 350S Elettronica (EL) was basically the 350B Sport with electronic ignition.

MZ (German 1953–)

Auction prices
Miller's only includes motorcycles declared sold. Our guide prices take into account the buyer's premium, VAT on the premium, and the extent of any published catalogue information relating to condition and provenance. motorcycles sold at auction are identified by the ⚲ icon; full details of the auction house can be found on page 167.

◄ **1990 MZ ETZ 125,** 124cc, 2-stroke single, 5-speed gearbox, 12 volt electrics, aftermarket screen, carrier and top box, needing cosmetic restoration.
£100–120 / €150–180 / $185–220 ⚲ PS

New Hudson *(British 1909–57)*

◄ **1914 New Hudson Model D,** 211cc, 2-stroke single, 2-speed gearbox, belt drive, external flywheels, front-mounted magneto, fully restored.
£3,800–4,550 / €5,700–6,800
$7,000–8,400 ✗ B(Kn)
New Hudson began production in 1909 at Parade Mills, Birmingham. Although now largely forgotten, the marque had an illustrious competition history, achieving many Brooklands successes and records, and recruiting such stars as Bert le Vack, Jimmy Guthrie and Fred Hutton to ride their machines. The majority of New Hudson production comprised side- and overhead-valve singles, but two-strokes also played a part.

New Imperial *(British 1910–39)*

1924 New Imperial Model 1, 2¾hp, side-valve single, all-chain drive, aluminium silencer, drum brakes, rear-mounted magneto, acetylene lighting, fully restored, concours condition.
£3,150–3,500 / €4,700–5,200 / $5,800–6,400 ⬤ NIO

1937 New Imperial 100 Clubmans, 346cc, overhead-valve single-port single, semi-unit construction, iron head and barrel, 70 x 90mm bore and stroke, foot-change gearbox, girder forks, chrome tank, restored.
£3,150–3,500 / €4,700–5,200 / $5,800–6,500 ⬤ NIO

1928 New Imperial 2.5hp, overhead-valve vertical single, magneto ignition, iron head and barrel, all-chain drive, rigid frame, saddle tank.
£2,700–3,250 / €4,100–4,900 / $5,000–6,000 ✗ B(Kn)
Builder of the last British-made machine to win the Lightweight 250 TT (in 1936), New Imperial was unsurpassed for innovation during the 1930s, with models featuring pivoted-fork rear suspension and unit construction of engine and gearbox. The marque was established in 1900, when Norman Downs acquired a cycle company in Birmingham, which he reorganized as New Imperial Cycles. The firm's first motorcycles, designed along Werner lines, were shown at the 1901 Stanley Show in London, but were not well received. Not until 1910 did Downs try again, launching a conventional JAP-powered model – the Light Tourist – that would prove an outstanding success. In racing, New Imperial concentrated on the 250 class, winning the Isle of Man TT trophy for 250cc machines in 1921, and the Lightweight TT in 1924, a feat repeated the following year. On the commercial front, the late 1920s saw production facilities expand, while proprietary engines were abandoned in favour of New Imperial's own power units.

Norman *(British 1937–62)*

◄ **1953 Norman B2 Rigid,** 197cc, Villiers 6E engine, 3-speed foot-change gearbox, rigid frame, telescopic front forks.
£1,050–1,200 / €1,600–1,800 / $1,950–2,200 ⬤ NORM
Charles and Fred Norman started a frame-making, enamelling and metal-plating business in a garden shed in Ashford, Kent, on their return from France at the end of WWI. During the 1920s and 1930s, they manufactured pedal cycles. Then, at the end of the 1930s, they began motorcycle production. In 1935, a new factory had been built in Beaver Road, Ashford, and during WWII a Norman motorcycle was presented to Guy Gibson, the legendary leader of 617 Squadron (the Dambusters). The post-war roadster range consisted of 122, 149 and 197cc singles, and twin-cylinder models powered by Anzani and Villiers engines.

Norton *(British 1902–)*

James Lansdowne Norton built his first motorcycle in 1902, using a French Clement engine.
The Energette, as it was called, was soon entered in reliability and speed trials.

In 1907, a Norton ridden by Rem Fowler had the distinction of winning the multi-cylinder class at the very first Isle of Man TT. Then came the first Norton designed engines, and by late 1907, the first of the 490cc (79 x 100mm bore and stroke) long-stroke, single-cylinder engines had been unveiled.

In 1911, following a long illness, James Norton lost control of the company to the Vandervell family, although he remained joint managing director with R. T. Shelley.He died in 1925 at the early age of 56.

The company relied on the side-valve layout until the 1920s, when its well-tried 490cc engine was used as the basis for its first overhead-valve design. Penned by James Norton himself, and first seen in prototype guise in 1922, the overhead-valve Norton made little impact in that year's Senior TT, but at Brocklands D. R. O'Donovan raised the world 500cc kilometre record to over 89mph. A road version, the Model 18, was listed for 1923 and quickly established a reputation for speed and reliability. Racing continued to improve the breed, the Model 18 gaining Webb forks and better brakes for 1925 – when Alec Bennett won the Senior TT for Norton.

In 1927, Norton produced its first overhead-camshaft engine, known as the CS1 (Cam Shaft 1). This led to a long association with sporting and camshaft singles.

A new 'cammy' engine was designed by Arthur Carroll, which achieved unparalleled racing successes throughout the 1930s, and led to the legendary International and Manx models. Team boss Joe Craig, and riders Stanley Woods, Jimmy Guthrie and Harold Daniel helped create the aura that surrounded the Birmingham marque in the days leading up to WWII. During the conflict, Norton became a major supplier to the British Army, with models such as the 16H and Big Four side-valve singles.

Post-war developments included the Roadholder front forks (1947), Dominator overhead-valve parallel twin (1948) and Featherbed duplex frame (1950). Geoff Duke and sidecar star Eric Oliver gave Norton several world road racing titles in the immediate post-war period.

However, all was not well, and rival AMC (Associated Motor Cycles) took over Norton in 1953. This signalled the end of the glory days. At the end of the 1954 season, Norton ceased racing factory specials and, from then on, only built the production Manx models.

In 1958, the lightweight twin, the 249cc Jubilee, was launched, followed by the 349cc Navigator (1960) and 400cc Electra (1962).

None of these could really be called successful, and with Norton's larger singles totally outdated in the marketplace, it was left to the Dominator family of big twins to keep the flag flying. Besides the already established 500, there was a 600, which was superseded by a 650 as the 1960s dawned, while the new 750 Atlas (originally for export only) arrived in 1961.

AMC went into receivership in 1966. Then came the Poore era of the Commando.

◄ **1924 Norton Model 16H,** 490cc, side-valve vertical single, hand-change gearbox, drum front/caliper rear brakes, all-chain drive, forward-mounted magneto, original, excellent condition.
£5,800–6,500 / €8,700–9,700 $10,800–12,000 ⊞ VER
The name 16H (Model 16, Home) made its debut in 1921 for the 1922 season. The designation was chosen to distinguish it from the 17C (Model 17, Colonial); the engine had its origins in WWI.

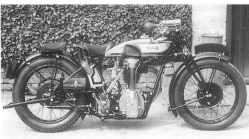

1928 Norton CS1, 490cc, overhead-camshaft single, 79 x 100mm bore and stroke, bevel-driven camshaft, coil valve springs, rear-mounted magneto, all-chain drive, Webb front forks, 8in drum brakes.
£9,500–10,500 / €14,200–15,700 / $17,600–19,500 ⊞ VER
The CS1 (Cam Shaft 1) was designed by Walter Moore and was Norton's first overhead-camshaft engine.

1930 Norton Model 19, 588cc, overhead-valve vertical single, iron head and barrel, forward-mounted magneto, Webb forks, rigid frame, restored, incorrect fuel tank for year.
£2,700–3,000 / €4,000–4,500 / $5,000–5,500 ⋏ CGC
The Model 19 was essentially a longer-stroke version of the better-known 490cc Model 18. Production ceased at the end of 1932.

1938 Norton Model 30 International, 490cc, overhead-camshaft single, 79 x 100mm bore and stroke, chain driven magneto, iron head and barrel, one-piece rockers, hairpin valve springs, 4-speed foot-change gearbox, excellent condition.
£8,000–9,000 / € 12,000–13,300 $14,800–16,500 ⊞ VER
Thanks to Norton's nemerous racing successes during the 1930s, the International was the dream bike for enthusiasts of the era.

1938 Norton Model 16H, 490cc, side-valve single, 79 x 100mm bore and stroke, 4-speed foot-change gearbox, Webb girder forks, rigid frame, top speed 65mph.
£2,500–2,800 / € 3,800–4,200 / $4,700–5,200 ⊞ BLM
As far removed as possible from Norton's race-winning overhead-camshaft racers, the Model 16H was, as one journalist described it, 'Dull but dependable, it was a slow, heavy plodder that kept on going'. That is probably why around 100,000 were subsequently supplied to the British armed forces during WWII.

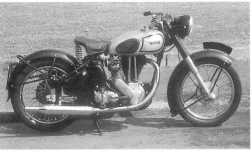

1947 Norton Model 30 International, 490cc, overhead-camshaft single, iron head and barrel, Amal TT carburettor, upright gearbox, 'Garden Gate' plunger frame, telescopic forks, excellent condition.
£10,000–11,000 / € 15,000–16,500 / $18,500–20,400 ⊞ VER

1951 Norton ES2, 490cc, overhead-valve vertical single, 'Garden Gate' plunger frame telescopic forks, single-sprung saddle, unrestored.
£2,000–2,200 / € 3,000–3,300 / $3,700–4,100 ⊞ PM

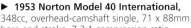

▶ 1953 Norton Model 40 International, 348cc, overhead-camshaft single, 71 x 88mm bore and stroke, 7.3:1 compression ratio, 19in wheels, 8in front/7in rear drum brakes, Featherbed frame, Roadholder forks, fully restored to concours condition.
£9,000–10,000 / € 13,500–15,000 $16,600–18,500 ⊞ MW
The International received the Featherbed frame (from the Dominator 88) for the 1953 season, together with improvements to the brakes, gearbox and carburettor.

◀ 1954 Norton Dominator 88, 497cc, overhead-valve vertical twin, 66 x 72.6mm, iron head and barrel, laid-down 4-speed foot-change gearbox, Featherbed frame, Roadholder front forks, 19in wheels, single-sided 8in front/7in rear brakes, restored, concours condition.
£5,000–5,500 / € 7,500–8,300 9,200–10,200 ⊞ VER
This was the last year of the iron-head engine.

NORTON Model	ENGINE cc/cyl	DATES	CONDITION		
			1	2	3
16H	490/1	1932–54	£2,600	£1,900	£1,000
Big Four	634/1	1932–54	£2,900	£2,200	£1,200
50	348/1	1933–63	£2,700	£2,000	£1,100
88*	497/2	1951–63	£3,000	£2,100	£1,600
99*	596/2	1956–62	£3,100	£2,200	£1,600
650SS	646/2	1961–70	£3,700+	£2,600	£2,000
Atlas	745/2	1962–68	£3,600	£2,500	£2,000
850 Commando	829/2	1973–78	£3,200	£2,200	£1,900
*SS Versions + 20 per cent					

1960 Norton Model 50, 348cc, overhead-valve single, 71 x 88mm bore and stroke, Amal Monobloc carburettor, alloy head, cast-iron barrel, 4-speed AMC gearbox, fully enclosed final drive chain, slimline Featherbed frame, Roadholder front forks, full-width brake hubs.
£2,250–2,500 / €3,400–3,750 / $4,150–4,600 ⬥ WCMC
The Model 50 was a smaller-engined version of the ES2.

1962 Norton Navigator, 349cc, overhead-valve vertical twin, 63 x 56mm bore and stroke, unit-construction, 4-speed gearbox, duplex primary chain, all original tinware.
£980–1,200 / €1,500–1,800 / $1,800–2,150 ⬈ CGC
Of the smaller Norton vertical twins, the 250 Jubilee, 350 Navigator and 400 Electrica, it is generally agreed that the Navigator was the best. This was due, in part, to the Roadholder forks and full-width 8in front brake from the Dominator 88.

1965 Norton Electra, 383cc, overhead-valve unit twin, 66 x 56mm bore and stroke, 24bhp at 7,000rpm, coil ignition, electric start, 19in front/18in rear wheels, bar-end indicators.
£2,200–2,600 / €3,300–3,900 / $4,000–4,800 ⊞ MW
The Electra was the largest of the small twin-cylinder range which began with the Jubilee (250) and continued with the Navigator (350). Like the latter, it sported the Roadholder forks and alloy front hub from the Dominator series.

► **1972 Norton 750 Commando,** 745cc, overhead-valve vertical twin, 60bhp at 6,800rpm, 73 x 89mm bore and stroke, triplex chain primary drive, diaphragm clutch, many extras and modifications, excellent condition.
£4,700–5,200 / €7,000–7,800 $8,700–9,700 ⊞ VER
The Commando was launched in September 1967 and was the work of Stefan Bauer, assisted by development engineers Bernard Hooper and Bob Twigg. It featured a new frame that carried the existing Atlas engine and AMC gearbox.

1974 Norton 750 Commando, 745cc, overhead-valve twin, 73 x 89mm bore and stroke, 68bhp, 19in wheels, disc front/drum rear brakes.
£3,350–4,000 / €5,000–6,000 / $6,200–7,400 ⊞ MW
This machine is a production racing version of the 750 Commando, known as the 'Yellow Peril'. It was built by Norvil race shop at Thruxton, using a Combat engine, clip-ons, rear-sets, nose fairing, racing seat and tank, and a hydraulically-operated disc front brake. This bike has an uprated (RGM) caliper and disc.

1977 Norton 850 Commando Interstate, 829cc, overhead-valve twin, 77 x 89mm bore and stroke, 8.5:1 compression ratio, triplex primary chain, 19in wheels, front and rear disc brakes, largely standard apart from uprated front brake.
£3,050–3,400 / €4,600–5,100 / $5,600–6,200 ⊞ MW

Miller's
Motorcycle Milestones

Norton Commando 750 (1967–73), 850 (1973–78)
Price Range: 750 £2,000–5,000 /€3,000–7,500 /
$3,700–9,200
850 £2,500–5,000 /€3,000–7,500 / $3,700–9,200

The Commando project began with the appointment of Stefan Bauer at Norton Villiers as director of engineering in January, 1967. Boss Dennis Poore wanted Bauer to lead a technical team to develop a new big twin to replace the ageing 750 Atlas.

Bauer was ably assisted by two well-known British engineers, Bernard Hooper and Bob Twigg. Actually, this was just as well, Bauer had no previous two-wheel experience at all, his background being in nuclear physics, and he had spent the previous 12 years with Rolls-Royce. Even so, his team was successful in creating a very marketable machine, which was launched, to much public acclaim, at the Earls Court Motorcycle Show in September, 1967.

The most innovative feature of the newcomer was its frame, the 745cc (73 x 89mm bore and stroke) Atlas engine (albeit with sloping cylinders) and four-speed AMC-type gearbox being retained in rubber mountings by a full-cradle duplex steel assembly.

There is no doubt that the Commando was a clever commercial design. It gave the appearance of being a very different motorcycle from the machine it replaced, yet actually, except for the frame and bodywork, most components were the same. Even so, it was a huge success, not only in the showroom, but also on the race track. It was voted Machine of the Year by *Motor Cycle News* in 1968, a title it went on to win no fewer than five years in a row, a feat that had never been bettered. The first model year was 1969, when it was sold as the 750 Fastback. The Roadster arrived for 1970, and for 1971 a new version of the Fastback and Roadster appeared, together with the Street Scrambler, Hi Rider and Production Racer; 1972 saw the Interstate, which featured a larger tank and a disc front brake (already used on the Production Racer). All models were fitted with disc brakes from the middle of the year.

Then, for 1973, the 850 (829cc, 77 x 89mm bore and stroke) version was launched in Roadster, Hi Rider and Interstate forms. In 1974, the John Player Norton café racer appeared. Finally, for 1975, the Roadster and Interstate 850s gained electric start, left-hand gear change and a disc rear brake.

In 1978, the final batch of 30 machines (Interstate 850s) was built.

◄ **1979 Norton 850 Commando Interstate Mk3,** 829cc, overhead-valve twin, 73 x 89mm bore and stroke, front and rear disc brakes, indicators, 12 volt electrics, electric start, fork gaiters, left-hand gear-change, original, very good condition.
£3,600–4,000 / €5,400–6,000 / $6,700–7,400 ⊞ NLM

1990 Norton F1, 588cc, twin Wankel rotary engine, 3-spoke cast-alloy wheels, inverted front forks, rising-rate monoshock rear suspension, only 20 miles from new, concours condition.
£10,300–12,400 / €15,500–18,600
$19,100–22,900 ⚙ B(Kn)

The F1 was Norton's last attempt to build a roadster around its rotary engine. Race-styled and painted in the John Player Specials livery of the works bikes ridden by Steve Spray and Trevor Nation, it made do with 94bhp, as opposed to the racer's 150-plus, a figure that put its performance (top speed was around 145mph) on a par with that of contemporary sports 600s from Japan. In the quality of its equipment though, the F1 was streets ahead of the opposition: Spondon alloy beam frame, White Power 'upside down' forks and rear shock, Brembo brakes all-round (floating discs at the front with four-pot calipers). The downside however, was the F1's cost, a staggering £12,700 / €19,000 / $23,500. Few were made before the factory hit yet another financial crisis and production ceased.

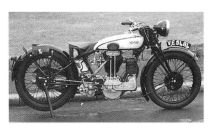

NSU *(German 1901–67)*

◀ **1960 NSU Supermax,** 247cc, overhead-camshaft single with 'Ultramax' connecting link for camshaft, 69 x 60mm bore and stroke, 4-speed gearbox, leading-link forks, swinging-arm rear suspension.
£3,000–3,600 / €4,500–5,400 / $5,500–6,600 ⚙ BB(L)
NSU had its roots in the bicycle industry and its first prototype motorcycle in 1900, production beginning in 1901. It went on to produce some outstanding and influential designs, one of the best being the Max two-fifty, introduced in 1952. The ultimate version, the Supermax, debuted in 1956. Production ceased in 1963.

OK-Supreme *(British 1899–1939)*

1931 OK-Supreme K32, 490cc, JAP overhead-valve twin-port single-cylinder engine, 85.7 x 85mm bore and stroke, hand-change gearbox, rear-mounted magdyno, girder forks, rigid frame, restored, but needing new wiring loom.
£2,200–2,650 / €3,300–3,950 / $4,100–4,900 ⚙ B(Kn)
A 1932 model manufactured in November 1931, this example has been renovated over the course of the past three years; it now needs only a new wiring loom to complete; comes with invoices showing restoration.
OK – the 'Supreme' came later – was founded by bicycle manufacturer Humphries & Dawes of Birmingham. The company experimented with powered two-wheelers in the 20th century's early years before exhibiting a Precision-engined range in 1911. When Charles Dawes and Ernie Humphries split in 1926, the latter continued motorcycle production using the name 'OK-Supreme'. The firm first entered the Isle of Man TT in 1912, but had to wait for its finest hour until 1928, when OK-Supremes filled four of the top six positions in the Lightweight race, Frank Longman scoring the marque's solitary TT victory. The majority of OK's 1930s range was JAP-powered, the exception being the overhead-camshaft models which used the inclined 'lighthouse' engine at first and a more conventional overhead-camshaft design from 1935.

Panther *(British 1900–66)*

◀ **1928 Panther Panthette,** 247cc, unit-construction overhead-valve transverse V-twin, vertically-split crankcase, 50 x 61.5mm bore and stroke, 4-speed gearbox, modified Pilgrim pump lubrication, forged steel H-section backbone frame.
£4,500–5,000 / €6,800–7,500
$8,300–9,200 ⚙ PAN
The Panthette was designed by Granville Bradshaw (formerly of ABC). In many ways it was an advanced design, but for various reasons did not become a sales success. The transmission was designed on car principles with bevel drive.

1936 Panther Model 100 Redwing, 598cc, overhead-valve single with sloping cylinder, 87 x 100mm bore and stroke, 6.5:1 compression ratio, iron head and barrel, high-level exhaust, foot-change gearbox, rigid frame.
£3,150–3,500 / €4,700–5,200 / $5,800–6,500 ⬧ PAN
In 1935, the Redwing had seen improvements, including a newly-finned sump and lubrication updates.

◄ **1938 Panther Red Panther,** 249cc, overhead-valve single cylinder, 60 x 88mm bore and stroke, single-port head, coil ignition, 3-speed hand-change gearbox, drum brakes, original.
£2,250–2,500 / €3,400–3,750 $4,150–4,600 ⊞ CotC
Early in 1933, Panther reached an agreement with London dealer Pride & Clarke, the result being the Red Panther, based on the existing 250, but with a red tank instead of a green one. They were available with a choice of acetylene or electric lighting.

► **1939 Panther M100 deluxe,** 598cc, overhead-valve single with sloping cylinder, twin-port head, 87 x 100mm bore and stroke, foot-change gearbox, front wheel speedometer drive, P & M Brampton heavy-duty girder forks, rigid frame, 8in drum front brake.
£3,600–4,000 €5,400–6,000 $6,700–7,400 ⬧ PAN

1958 Panther Model 100, 594cc, overhead-valve inclined twin-port single, 87 x 100mm bore and stroke, 4-speed foot-change gearbox, full-width hub, telescopic forks, swinging-arm frame, top speed 85mph (70mph with sidecar).
£2,800–3,100 / €4,200–4,650 / $5,200–5,700 ⊞ BLM
The one feature that P & M, the maker of Panther motorcycles, retained throughout its long history was the use of the engine in place of the frame downtube for at least one model. Back in 1924, the marque adopted an overhead-valve sloping single, a design feature that was to remain until the last motorcycle was built in 1968.

► **1962 Panther M120 deluxe,** 649cc, overhead-valve twin-port single, 88 x 106mm bore and stroke, 6.5:1 compression ratio, 28bhp at 4,500rpm, 4-speed foot-change gearbox, swinging-arm frame, telescopic front forks.
£2,700–3,000 / €4,050–4,500 / $5,000–5,500 ⬧ PAN
Last of the famous Panther big singles, the Model 120 ran from 1959 through to the end of production in 1966. It was equipped with Lucas magdyno ignition/lighting and full-width interchangeable 8in alloy brake hubs.

Parilla *(Italian 1946–67)*

◀ **1963 Parilla Olympia,** 97.7cc, overhead-valve horizontal single, 52 x 46mm bore and stroke, 6.5bhp at 7,200rpm, 4-speed foot-change gearbox, top speed 53mph, fully restored.
£900–1,000 / €1,350–1,500 / $1,650–1,850 ⊞ MW
Giovanni Parrilla (an 'r' was dropped for the marque name) joined the ranks of motorcycle manufacturers in 1946, with the first truly all-new Italian racing design of the post-WWII era. Over the next two decades there followed an array of interesting machines with both four- and two-stroke engines. After motorcycle production ceased in 1967, Parilla continued building its highly successful kart engines for many years.

Peugeot *(French 1899–)*

The French Peugeot Company is one of the most famous names in the four-wheel world, but it has also played an important role in the development of powered two-wheelers, manufacturing motorcycles, mopeds and scooters.

Jean Frederic and Jean Pierre Peugeot opened a small foundry in 1810, which acted as a launch pad for its subsequent manufacturing empire. In 1885 the brothers Eugene and Armund, the third generation of the Peugeot family, transformed the company's fortunes, which up to that time had relied on making bicycles and tricycles, by starting car manufacture.

Peugeot's first motorcycles appeared in 1899, while the brothers began making their own engines in 1903. By 1906, there was a range of V-twins, displacing 345, 726 and 994cc. These engines were so highly respected that they were also used by rival manufacturers. For example, the Norton that Rem Fowler rode to victory in the first Isle of Man TT in 1907 had a Peugeot V-twin engine.

Car production began in 1913. That year saw the arrival of Swiss engineer Ernst Henry who, having built successful Grand Prix cars, had joined the company to design a new racing motorcycle. This was a parallel twin with a capacity of 498cc. A novelty was the valve gear, which not only employed double overhead camshafts, but four-valves per cylinder.

At the beginning of the 1920s, the Romanian engineer Lessman Antionescu was hired to redesign the 1913 twin. The result was a simplified engine with only one camshaft and half the number of valves, while the gear train driving these components featured bevel gears and a vertical shaft. Although these measures appeared a backwards step, they worked, resulting in victory for Peugeot in the 1923 Grand Prix des Nations at Monza in Italy at a speed of 75mph.

Production models centred upon a unit-construction, 350cc side-valve single, plus a 125cc two-stroke and a 500cc four-stroke.

In 1927, the five hundred racing twin was dropped, and Peugeot concentrated on its roadster models.

After WWII, production did not resume until the end of the 1940s, and when it did the company concentrated very much on the commuter market, in particular mopeds and scooters.

Peugeot's motorcycle range suffered as the 1950s wore on, and production was finally halted in 1959. However, moped sales boomed, which helped Peugeot back into profitability and a return for a short period to motorcycle manufacture in 1980.

Then it was back to mopeds. Later still, in the mid-1990s, with scooters coming back into fashion, Peugeot became a major producer of powered two-wheelers once more.

1934 Peugeot Type 515 De Luxe, 500cc, overhead-valve twin-port single, unit construction, 4-speed gearbox, girder forks, rigid frame, finned brake drums, front wheel speedometer drive, aluminium fishtail silencer.
£3,050–3,400 / €4,600–5,100 / $5,600–6,200 ⊞ MW

1934 Peugeot P111, 350cc, side-valve single, iron head and barrel, hand-change 3-speed gearbox, magneto at rear of cylinder, dynamo at front.
£1,800–2,000 / €2,700–3,000 / $3,350–3,700 ⊞ MW

1952 Peugeot 55AL, 125cc, 2-stroke single, girder forks, rigid frame, fully restored, concours condition.
£1,450–1,600 / €2,200–2,450 / $2,700–3,000 ⊞ MW

1956 Peugeot Model 56 TL4, 125cc, single-cylinder 2-stroke, twin-port cylinder head, unit construction, telescopic front forks, plunger rear suspension, pillion saddle.
£1,450–1,600 / €2,200–2,450 / $2,700–3,000 ⊞ MW

Premier *(British 1908–20)*

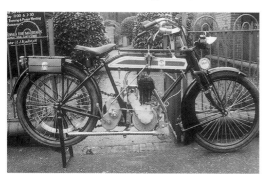

Restored values

The cost of a professional restoration will have an influence on, but no direct relation to, a motorcycle's market value. A restored motorcycle can have a market value lower than the cost of its restoration.

◀ **1913 Premier,** 499cc, side-valve single, magneto ignition, 3-speed hand-change countershaft gearbox, clutch, belt drive, lighting equipment, fully restored.
£7,600–8,500 / €11,400–12,700 / $14,100–15,700 ⊞ VER

Puch *(Austrian 1903–87, Italian 1987–)*

1952 Puch SG125, 123cc, 2-stroke split-single, 4-speeds, twin carburettors, telescopic forks, swinging-arm frame, fully restored.
£1,700–1,900 / €2,550–2,800 $3,150–3,500 ⊞ MW
Puch has a particularly complex history. Johann Puch built his first motorcycle in 1903 after starting out as an armaments manufacturer. Puch amalgamated with Austro-Daimler in 1928 and Steyr in 1934.

1965 Puch Allstate SGS 250, 247cc, 2-stroke split-single, alloy head, cast-iron barrel, twin carburettors, full-width hubs, telescopic front forks, swinging-arm frame, excellent condition.
£1,450–1,600 / €2,150–2,400 $2,700–3,000 ⊞ MW
The Allstate is the American-market version of the SGS 250.

Raleigh (British 1901–06, 1920–33, 1958–71)

1925 Raleigh 250, 247cc, side-valve single, oil-bath primary chaincase, magneto ignition, acetylene lighting, original.
£1,600–1,800 / €2,400–2,650 / $3,000–3,300 ⊞ CotC

1926 Raleigh Model 17, 174cc, side-valve single, unit-construction, 2-speed gearbox, chain final drive, recently restored.
£2,250–2,500 / €3,350–3,700 / $4,150–4,600 ⊕ VMCC

◀ **c1930 Raleigh Model MH Sports,** 495cc, overhead-valve twin-port single, coil valve springs, iron head and barrel, Sturmey-Archer hand-change gearbox, all-chain drive, fully restored.
£4,600–5,500 / €6,900–8,200 / $8,500–10,200 ⚙ B(Kn)
During the 1920s, the Raleigh range expanded to include machines of a wide variety of capacities and types, ranging from a 175cc unit-construction lightweight to a hefty 998cc V-twin. Traditionally, trials had been Raleigh's favoured area of motorcycle competition, but in 1928 the firm entered the Isle of Man Senior TT with a team of new 495cc overhead-valve long-stroke singles, one of which finished eighth, a creditable first effort.

Ratier (French 1959–62)

1958 Ratier, 600cc, overhead-valve flat-twin, shaft final drive, swinging-arm frame, telescopic front forks, full-width drum brakes, fully restored.
£5,400–6,000 / €8,100–9,000 / $10,000–11,100 ⊞ MW
Established in 1945 as CMR, the marque was renamed Cemac in 1948 and finally became Ratier in 1955. The machines were based around the BMW flat-twin engine with shaft final drive, although the cycle parts were French.

Rickman (British 1959–80s)

◀ **c1972 Rickman Triumph Metisse,** 649cc, Triumph T120 Bonneville engine, Rickman cycle parts, including frame, forks and disc brakes, alloy rims, swept-back pipes with short Daytona megaphone silencers.
£4,250–4,700 / €6,300–7,000 / $7,900–8,700 ⊞ BLM
Brothers Don and Derek Rickman made a name for themselves with their Metisse scramblers – powered by either Triumph twin or AMC single-cylinder engines. Then, in 1966, they built a series of road racers, again with Triumph and AMC engines. Finally, in the late 1960s, they began offering both frame kits and complete machines for road use.

Rover *(British 1902–25)*

◀ **1914 Rover,** 550cc, side-valve single, iron top end, belt final drive, pedalling gear, hand-pump lubrication, caliper brakes.
£6,100–7,300 / €9,100–10,900 / $11,300–13,500 ➴ B(Kn)

Royal Enfield *(British 1901–70)*

The first Royal Enfield motorcycle was built in 1901, in Redditch, which would be the marque's home for the next 65 years. Today, the company's most famous model, the Bullet, continues to be produced in India and is sold in many countries, including Britain, the United States of America, France and Germany.

For the first half of the 20th century, Royal Enfield pioneered such features as dry-sump lubrication, quickly-detachable wheels, the countershaft gearbox, three and four valves per cylinder, and swinging-arm rear suspension. Although most enthusiasts will remember the company for its four-stroke singles and parallel twins, it also designed and built many other layouts, including V-twins, a whole family of two-strokes and even an inline three-cylinder prototype (1915).

In WWI the British War Department commissioned Royal Enfield to supply motorcycles for the military. Notable was a series of large-displacement, JAP-engined V-twins equipped with sidecars. These performed a variety of duties, including machine-gun mount and even ambulance.

Right from Royal Enfield's earliest days as a motorcycle manufacturer, the Smith family had been involved in its affairs. Robert Walker Smith was appointed managing director in 1923.

His three sons had served in the war, and all had survived.

The oldest, Frank, who had served as a Royal Flying Corps pilot in France – 'Major Frank', as everyone called him – took over the reigns when his father died in 1933 (after serving as assistant MD). All the brothers were keen motorcyclists. This not only led to a hands-on approach, but also meant that the Smith family was closely involved with developments of new innovations and models, and that the company was one of the very best British bike firms to work for.

The famous Bullet name was first used during the early 1930s for a range of 248, 346 and 488cc overhead-valve singles. The most famous Royal Enfield of WWII was the 125cc Flying Flea, a two-stroke that served with the Allied airborne troops on D-Day.

Post-war came a new Bullet overhead-valve single with swinging-arm rear suspension (for the 1949 model year), together with the 496cc 500 twin, which debuted in November 1948. From then until production ceased at Redditch during the late 1960s, there were four Enfield model series: Bullet singles (350 and 500cc), parallel twins (500, 700 and 750cc), Crusader (250) and two-strokes (125, 150 and 250cc).

▶ **1926 Royal Enfield Model K,** 976cc, side-valve V-twin, 85.5 x 85mm bore and stroke.
£5,200–6,200 / €7,800–9,300 $9,600–11,500 ➴ B(Kn)
In 1912 Royal Enfield produced the successful 6hp motorcycle combination, with JAP V-twin engine, two-speed gear and all-chain drive. Enfield's characteristic cush-drive rear hub appeared for the first time on this model. When motorcycle production resumed after WWI, the Enfield combination reappeared with an 8hp JAP engine, although this was soon superseded by one of Enfield's own design, manufactured for them by Vickers. The 8hp engine had been redesigned and was being built at Enfield's Redditch works by 1925.

1935 Royal Enfield B35, 248cc, side-valve single, 64 x 77mm bore and stroke, 3-speed gearbox, blade girder forks, rigid frame, tank-mounted instruments, fully restored.
£1,600–1,800 / €2,450–2,700 / $3,000–3,300 ⊞ BLM

1954 Royal Enfield Clipper, 248cc, overhead-valve single, 64 x 77mm bore and stroke, iron head and barrel, 11bhp at 5,500rpm, 4-speed Albion foot-change gearbox, telescopic forks, swinging-arm rear suspension.
£850–950 / €1,300–1,450 / $1,600–1,800 ⊞ BLM
The pre-unit Clipper ran from 1953 until 1957, when it was effectively replaced by the new unit-construction Crusader model.

1959 Royal Enfield Prince, 148cc, 2-stroke piston-port single, alloy head, cast-iron cylinder, 6.5:1 compression ratio, 7.5bhp, top speed 53mph.
£800–900 / €1,200–1,350 / $1,500–1,650 ⊞ MW
The Prince was the final development of the famous wartime Flying Flea design, which had been developed into the 148cc Ensign for 1952. The Prince ran from 1959 until the end of 1962. For the first time, an Enfield production two-stroke featured hydraulically-damped rear shocks (manufactured by Armstrong). This machine is fitted with an earlier tank badge.

1960 Royal Enfield 500 'Big Head' Bullet, 499cc, overhead-valve single, alloy head and barrel, Amal Monobloc carburettor, double-sided front brake, non-standard front mudguard, otherwise original, unrestored.
£2,350–2,600 / €3,500–3,900 / $4,400–4,850 ⊞ MW

1948 Royal Enfield Model G, 346cc, overhead-valve single, oil-bath primary chaincase, telescopic front forks, rigid frame, unrestored.
£1,500–1,800 / €2,250–2,700 / $2,800–3,350 ⋏ B(Kn)
Royal Enfield's range for 1946 comprised three related models: G, J and C/CO. The G and J were of 350cc and 500cc respectively, and used the same overhead-valve engine with different bore sizes, while the CO used the G motor and the C likewise, but with side, rather than overhead, valves. Models G and J had new telescopic front forks, whereas the C/CO retained the pre-war girders. All had cast-iron engine top-ends, plain big-end bearings, four-speed Albion gearboxes featuring Enfield's characteristic neutral selector lever, and rigid frames.

1955 Royal Enfield Bullet, 346cc, overhead-valve single, 70 x 90mm bore and stroke, alloy head, iron barrel, 4-speed Albion gearbox, double-sided front brake, telescopic forks, swinging-arm, fully restored.
£2,100–2,500 / €3,150–3,750 / $3,900–4,600 ⋏ BRIT
The Bullet designation was first used in 1930 and was befitting for a machine with a little extra performance from a company with the slogan 'made like a gun'. Post-war, the name was reinstated for a new single-cylinder machine. Introduced for 1949, the Bullet had been proven the previous year, a prototype having raised eyebrows on the trials scene by using rear suspension, the first post-war machine to be so equipped. The 350cc machine was made available in road, trials and scrambles forms, all essentially the same, but with different finishing kits. For 1954, the Bullet gained the distinctive cowl at the top of the forks with the trademark Enfield pilot lights at each top corner, and the following year a dualseat was added. With various revisions, the Bullet was to continue as a mainstay of the Royal Enfield line right through to the 1950s, and production has continued in India to this day.

1961 Royal Enfield Constellation, 692cc, overhead-valve vertical twin, semi-unit construction with separate cylinders and heads, 70 x 90mm bore and stroke, twin Amal Monobloc carburettors, 51bhp at 6,250rpm, top speed 112mph, excellent condition.
£4,050–4,500 / €6,100–6,700 / $7,500–8,300 ⊞ BLM

Rudge *(British 1911–40)*

1912 Rudge Multi, 499cc, inlet-over-exhaust vertical single, 85 x 88mm bore and stroke, variable gear ratios, totally original, unrestored.
£8,000–9,650 / €12,000–14,400 / $14,800–17,700 ⚒ CGC

Fully established as a manufacturer of bicycles, Rudge started to move towards the production of motorcycles in 1909. At the end of 1911, the majority of machines produced were only of single gear drive, but nevertheless were fitted with a clutch. For buyers in need of more flexibility of performance, the NSU two-speed gearbox was offered as an option, and one or two machines made use of the Mabon gear, although this was prone to premature wear. Quick to address the shortcomings of an otherwise fine machine, John Pugh developed a variable drive system that was to become a classic and remain in production for ten years, the Multi gear. Instantly recognisable by its long celluloid-covered lever, the Multi allowed gear ratios from 3½ : 1 to 7 : 1 by a series of infinitely small variations. Testing of the new gear took less than four months, and by February 1912 the first production models went on sale. The Multi soon became a staple model in the Rudge range, and by mid-summer 1912, roughly 60 machines a week were being produced, most of them Multis.

1937 Rudge Ulster, 499cc, semi-radial 4-valve single, twin-port head, 85 x 88mm bore and stroke, concours condition.
£5,400–6,400 / €8,100–9,700 / $9,900–11,900 ⊞ MW

1937 Rudge 500 Special, 493cc, pent-roof 4-valve single, twin-port head, 84.5 x 88mm bore and stroke, 4-speed foot-change gearbox, rigid frame, girder forks, unrestored.
£3,000–3,300 / €4,500–5,000 / $5,500–6,100 ⊞ NLM

The Special ran throughout the 1930s; until 1936. It had a 499cc (85 x 88mm bore and stroke) engine; from then until production ceased in 1939, it displaced 493cc.

1937 Rudge Special, 493cc, overhead-valve pent-roof 4-valve single, twin-port, 4-speed foot-change gearbox, restored.
£4,400–4,900 / €6,600–7,900 / $8,150–9,750 ⊞ BLM

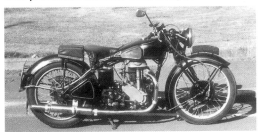

1938 Rudge Ulster 499cc, overhead-valve single, semi-radial 4-valve head, 4-speed foot-change gearbox, 8in coupled brakes, unrestored, missing logos on fuel tank.
£3,700–4,100 / €5,500–6,100 / $6,800–7,600 ⊞ PM

Rumi *(Italian 1949–early 1960s)*

◀ **1955 Rumi 125 Turismo,** 124cc, twin-cylinder 2-stroke, piston-port induction, 4-speed gearbox, telescopic forks, plunger frame.
£5,000–5,500 / €7,500–8,300 $9,200–10,200 ⊞ NLM

Donnino Rumi began trading just prior to the outbreak of WWI. During the 1920s, his company manufactured components and later complete machines for the textile industry. During WWII Rumi built two-men submarines and torpedos. In 1949, Rumi built its first motorcycle. A characteristic of its two-wheel vehicles was the 125 horizontal twin-cylinder two-stroke engine. This powered a range of high-quality lightweight motorcycles and scooters, production of which continued until the early 1960s.

Sanglas (Spanish 1942–82)

1980 Sanglas 500 S2, 497cc, overhead-valve unit-construction single, 89.5 x 79mm bore and stroke, 4-speed gearbox, cast-alloy wheels, triple Brembo disc brakes, electric start.
£1,450–1,600 / €2,150–2,400 / $2,700–3,000 ⊞ MW
Formed by Martin and Camps, Sanglas opened for business in 1942, and was based in Barcelona. The company's first motorcycle was a three-fifty overhead-valve twin-port single with a long-stroke (69 x 93mm) engine – very much like British bikes of the period. However, unlike the majority of British designs, the Sanglas featured unit construction. By the mid-1950s the range included a five-hundred engine (achieved by increasing the cylinder size to 82.5mm). Also, around the same time, the Spanish police began using the larger single. Nineteen-sixty saw a wider range of models, including smaller-capacity two-strokes. For the latter, British Villiers and German Zündapp engines were used, both built under licence in Spain, as were British Amal carburettors. During the 1970s came yet more models, including, in 1973, the 400E ('E' for electric starter), the first Sanglas to feature push-button starting. A new short-stroke five-hundred was developed from the four-hundred. At the end of 1979 came the first co-operation with Yamaha, resulting in the XS400-powered 400Y, but this proved very much a Trojan horse, Yamaha taking over Sanglas in 1982.

Scott (British 1909–late 1960s)

1911 Scott 2-Speed, 486cc, water-cooled twin-cylinder 2-stroke, 2-speed gearbox, chain drive, open frame.
£14,000–16,500 / €21,000–25,200 $25,900–31,000 ↗ B(Kn)
By 1911, Alfred Scott's original design had undergone a number of refinements. The handful of machines built by Jowett had been deemed under-powered, leading to an increase in engine capacity from 333cc to 450cc for the first of the Scott-built models. Soon after, the engine capacity was raised again, this time to 486cc. Water-cooling was adopted for both cylinder head and barrel – previously the latter had been air-cooled – together with a 'honeycomb' radiator of Scott's own design. Ever the innovator, Scott fitted a kickstart, the first time such a device has been used on a motorcycle. Lightweight, ample power and sure-footed handling, thanks to a low centre of gravity, were virtues of the Scott motorcycle right from the outset. Not surprisingly, it soon made a name for itself in the trials of the day, often with its inventor at the controls. In 1909, the marque made its first appearance at the Isle of Man TT. Ridden by works tester Eric Myers, the lone Scott was eliminated on lap seven when Myers fell. An inauspicious beginning to Scott's Isle of Man adventure, but greater times were just around the corner.

1930 Scott TT Replica, 596cc, liquid-cooled, twin-cylinder, piston-port.
£6,000–7,200 / €9,000–10,800 / $11,100–13,300 ✈ B(Kn)
One of the major changes at the Scott Engineering company in the 1920s was the introduction in 1926 of a new duplex frame in a long-wheelbase form, soon recognized by riders as a strong and stiff device. In 1928, a short-wheelbase version was introduced and, in 1929, the TT Replica commemorating a third place in the 1928 TT. The engine was a tuned long-stroke version of the Flying Squirrel's with much more power, and the chassis was fitted with Scott's own triangulated and externally damped taper-tube teleforks.

1921 Scott Standard Tourer, 532cc, water-cooled twin-cylinder 2-stroke, Scott teleforks, kickstarter, acetylene lighting, completely restored, excellent condition.
£7,800–9,400 / €11,700–14,100 / $14,400–17,300 ✈ B(Kn)
The Scott company was restructured in 1918 after the departure of Alfred Scott. The first machines left the new company's factory in 1919. The Standard Tourer, virtually unchanged from A. A. Scott's original design for 1914, was the mainstay of the company, producing smooth power through the two-speed gear and foot clutch.

◀ **1935 Scott Flying Squirrel,** 498cc, water-cooled twin-cylinder 2-stroke, foot-change gearbox, duplex girder front forks, fully triangulated frame, concours condition.
£5,800–6,500 / €8,700–9,600
$10,700–11,800 ⊞ VER

Seeley *(British 1966–78)*

A known continuous history can add value to and enhance the enjoyment of a motorcycle.

▶ **1976 Seeley Dixon Honda,** 820cc, overhead camshaft across-the-frame four cylinder, 5-speed gearbox, twin-disc front brakes, single-disc rear brake, 4-into-1 exhaust.
£2,300–2,600 / €3,450–3,800 / $4,250–4,700 ⊞ MW
This machine is a big-bore version of the overhead-camshaft Honda CB750 with Seeley body parts, built in conjunction with Dixon Racing.

Sparkbrook *(British 1912–25)*

◀ **c1922 Sparkbrook,** 247cc, Villiers single-cylinder 2-stroke engine, belt final drive, older restoration.
£1,150–1,400 / €1,700–2,050
$2,100–2,550 ✈ CGC
Manufacturing motorcycles between 1912 and 1925, Sparkbrook moved post-WWI from large-capacity JAP V-twins to Villiers two-stroke engines of 247, 269 and 346cc, as well as 346cc side-valve JAP and sleeve-valve Barr and Stroud units.

Sunbeam *(British 1912–57)*

◀ **1927 Sunbeam Model 1,** 346cc, side-valve single, 70 x 90mm bore and stroke, hand-change gearbox, fully-enclosed final drive chain, footboards, very original.
£4,900–5,500 / € 7,300–8,100
$9,100–10,100 ⊞ VER
This was the last year before Sunbeam was sold to ICI in 1928. Many consider that the previous industry-leading quality began to lower its standards thereafter.

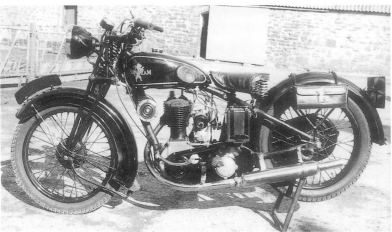

1930 Sunbeam Lion, 489cc, side-valve single, cast-iron head and barrel, 77 x 105mm bore and stroke, all-chain drive, rear chaincase, girder forks, rigid frame, electric lighting, original, unrestored.
£3,750–4,200 / € 5,600–6,200 / $6,900–7,600 ⊞ MW
The Lion ran until the end of 1937, when it was replaced by the A29.

1932 Sunbeam Model 9, 493cc, overhead-valve single, twin-port iron head, iron barrel, girder forks, rigid frame, oil-bath chaincase, magdyno, electric lighting, original, unrestored.
£3,600–4,000 / € 5,400–6,000 / $6,700–7,400 ⚙ CMT
The Model 9 was produced throughout most of the 1930s, until replaced by the A27 for 1938.

◀ **1936 Sunbeam Model 6 Lion,** 489cc, side-valve single, alloy head, iron barrel, saddle tank, girder forks, rigid frame, hand-change gearbox, oil-bath chaincases.
£3,800–4,550 / € 5,700–6,800 / $7,000–8,400 ⚒ B(Kn)
Sunbeam's famous 'longstroke' side-valve engine first appeared at the 1921 French Grand Prix, scoring a debut win in the hands of Alec Bennett; in road-going form, this remarkable engine remained in production right up until WWII. A version of it powered the new-for-1931 Model 6 Lion. Introduced in the summer of 1930, the revamped Lion replaced the old Model 6 and featured innovations – for Sunbeam – such as a chrome-plated fuel tank and Webb-pattern girder forks.

1938 Sunbeam Model 8, 346cc, overhead-valve single, 70 x 90mm bore and stroke, 4-speed foot-change gearbox, central-spring girder forks, rigid frame, fully restored to original specification.
£3,100–3,700 / €4,650–5,500 / $5,700–6,800 ⚒ B(Kn)

1939 Sunbeam B24, 348cc, overhead-valve single, 69 x 93mm bore and stroke, dry-sump lubrication, 4-speed foot-change gearbox, girder front forks, rigid frame.
£3,350–3,750 / €5,000–5,500 / $6,200–6,900 ⊞ BLM
AMC took over Sunbeam in late 1937, and the B24 was one of a series of new engines. It employed chain drive for its high-camshaft.

◀ **1950 Sunbeam S8,** 489cc, overhead-camshaft inline twin, 70 x 63.5mm bore and stroke, 4-speed foot-change gearbox, shaft final drive, fully restored 1991.
£2,300–2,750 / €3,500–4,200 $4,250–5,100 ⚒ CGC

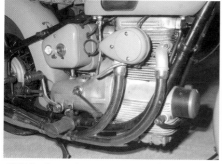

1953 Sunbeam S7, 487cc, overhead-camshaft inline twin, 25bhp, 4-speed foot-change gearbox, shaft final drive, 43.5lb (197kg), top speed 72mph.
£2,250–2,500 / €3,350–3,700 / $4,150–4,650 ⚙ T&DC
The Sunbeam name was purchased from AMC by BSA in 1943. The first new model under the new regime was the radical Erling Poppe-designed S7.

Suzuki (Japanese 1952–)

1961 Suzuki TA250, 246cc, 2-stroke twin, 52 x 58mm bore and stroke, 4-speed gearbox, pressed-steel frame, leading-link front forks, 16in wheels, 7in full-width brake drums, concours condition.
£3,000–3,300 / €4,500–4,950 / $5,550–6,100 ⊞ MW
Now extremely rare, this model was never officially imported into the UK.

◀ **1963 Suzuki T10,** 247cc, 2-stroke twin, piston-port induction, 52 x 58mm bore and stroke, 4-speed gearbox, fully-enclosed final drive chain, electric start, hydraulic rear brake, 17in wheels, top speed 80mph, concours condition.
£3,000–3,300 / €4,500–4,950 $5,500–6,100 ⊞ MW
The T10 was a luxury touring mount and is much rarer than the T20 Super Six sportster that followed.

1972 Suzuki GT550J, 544cc, 2-stroke triple, 50bhp at 6,500rpm, piston-port induction, 61 x 62mm bore and stroke, early model with drum front brake, electric start.
£2,500–2,750 / €3,750–4,150 / $4,600–5,100 ⊕ VJMC
The GT550 series ran from 1972 until 1977.

1976 Suzuki GT380A, 371cc, across-the-frame triple, 54 x 54mm bore and stroke, pump lubrication, 6-speed gearbox, kickstart, disc front and drum rear brakes.
£900–1,000 / €1,350–1,500 / $1,650–1,850 ⊞ MW

1977 Suzuki GT250, 247cc, 2-stroke twin, 54 x 54mm bore and stroke, ram air-cooling, 6-speed gearbox, disc front and drum rear brakes, duplex cradle frame, original, unrestored.
£630–700 / €950–1,050 / $1,150–1,300 ⊞ MW
The GT250 ran from the beginning of 1973 through to the end of 1978, bridging the old T250 and the new X7.

1977 Suzuki TS185, 185cc, 2-stroke single, 64 x 57mm bore and stroke, 17.5bhp at 7,000rpm, pump lubrication, 5-speed gearbox, 19in front/18in rear wheels, drum brakes, only 163 miles recorded, original 'as new' condition.
£630–700 / €950–1,050 / $1,150–1,300 ⊞ MW

1980 Suzuki TS50 ER, 49cc, 2-stroke single, 41 x 37.8mm bore and stroke, 5-speed gearbox, pump lubrication, telescopic front forks, swinging-arm rear suspension, fully restored, concours condition.
£360–400 / €540–600 / $660–730 ⊞ MW

▶ **1984 Suzuki XN85 Turbo,** 650cc, turbocharged double-overhead-camshaft across-the-frame four, 85bhp, anti-dive front forks, monoshock rear suspension, cast-alloy wheels, triple disc brakes, top speed 138mph.
£1,050–1,200
€1,500–1,650
$1,950–2,150
⊞ MW

1985 Suzuki GP125, 125cc, 2-stroke single, pump lubrication, 12bhp, 5-speed gearbox, disc front and drum rear brakes, 70mph, concours condition.
£500–550 / €750–830 / $930–1,050 ⊞ MW
The GP125 ran from the late 1970s until the mid-1980s. It was surprisingly powerful and comfortable for such a small bike.

1987 Suzuki Savage, 650cc, overhead-camshaft single, alloy head and barrel, unit construction, 5-speed gearbox, belt final drive, disc front and drum rear brakes, 19in front wheel, 16in rear wheel, 'King & Queen' seat, rear grab rail, electric start, tank-mounted speedometer.
£850–950 / €1,250–1,400 / $1,550–1,750 ⊞ MW

1992 Suzuki GS500, 498cc, double-overhead-camshaft twin, 6-speed gearbox, chain final drive, front and rear disc brakes, monoshock rear suspension, full cradle frame.
£450–500 / €670–740 / $830–920 ⊞ NLM

SWM *(Italian 1971–85)*

◀ **1981 SWM 315GTS,** 315cc, 2-stroke single, 5-speed gearbox, conical brake hubs, twin rear suspension shock absorbers, telescopic front forks with gaiters, indicators, rear carrier, original, unrestored.
£900–1,000 / €1,350–1,500
$1,650–1,850 ⊞ NLM
SWM (Speedy Working Motors) was one of the success stories of the 1970s Italian motorcycle industry. In the 1980s, however, its fortunes waned and it closed in 1985.

Terrot *(French 1901–early 1960s)*

◀ **1956 Terrot 47,** 124cc, overhead-valve single, unit construction, iron barrel, alloy head, dry-sump lubrication, telescopic front forks, rigid frame, front crashbars.
£1,600–1,900 / €2,400–2,850 / $2,950–3,500 ⊞ MW

Triumph *(British 1902–)*

c1907 Triumph 3½hp, 453cc, side-valve vertical single, 82 x 86mm bore and stroke, total-loss lubrication, restored.
£6,900–8,250 / €10,350–12,400 / $12,800–15,300 ⚒ B(Kn)
The 3½hp appeared in 1907. Originally of 453cc, the engine was enlarged to 476cc in 1908 and to 499cc in 1910, before being superseded by the 4hp model in 1914. Magneto ignition and lighting equipment were listed as cost options.

1914 Triumph 4hp, 550cc, side-valve single, Bosch magneto, belt drive, 3-speed hand-change hub, caliper rear brake, rear carrier, unrestored.
£5,200–6,200 / €7,800–9,300 / $9,600–11,500 ⚒ CGC
During WWI, the 4hp became the Model H, and some 30,000 were supplied to the Allied forces. It was so successful that it earned the nickname 'Trusty Triumph', which stuck for years.

◀ **1922 Triumph LW Junior,** 225cc, 2-stroke single, magneto ignition, outside flywheel, sprung forks, rigid frame, belt final drive, acetylene lighting, original, excellent condition.
£4,000–4,400
€6,000–6,600
$7,400–8,200
⚙ WCMC

▶ **1922 Triumph Type IR Ricardo,** 498cc, overhead-valve single, 4-valve head, magneto, hand gear-change, chain drive, caliper rear brake, block front brake, kickstart.
£8,100–9,000 / €12,150–13,400
$15,000–16,500 ⊞ VER
The Triumph factory entered six machines for the 1921 Senior TT. The top halves of their engine sported four-valves and had been designed by Harry Ricardo; consequently the design was soon nicknamed the 'Ricky'. Although the TT result were disappointing, after more development the Type IR became a success, both on the circuit (second in the 1922 TT) and in the showroom.

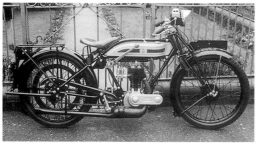

◄ **1926 Triumph Model P MkII,** 494cc, side-valve single, magneto ignition, hand-change gearbox, all-chain drive, drum front/caliper rear brake, fully restored, concours condition.
£4,500–5,000 / €6,750–7,500 / $8,300–9,200 ⊞ VER
The original Model P was introduced for the amazingly low price of £42.17s.6d at the 1924 London Olympia show. This made it a top seller the following year, but cost cutting produced a crop of problems, including poor brakes, clutch and big-end bearing. However, a Mark II version was built, which did a great deal to restore Triumph's reputation.

► **1934 Triumph Model XO5,** 148cc, overhead-valve single with inclined cylinder, horizontal cooling fins, 56.6 x 59mm bore and stroke, 3-speed hand-change gearbox, duplex frame, drum brakes, largely original.
£2,450–2,750 / €3,700–4,100
$4,500–4,950 ⊞ VER
The XO series began for the 1933 season. It was designed to fall within a low-cost tax class. For 1934, it became the XO5/1 in standard guise, and the XO5/5 when fitted with a four-speed gearbox. The /5 suffix indicated a sports model with a tuned engine.

◄ **1934 Triumph XV/1,** 148cc, Villiers 2-stroke single-cylinder engine, 3-speed hand-change gearbox, all-chain drive, drum brakes, largely original, unrestored.
£850–990 / €1,250–1,500
$1,600–1,900 ⚒ PS
This model ran for only one year and is now quite rare.

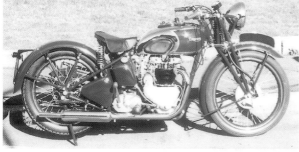

► **1935 Triumph 6/1,** 647cc, vertical twin, 70 x 84mm bore and stroke, hand-change gearbox, magdyno, dry-sump lubrication with oil tank built into crankcase, double-helical-gear primary drive, chain final drive, restored to original specification, concours condition.
£10,800–12,000 / €16,200–17,800
$20,000–22,000 ⊞ CotC
The 6/1 was Triumph's first parallel twin and was designed by Val Page. The overhead valves were operated by a single gear-driven camshaft mounted at the rear of the crankcase.

◄ **1938 Triumph Speed Twin,** 498cc, overhead-valve vertical twin, 63 x 80mm bore and stroke, dry-sump lubrication, magdyno, single Amal carburettor, rigid frame, girder forks, concours condition.
£6,000–6,600 / €9,000–9,900
$11,100–12,100 ⊞ PM
The 1938 Speed Twin, designed by Edward Turner, altered the course of motorcycle engineering history. It was a masterpiece of 'compact power', as Triumph's PR chief, Ivor Davies, described it in his book *Triumph – The Complete Story.*

TRIUMPH Model	ENGINE cc/cyl	DATES	CONDITION		
			1	2	3
T15 Terrier	149/1	1953–56	£900	£600	£250
T20 Tiger Cub	199/1	1954–65	£1,100	£800	£400
5T Speed Twin	499/2	1937–39	£6,000	£4,000	£2,600
6T Thunderbird	649/2	1949–54	£3,600	£2,200	£1,800
3TA Twenty-One	349/2	1957–66	£2,600	£1,800	£1,200
5TA Speed Twin	490/2	1958–66	£2,800	£1,800	£1,200
T120 Bonneville	649/2	1958–62	£7,000+	£4,000	£3,000

1938 Triumph Tiger 80, 343cc, overhead-valve vertical single, 70 x 89mm bore and stroke, dry-sump lubrication, 4-speed foot-change gearbox, girder forks, rigid frame, fully restored, concours condition.
£4,500–4,950 / €6,700–7,500 / $8,300–9,200 ⚙ **EWC**
The Tiger 80 was offered in the period 1936 to 1940, and proved a popular machine, thanks to its combination of sparkling performance, smart appearance and the Triumph name.

Miller's
Motorcycle Milestones

Triumph Speed Twin 499cc pre-unit (1937–58)
490cc unit-construction (1959–65)
Price Range: Pre-unit £2,500–6,000 / €3,750–9,000 / $4,600–11,100
Unit £1,800–3,000 / €2,700–4,500 / $3,300–5,500
Although he was responsible for many other designs, Edward Turner's real masterpiece was the Speed Twin, which he penned shortly after he joined Triumph as chief designer in 1936. The machine would prove a real trend-setter, reshaping motorcycle design in the decades that followed.

Over 20 years earlier, WWI had dashed Triumph's hopes of constructing its first parallel twin, a 600 side-valve job. The company's second effort, designed by Val Page, failed to sell in any real quantity. Debuting in 1932, it featured a semi-unit-construction, overhead-valve 647cc engine with a one-piece crankshaft, which ran backwards and a four-speed gearbox with dual helical primary-drive gears. Its robustness was proved by Harry Perrey, who used an example to win a sidecar gold medal in the 1933 ISDT. Its weaknesses were its bulk and the cost of production, which conspired to kill it off after a mere 40 had been built. Turner joined Triumph from Ariel, where he had penned the Square Four. On moving to Triumph, he set about designing a parallel twin. His initial

idea had been for an overhead-camshaft engine, but this was abandoned in favour of a more basic pushrod unit. The latter had the same bore and stroke dimensions (63 x 80mm) as Triumph's contemporary 250 single, thus maximizing production facilities.

An iron cylinder head and barrel were specified, the latter with a six-stud base flange, which was changed to an eight-stud arrangement in 1939 after some had cracked. In prototype guise, the engine developed 30bhp, while the early production versions, built in 1937, gave 3–4bhp less, but this was still enough to reach 90mph. Compared to rival single-cylinder bikes of the period, the Speed Twin was a superb piece of kit, being flexible, quicker and easier to start. Triumph had really struck gold.

The Speed Twin continued after the war, the most notable changes being telescopic front forks, rear suspension (at first, Triumph's patented sprung hub and later swinging arm) and improved electrics.

Then, as the 1950s neared their end, came the brand-new 5TA version with unit-construction engine and 'bathtub' rear enclosure. This machine was essentially a larger-engined version of the 350 3TA Twenty One.
Production of the 5TA continued until the mid-1960s.

1946 Triumph Speed Twin, 498cc, overhead-valve vertical twin, 4-speed foot-change gearbox, handlebar-mounted speedometer, rest of switches/instruments on tank, restored.
£4,500–4,950 / €6,700–7,500 / $8,300–9,200 ⊞ **CotC**
This is an example of the first post-war Speed Twin models with telescopic front forks and rigid frame.

Cross Reference
See Colour Review (pages 122–125)

1947 Triumph 3T, 349cc, overhead-valve vertical twin, 55 x 73.4mm bore and stroke, 19bhp at 6,500 rpm, 4-speed foot-change gearbox, telescopic forks, rigid frame.
£2,500–3,000 / €3,750–4,500 / $4,600–5,500 🔧 **B(Kn)**
Triumph's first 350cc vertical twin was built for military purposes in wartime and would form the basis for a civilian version when hostilities ceased. The basic engine design followed that laid down pre-war by Edward Turner for the trend-setting Speed Twin, but featured rocker boxes incorporated into the cylinder-head casting and a built-up crankshaft with one-piece connecting rods, like the military 3TW. The running gear was essentially that of the Speed Twin and featured Triumph's new telescopic front forks.

1953 Triumph Tiger 100C, 499cc, overhead-valve vertical twin, 63 x 80mm bore and stroke, close-fin alloy head and barrel, 40bhp at 7,000rpm, sprung hub, telescopic forks, 19in wheels, top speed 112mph.
£4,500–5,000 / €6,800–7,500 / $8,300–9,200 ⚙ **EWC**
The T100C only ran for 1953, replacing the separate race kit that owners could bolt on to their existing T100s. It came with all the goodies, including twin carburettors, race cams and a large-capacity oil tank.

1955 Triumph 6T Thunderbird, 649cc, overhead-valve pre-unit twin, iron head and barrel, 4-speed foot-change gearbox, single-sided brakes, headlamp nacelle, tank-top parcel grid, original, unrestored.
£3,400–4,100 / €5,100–6,100 / $6,300–7,500 🔧 **CGC**
The 6T Thunderbird was given the swinging-arm frame for the 1955 model year.

c1957 Triumph Tiger 110, 649cc, overhead-valve pre-unit parallel twin, single carburettor, alloy head, 4-speed foot-change gearbox, swinging-arm frame, 8in ventilated front brake, headlamp nacelle, tank-top grid, restored.
£3,900–4,400 / €5,800–6,400 / $7,200–8,000 ⊞ **BLM**
The Tiger 110 was Triumph's top-of-the-range sportster until the Bonneville arrived.

1959 Triumph Tiger Cub, 199cc, overhead-valve unit single, 63 x 64mm bore and stroke, 7:1 compression ratio, 10bhp, distributor, dry-sump lubrication, 4-speed gearbox, 16in wheels, top speed 65mph, original, very good condition.
£1,250–1,400 / €1,900–2,100 / $2,350–2,600 ⊞ **CotC**

1954 Triumph Tiger 100, 498cc, overhead-valve pre-unit twin, 63 x 80mm bore and stroke, close-fin alloy head and barrel, single carburettor, sprung hub, telescopic forks, dualseat, concours condition.
£3,800–4,600 / €5,700–6,300 / $7,000–7,700 ⊞ **PM**

1955 Triumph TR5, 499cc, overhead-valve vertical twin, 63 x 80mm bore and stroke, siamesed exhaust, 33bhp, 4-speed foot-change gearbox, knobbly tyres.
£3,600–4,000 / €5,400–6,000 / $6,650–7,350 ⚙ **CMT**
The swinging-arm-framed TR5 arrived in 1955 and was fitted with the all-alloy Tiger 100-type engine, but with 'softer' cams.

1959 Triumph 3TA, 349cc, overhead-valve unit twin, 58.25 x 65.5mm bore and stroke, single carburettor, alloy head, cast-iron barrel, distributor, 18.5bhp at 6,500rpm.
£2,000–2,250 / €3,000–3,300 / $3,700–4,100 ⊞ **BLM**
This 3TA has been given the 'Bonneville' treatment. Although nicely done, it's still 350!

1959 Triumph 5TA Speed Twin, 490cc, overhead-valve unit twin, 69 x 65.5mm bore and stroke, alloy head, iron barrel, distributor, 17in wheels, full rear enclosure, unrestored, good condition.
£2,800–3,200 / €4,200–4,700 / $5,200–5,800 ⊞ **BLM**
The new unit-construction Speed Twin arrived for 1959 and essentially was a larger-displacement 3TA Twenty-One.

1960 Triumph T120 Bonneville, 649cc, overhead-valve pre-unit twin, 71 x 82mm bore and stroke, dry-sump lubrication, 4-speed foot-change gearbox.
£6,200–7,400 / €9,300–11,100 / $11,500–13,800 ✗ CGC
Launched in 1958 amid claims from Triumph that it would offer 'the highest performance available from a standard production motorcycle', the T120 Bonneville created a furore. No doubt helped by the fact that its name recalled Johnny Allen's 1956 AMA Land Speed Record run of 214.4mph in a Triumph streamliner at the Bonneville Salt Flats. Initially inspired by demand from the US market, it was based on the successful Tiger 110, its performance advantage coming from splayed inlet ports, a single-piece camshaft and twin Amal carburettors. Producing 47bhp at 6,500rpm, its 649cc twin-cylinder engine drove through a four-speed gearbox and was capable of propelling the swinging-arm-framed machine to over 110mph. Its speed, light weight and good handling helped it to become arguably Britain's best-loved big twin and one of the world's most famous motorcycles. Initially sold with a pearl grey and tangerine colour scheme, bulbous headlamp nacelle and heavily-valanced mudguards, the Bonneville was less of a sales success than expected. Thus, late in 1959, the tangerine gave way to royal blue, slimmer mudguards and a chromed bullet headlamp were adopted for 1960.

◄ **1960 Triumph Speed Twin,** 490cc, overhead-valve unit twin, alloy head, iron barrel, distributor, 4-speed foot-change gearbox.
£1,850–2,200 / €2,800–3,350 / $3,400–4,000 ✗ B(Kn)
Introduced in September 1958, the 5TA Speed Twin was the second of Triumph's new family of unit-construction vertical twins, joining the 350cc Twenty One/3TA launched the previous year. The 500 closely followed the lines of its 350 predecessor, there being little to distinguish it mechanically apart from a larger bore, raised gearing and larger-section rear tyre. The 'bathtub' rear enclosure introduced on the Twenty One was retained and the Speed Twin was finished in the model's traditional Amaranth Red. In use until recently, this well presented 5TA Speed Twin is fitted with Craven-type rear carrier and 'bar-end' mirror.

1960 Triumph Tiger 100A, 490cc, overhead-valve unit twin, 69 x 65.5mm bore and stroke, single Amal monobloc carburettor, distributor, alloy head, iron barrel, 32bhp at 7,000rpm, twin exhausts, 7in brakes, swinging-arm frame, telescopic front forks, original, excellent condition.
£3,150–3,500 / €4,700–5,200 / $5,800–6,400 ⊶ WMC

► **1961 Triumph T20 Tiger Cub,** 199cc, overhead-valve unit single, 63 x 64mm bore and stroke, 7:1 compression ratio, distributor, swinging-arm frame, headlamp nacelle.
£1,350–1,500 / €2,000–2,200 / $2,500–2,750 ⊞ BLM
With many Cubs being converted to Trials Cub Replicas, bikes in original condition like this example are rare.

A known continuous history can add value to and enhance the enjoyment of a motorcycle.

◀ **1963 Triumph 6T Thunderbird,** 649cc, overhead-valve unit twin, 71 x 82mm bore and stroke, 34bhp at 6,300rpm, duplex primary chain, 18in wheels, 8in front and 7in rear brakes, concours condition.
£4,000–4,400 / €6,000–6,600 $7,400–8,200 ♙ B(Kn)

1963 Triumph Tiger 90, 349cc, overhead-valve unit twin, 58.25 x 65.5mm bore and stroke, 9:1 compression ratio, 27bhp at 7,500rpm, duplex primary chain, points in timing cover, 18in wheels, 7in brakes, top speed 94mph.
£3,000–3,300 / €4,500–5,000 / $5,500–6,100 ⊞ BLM

1964 Triumph T100SS, 490cc, separate exhausts, fitted optional rev-counter.
£1,900–2,250 / €2,850–3,400 / $3,500–4,200 ♙ B(Kn)
Introduced for 1962, the Tiger 100SS replaced the T100A as Triumph's sports 500 twin. A comprehensive restyle saw the 'bathtub' rear enclosure of its predecessor replaced by an abbreviated version, while the headlamp nacelle gave way to a separate chromed shell. Sports mudguards were fitted, wheel sizes were increased, and the engine gained a few more horsepower courtesy of redesigned camshafts and a siamesed exhaust system. Top speed was now within a whisker of 100mph.

1966 Triumph 3TA Twenty-One, 349cc, overhead-valve unit twin, single Amal Monobloc carburettor, points in timing cover, 18in wheels, headlamp nacelle, 12 volt electrics, original specification.
£2,650–2,950 / €4,000–4,400 / $4,900–5,400 ⊞ BLM
Production of the 3TA was discontinued in July 1966 together with the 5TA and 6T.

1967 Triumph T120R Bonneville, 649cc, overhead-valve vertical twin, twin carburettors, 4-speed foot-change gearbox, 8in front brake, separate exhausts, export model with high handlebars and smaller capacity fuel tank.
£4,300-4,800 / €6,500–7,200 / $8,000–8,800 ⊞ BLM

1967 Triumph T100T, 490cc, overhead-valve unit twin, twin Amal 376 Monobloc carburettors, 39bhp at 7,400rpm, twin-leading-shoe front brake, in need of chromework and aluminium attention.
£1,800–2,000 / €2,700–3,000 / $3,350–3,700 ⊞ BLM

▶ **1968 Triumph T120 Bonneville,** 649cc, overhead-valve unit twin, 71 x 82mm bore and stroke, twin Amal Concentric carburettors, twin-leading-shoe front brake, matching speedometer and rev-counter.
£4,300–4,800 / €6,500–7,200 / $8,000–8,800 ⊞ BLM

1969 Triumph T100T Daytona, 490cc, overhead-valve unit twin, 69 x 65.5mm bore and stroke, twin Amal Concentric carbs, twin-leading-shoe front brake, unrestored, in need of some attention.
£2,500–3,000 / €3,750–4,500 / $4,600–5,500 ⚒ B(Kn)
Triumph revamped their motorcycle range in November 1967 with the launch of the new super sports 500cc twin, the Daytona Tiger. Coded the T100T, the new bike was race bred from the laurels-winning bike at Daytona that year. Its twin-carburettored engine was to an all-new design and mounted in an all-new frame with a slightly lower seat height. In standard form the Daytona Tiger developed 39bhp at 7,400rpm and retailed at £345 / €520 / $640 in 1969, a price soon to be challenged by the influx of Japanese machinery.

▶ **1969 Triumph T150 Trident,** 740cc, overhead-valve across-the-frame triple, 67 x 70mm bore and stroke, 4-speed foot-change gearbox, several non-standard parts, including 3-into-1 exhaust, in need of attention.
£1,700–2,000 / €2,500–3,000 / $3,150–3,750 ⚒ B(Kn)

1969 Triumph T100C, 490cc, overhead-valve unit twin, 4-speed foot-change gearbox, upswept exhausts, single Amal Concentric carburettor, side and centre stands, restored in 1997.
£3,500–4,200 / €5,250–6,300 / $6,500–7,800 ⚒ B(Kn)
American street scrambler export model.

◀ **1970 Triumph T120R Bonneville,** 649cc, overhead-valve vertical twin, twin carburettors, twin-leading-shoe front brake, fully restored in 2002.
£11,500–13,800 / €17,200–20,700 $21,300–25,500 ⚒ BB(L)
This machine is a US-market export model. Nineteen-seventy was the last year of production before the introduction of the infamous Umberslade Hall oil-in-frame model.

▶ **1970 Triumph TR6 Trophy,** 649cc, overhead-valve unit twin, single Amal Concentric carburettor, 4-speed gearbox, twin-leading-shoe front brake, rev-counter, fully restored, concours condition.
£4,800–5,400 / €7,200–8,000 / $8,900–9,700 ⊞ BLM
Many riders prefer the smoother performance Trophy than its twin-carb, hot-shot brother, the Bonneville.

1971 Triumph TR25SS Blazer, 247cc, overhead-valve single, 67 x 70mm bore and stroke, 10:1 compression, 22.5bhp at 8,250rpm, 8in twin-leading-shoe front brake, 7in rear brake, top speed 80mph.
£1,300–1,600 / €2,000–2,200 / $2,400–2,700 ⚒ CGC
The TR25SS was only offered in 1970 and 1971. It came at the time of Triumph's problems as part of the doomed BSA Group.

1971 Triumph TR6C Trophy, 649cc, overhead-valve unit twin, 4-speed gearbox, fork gaiters, conical hubs, side and centre stands, high-level exhaust, high bars, excellent condition.
£3,500–3,900 / €5,250–5,800 / $6,500–7,200 ⊞ BLM

1972 Triumph Tiger, 649cc, overhead-valve unit twin, single Amal Concentric carburettor, disc front brake, drum rear brake, export model with small tank and high bars, unrestored.
£2,400–2,700 / €3,600–4,000 / $4,450–4,900 ⊞ BLM

1974 Triumph T150 Trident, 740cc, overhead-valve vertical twin, 4-speed gearbox, disc front and drum rear brakes, conical hub, kickstart, original specification apart from Burgess-type silencers and headlamp peak, export model.
£3,150–3,500 / €4,700–5,200 / $5,800–6,400 ⊞ BLM

1975 Triumph T160 Trident, 740cc, overhead-valve across-the-frame triple, 5-speed gearbox, left-hand gear-change, electric start, indicators, only 4,000 miles recorded, excellent condition.
£4,100–4,600 / €6,100–6,800 / $7,600–8,400 ⊞ BLM

1979 Triumph T140 Bonneville, 744cc, overhead-valve unit twin, 5-speed gearbox with left-hand gear-change, front and rear disc brakes, in need of attention.
£1,100–1,300 / €1,650–1,950 / $2,000–2,400 ⚒ PS

1978 Triumph T140V Bonneville, 744cc, updated with 3-phase electrics, stainless steel rear wheel rim, new mudguard and Avon Roadrunner II tyres, otherwise unrestored.
£1,600–1,900 / €2,400–2,850 / $3,000–3,600 ⚒ B(Kn)
The final phase of Triumph twin development began in 1972 with the appearance of the new 750cc version of the Bonneville, the increase in bore size necessitating a new crankcase to accommodate the larger barrel. Other improvements included a ten-stud cylinder head, triple primary chain, stronger transmission and disc front brake. A five-speed gearbox, introduced on the preceding six-fifty Bonneville, was standard equipment. Despite the age of the basic design, and strong competition from Japanese and European manufacturers, the Bonnie remained for many years the UK's top-selling seven-fifty and was voted *Motor Cycle News* 'Machine of the Year' in 1979.

1981 Triumph Thunderbird 650, 649cc, overhead-valve vertical twin, 76 x 71.5mm bore and stroke, single carburettor, 5-speed gearbox, disc front and drum rear brakes.
£2,000–2,500 / €3,000–3,300 / $3,700–4,100 ⊞ BLM
This machine was one of the last models to come from the Meriden Workers' Co-operative.

Velocette *(British 1904–68)*

1923 Velocette G3, 249cc, 2-stroke single, mechanical oil pump, twin-port exhaust, clutch, 3-speed hand-change gearbox, drum brakes.
£2,250–2,500 / €3,350–3,750 / $4,150–4,600 ⚙ **Velo**

c1933 Velocette KSS MkI, 349cc, overhead-camshaft vertical single, iron cylinder head, exposed valve gear, foot-change gearbox, drum brakes.
£2,800–3,350 / €4,200–5,000 / $5,200–6,200 ➤ **B(Kn)**
Introduced in 1925, the KSS was the 'super sports' version of Velocette's first post-WWI four-stroke, the overhead-camshaft Model K. The work of Percy Goodman, the Model K, with its shaft-and-bevel drive to the 'upstairs' cam was ahead of its time and would prove extremely influential. It was a superb high-performance motorcycle that established the marque's sporting reputation almost overnight. Along with the other K models, the 80mph KSS was offered with the revolutionary positive-stop, foot-controlled gear-change from 1929. Introduced for the 1936 season, the MkII KSS represented a major redesign of the roadster overhead-camshaft single. It featured many improvements, including a new aluminium cylinder head with enclosed valve gear (which replaced the old cast-iron head with exposed springs), and the cradle frame and heavyweight Webb forks of the new MSS.

1954 Velocette MSS, 499cc, overhead-valve single, 86 x 86mm bore and stroke, 4-speed foot-change gearbox, telescopic forks, swinging-arm frame, original specification, excellent condition.
£3,000–3,300 / €4,500–5,000 / $5,500–6,100 ⊞ **CotC**

◀ **1936 Velocette KSS MkII,** 349cc, overhead-camshaft single, alloy cylinder head, 74 x 81mm bore and stroke, 4-speed foot-change gearbox.
£5,000–6,000 / €7,500–9,000 / $9,200–11,100 ➤ **B(Kn)**

1936 Velocette KTS, 349cc, overhead-camshaft single, 74 x 81mm bore and stroke, original, unrestored.
£4,000–4,400 / €6,000–6,600 / $7,400–8,200 ⊞ **CotC**

◀ **1938 Velocette MOV,** 248cc, overhead-valve single, 68 x 68.25mm bore and stroke, 4-speed foot-change gearbox, older restoration, 1 owner for 33 years.
£2,000–2,250 / €3,000–3,350 / $3,700–4,150 ⚙ **Velo**
The MOV was introduced for the 1933 season, and soon became popular with both road riders and racers.

▶ **1939 Velocette KTS,** 349cc, overhead-camshaft single, 74 x 81mm bore and stroke, 4-speed foot-change gearbox, spring girder forks, rigid frame, original, unrestored.
£5,600–6,300 / €8,400–9,400 $10,300–11,400 ⊞ **VER**

◀ **1946 Velocette MAC,** 349cc, overhead-valve single, 68 x 96mm bore and stroke, 4-speed foot-change gearbox, iron head and barrel.
£2,400–2,800 / €3,600–4,300 $4,400–5,200 ⚡ B(Kn)
Developed from the pre-war MOV 250, the MAC proved popular until the three-fifty size was dropped by the company. This is a very early post-WWII machine, effectively to pre-war specification, with Webb girder forks and the 'kipper' silencer. Dowty AV telescopic forks were to be introduced in 1948.

1954 Velocette MSS, 499cc, overhead-valve single, 4-speed foot-change gearbox, telescopic forks, swinging-arm rear suspension, dualseat, unused for a number of years and museum displayed.
£1,500–1,800 / €2,250–2,700 / $2,800–3,350 ⚡ PS

1956 Velocette MAC, 349cc, overhead-valve single, 4-speed foot-change gearbox, correct stepped seat, original, excellent condition.
£2,300–2,700 / €3,500–4,200 / $4,250–5,100 ⚡ CGC
First introduced in 1933, the MAC model line soon became a mainstay of Velocette production. Subjected to continual modification and improvement, it was relaunched in civilian guise following WWII. Updated with Velocette-designed telescopic forks (1951), a new cylinder head (1952) and swinging-arm rear suspension (1953), it developed a reputation as a charming bike with good steering and enviable reliability. Performance was a strong point, too, its 349cc, overhead-valve single-cylinder engine giving a near 80mph top speed.

1956 Velocette Venom, 499cc, Thruxton-type swept-back exhaust pipe, non-standard paintwork to tank.
£3,700-4,100 / €5,500–6,100 / $6,800–7,500 ⊞ BLM
The Venom and smaller-engined Viper were the high-performance sports models of the Velocette range, each having a 7½in front brake, full-width hubs and a deep headlamp shell that carried the instruments in its top surface.

▶ **c1958 Velocette Venom,** 499cc, overhead-valve single, 86 x 86mm bore and stroke, 4-speed foot-change gearbox, chrome mudguards, tank and Thruxton-type swept-back exhaust pipe.
£3,800–4,300 / €5,700–6,800 / $7,000–8,400 ⚡ B(Kn)

1959 Velocette MAC, 349cc, overhead-valve single, 68 x 96mm bore and stroke, 4-speed foot-change gearbox, swinging-arm rear suspension, telescopic front forks, fishtail silencer.
£2,700–3,000 / €4,000–4,400 / $5,000–5,500 ⚙ T&DC
The later MAC, produced from the mid-1950s, was very much in the style of the more sporting Viper. However, beside having a lower state of tune it used single-sided brakes rather than the full-width type found on the Viper.

1961 Velocette MSS Veeline, 499cc, overhead-valve single, telescopic front forks, swinging-arm frame, fishtail silencer, lower engine enclosure, original apart from aftermarket rear shocks, fewer than 10,000 miles from new and fewer than 200 miles in the last 20 years.
£3,100–3,700 / €4,650–5,500 / $5,700–6,800 ⚒ CGC

▶ **1961 Velocette Viper,** 349cc, overhead-valve single, chrome mudguards, full-width hubs, non-standard paintwork to tank.
£2,900–3,250 / €4,350–4,800 / $5,400–6,000 ⊞ CotC

1963 Velocette Venom, 499cc, overhead-valve single, alloy head, iron barrel, chrome mudguards, uprated with Amal Concentric carburettor, separate headlamp and revised headlamp brackets.
£4,000–4,500 / €6,000–6,600 / $7,400–8,200 ⊞ VER

1965 Velocette Venom Clubman, 499cc, overhead-valve single, close-ratio gears, 86 x 86mm bore and stroke, tuned engine, GP carburettor, twin-leading-shoe front brake, alloy rims, large tank, swept-back pipe, dualseat.
£4,900–5,500 / €7,350–8,100 / $9,000–10,000 ⊞ CotC

◀ **1967 Velocette LE MkIII,** 192cc, side-valve flat-twin, foot-change gearbox, shaft final drive, single seat, screen, legshields, panniers, footboards.
£900–1,000
€1,350–1,500
$1,700–1,900 ⚙ EWC

1969 Velocette Thruxton, 499cc, overhead-valve single.
£9,400–10,500 / €14,100–15,550
$17,400–19,200 ⊞ VER
The Thruxton went on sale in 1965 as a high-performance variant of the Venom. It featured an 8:1 compression ratio cylinder head with a 2in (50mm) inlet valve fed by a 1⅜in Amal GP carburettor. Other features included close-ratio gears, alloy rims and a twin-leading-shoe front brake.

1969 Velocette Thruxton, 499cc, overhead-valve single, 86 x 86mm bore and stroke, Amal GP carburettor, oil tank heat guard, twin-leading-shoe front brake, fork gaiters, correct Avon nose-cone fairing.
£9,400–10,500 / €14,100–15,600
$17,400–19,200 ⊞ CotC

Vincent-HRD *(British 1928–55)*

Philip Conrad Vincent (PCV) was born in 1908 and grew up on a ranch in Argentina, owned by his wealthy British parents. He was sent to study in England at Harrow School, and it was there that his interest in motorcycles began to grow. In 1927, at 18, he left Harrow to study Mechanical Sciences at Cambridge. Before leaving Harrow, PCV had designed an ingenious cantilever system of rear suspension, with near-horizontal springs positioned beneath the saddle. This system, modified over the years and patented, would become a feature of all his future motorcycle designs. To appreciate the forward thinking of the young Vincent, one has to understand that the vast majority of motorcycles remained un-sprung for the following two decades, and that it would be half a century before cantilever systems began to appear on Japanese motorcycles! In his first year at Cambridge, PCV built the first Vincent motorcycle, incorporating the spring frame.

With his Cambridge course unfinished, Vincent persuaded his father to assist him financially in his bid to set up as a motorcycle manufacturer. This included providing the sum of £400 (some £40,000 / €60,000 / $74,000 at today's values) to purchase the name and stock of HRD. In 1925, Howard R. Davis had been the only rider to have won the Senior TT on a machine of his own design. The Vincent-HRD Company was set up in Stevenage, Hertfordshire.

In 1932, PCV hired the Australian engineer Phil Irving as chief designer, and together they designed the first brand-new model in a hectic 11 weeks.

As a sign of his commitment to his company during these early years, Philip Vincent lived in an old half-timbered house adjoining the factory's main office block, with only an ageing aunt as company.

Underfunding was always a problem, such that the combined genius of PCV and Irving was often stunted by a lack of finance. However, in many ways, Vincent-HRD was a firm which showed the rest of the British industry how it should be done. Its best-known bikes were the 499cc single and later 998cc V-twin motorcycles, but there were other projects. For example, there was a superb 500cc opposed-piston, two-stroke twin-cylinder marine engine that so completely outperformed the Admiralty's existing engine that the tester concluded, 'It's far too good to be true.' There was also a light industrial engine, a superb three-wheeler with a V-twin bike engine, and a remarkably efficient water scooter – in effect, a jet ski four decades before the advent of the modern marine vehicle.

Unfortunately, following an accident on the airfield where the company tested its motorcycles in the immediate post-war period, Philip Vincent was never really himself again. This led to a financial crisis, which resulted in the appointment of E. C. Baillie, the official receiver, who took over control of the company in September 1949. 'To save costs', Phil Irving departed shortly thereafter, to be followed over the next few years by the majority of the key engineering staff. Eventually, only PCV remained, and the last Vincent motorcycle was built in late 1955.

In 1971, Philip Vincent suffered the first of a series of strokes and he died in April 1979.

1937 Vincent-HRD Comet Series A, 499cc, overhead-valve single, 84 x 90mm bore and stroke, 4-speed Burman gearbox, short pushrods.
£20,700–23,000 / €31,000–34,100
$38,000–42,000 ⚙️ **VOC**
The Series A Vincent was born in 1934. It was jointly designed by Philip Vincent and the brilliant Australian engineer, Phil Irving.

▶ **1948 Vincent-HRD Rapide,** 998cc, overhead-valve V-twin, 84 x 90mm bore and stroke, 4-speed foot-change gearbox, cantilever rear suspension, Brampton front forks, fully restored.
£13,000–14,500 / €19,500–21,500
$24,000–26,400 ⊞ **CotC**

1951 Vincent-HRD Black Shadow, 998cc, overhead-valve V-twin, twin Amal carburettors, 4-speed foot-change gearbox, correct large-diameter 150mph speedometer, black engine casings, non-standard footrest hangers and alloy rims.
£18,000–20,000 / €27,000–30,000 / $33,000–37,000 🏍 **VOC**

1951 Vincent-HRD Series C, 499cc, overhead-valve single, 4-speed Burman gearbox, sprung frame, Girdraulic front forks, dual front brake, polished engine casings.
£5,400–6,000 / €8,100–9,000 / $10,000–11,100 🚲 **WCMC**

1951 Vincent-HRD Series C Rapide, 998cc, overhead-valve V-twin, 4-speed foot-change gearbox, alloy mudguards, older restoration, updated with Amal MkII carburettors and Akront wheel rims.
£10,800–13,000 / €16,200–19,500 $20,000–24,000 ⚖ **BB(L)**

Ever since the Series A's arrival in 1934, the Vincent V-twin was synonymous with design, innovation, engineering excellence and high performance. From Rollie Free's capture of the 'world's fastest production motorcycle' record in 1948 on a specially prepared machine from the Vincent race department, to the fully-enclosed Black Knight and Prince models, Phil Vincent's stress on performance and appearance is legendary. His machines bristled with innovative features: adjustable brake pedal, footrests, seat height and gear change levers. The finish was to a very high standard commensurate with the cost of the machine, which was double that of any of its contemporaries.

1953 Vincent-HRD Touring, 998cc, carrier, additional mirrors, export model with valanced mudguards and other differences compared to standard Rapide.
£16,200–18,000 / €24,300–26,800 / $30,000–33,000 🏍 **VOC**

1955 Vincent-HRD Black Prince, 998cc, overhead-valve V-twin, 84 x 90mm bore and stroke, 4-speed gearbox, dual front brakes.
£22,500–25,000 / €33,000–37,000 / $41,000–46,000 ⬥ VOC
The 1955 Vincent range included the Series D machines, such as the Black Shadow, Black Knight and fully-enclosed Black Prince. This particular motorcycle was the 13th to last made.

Wilkinson *(British 1908–15)*

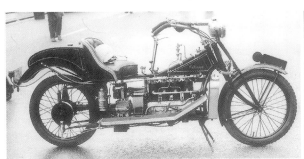

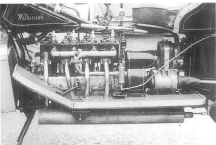

1914 Wilkinson TMC Four Cylinder, 848cc, inlet-over-exhaust inline 4-cylinder engine, shaft final drive, total-loss lubrication, twin-drum rear brake, front and rear suspension.
£10,000–11,000 / €15,000–16,500 / $18,500–20,400 ⊞ MW
TMC stood for Touring Motor Cycle and was developed from the earlier TAC (Touring Auto Car). Both were built by the Wilkinson Sword company of London, long-established firm of military cutlers, and now world famous for its razor blades.

Yale *(American 1902–15)*

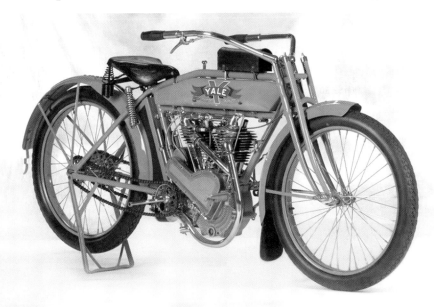

1914 Yale V-twin, 950cc, girder front forks, rigid frame, chain final drive.
£26,000–31,200 / €39,000–46,800 / $48,100–57,700 ⤢ BJ
Initially, Yale built a single-cylinder machine with the engine mounted over the pedals within a strenghtened bicycle frame. In 1910 it switched to manufacturing an all-chain drive V-twin which had two speeds and a displacement of 950cc.

Yamaha *(Japanese 1954–)*

Yamaha conjures up a sporting image with any motorcycle enthusiast, although actually, if its successes in road racing, motocross, trials and the like are combined, both Honda and Suzuki could probably boast as many, if not more, victories. The reason for Yamaha's image lies in its unwavering commitment to racing since the early 1960s, which has included the production of both pukka works machinery and 'over-the-counter' customer bikes for club and national riders around the globe.

The company has also manufactured musical instruments (including some of the best pianos in the world), snowmobiles, industrial engines, marine engines, lawnmowers, unmanned helicopters, Formula 1 car engines, industrial robots and even swimming pools!

Although Yamaha only began building motorcycles in the 1950s, its origins actually go back to the 19th century, when Torakysa Yamaha started repairing organs in 1887. This set him on a course that eventually would lead his company, Nippon Gakki, to become one of the world's foremost manufacturers of musical instruments. Before the turn of the 20th century, the company was not only a major supplier on the home market, but also had begun an export drive, which included shipping some 80 organs to Britain in 1892.

Although Torakysa Yamaha died in 1916, Nippon Gakki continued to expand, even when its production facilities were badly damaged by Allied bombing in 1945. The company managed to struggle back to manufacturing musical instruments in 1948.

During 1950, control of the company passed to Genichi Kawakami. One of his first moves was to begin motorcycle production, even though the company had no previous experience. The first model closely followed the German DKW RT125.

From this came a long line of ever improving two-stroke machines, culminating in the RD series of twin-cylinder sportsters in the 1970s. Later, from 1979, came the LC (Liquid Cooled) range. Running parallel with these developments was a policy of racing similar models. So, from the early 1960s came successively the TD1A, TD1B, TD1C, TD2 and TD2B air-cooled two-fifties, followed by the TR2 and TR2B. Then came the new TZ series in both 250 and 350cc guises with liquid cooling.

Like its great rival Suzuki, Yamaha had largely switched to four-strokes (except for racing) from the late 1980s. There has been a whole series of four-cylinder models with either four or five valves per cylinder. In the late 1990s came the R6 (600) and R1 (1000), both class leaders for road and track.

1965 Yamaha YDS3, 246cc, 2-stroke parallel twin, 28bhp at 8,000rpm, 5-speed gearbox, transmission-driven autolube, twin-leading-shoe drum front brake, 18in wire wheels, fully restored, concours condition.
£1,850–2,100 / €2,700–3,000 / $3,300–3,700 ⊞ MW
The YDS3 ran from mid-1964 through to the end of 1966.

1972 Yamaha YR5, 347cc, 2-stroke parallel twin, reed-valve induction, 64 x 54mm bore and stroke, 36bhp at 7,000rpm, pump lubrication, 5-speed gearbox, twin-leading-shoe drum brakes, top speed 95mph.
£1,600–1,800
€2,400–2,700
$3,000–3,300 ⊞ MW
The neatly styled YR5 was unveiled in 1970. Its descendents included the six-speed RD350 of 1974 and the RD400 of 1976.

1979 Yamaha RD200, 196cc, 2-stroke twin, 52 x 46mm bore and stroke, 22bhp at 7,500rpm, pump lubrication, 5-speed gearbox, twin-shock frame, 12 volt electrics, disc front brake, electric start, cast-alloy wheels, top speed 80mph, fully-restored, concours condition.
£1,350–1,500 / €2,000–2,200 / $2,500–2,750 ⊕ WMC
The RD200 was built from 1973 through to 1980.

Restored values

The cost of a professional restoration will have an influence on, but no direct relation to, a motorcycle's market value. A restored motorcycle can have a market value lower than the cost of its restoration.

1981 Yamaha TR1, 981cc, overhead-camshaft V-twin, 95 x 69.2mm bore and stroke, 8.5:1 compression ratio, 70bhp at 6,500rpm, 5-speed gearbox, telescopic forks, monoshock rear suspension, 70bhp at 6,500rpm.
£1,900–2,100 / €2,850–3,150 / $3,500–3,900 ⊞ MW
The TR1 was sold in the USA as the VX920 (920cc – 83 x 69.2mm bore and stroke).

► **1981 Yamaha XS1100 Martini Hailwood,** 1101cc, double-overhead-camshaft across-the-frame four, 5-speed gearbox, shaft final drive.
£3,200–3,800 / €4,800–5,700 / $5,900–7,000 ⚒ B(Kn)
Yamaha's big shaft-drive 1100 was a formidable tour de force at the end of the 1970s, with its double-overhead-camshaft four-cylinder engine producing almost 100bhp, a five-speed gearbox and shaft drive. In preparation for his comeback win at the 1978 TT, Mike Hailwood used one of the four-cylinder bikes, in modified guise, to put in training laps, and Yamaha produced this special edition in commemoration. Fitted with a John Mockett-designed downforce fairing finished in Martini colours, a run of 500 was proposed, although few are thought to have been sold in the UK.

◄ **1981 Yamaha DT175,** 175cc, 2-stroke single, reed-valve induction, high-level exhaust, monoshock rear suspension, telescopic forks, gaiters, conical hubs, good condition.
£1,050–1,200 / €1,550–1,800 / $1,950–2,200 ⊞ NLM

1985 Yamaha RD500LC, 499cc, 2-stroke V4, 56.4 x 50mm bore and stroke, 87bhp at 9,500rpm, 6-speed gearbox, triple disc brakes, cast-alloy wheels, fairing, top speed 150mph, concours condition.
£2,700–3,000 / €4,000–4,400 / $5,000–5,500 ⊞ MW

1986 Yamaha SRX-6, 608cc, 4-valve single, 96 x 84mm bore and stroke, 45bhp at 6,500rpm, square-section tube frame, monoshock rear suspension, triple disc brakes, cast-alloy wheels, top speed 110mph, original, very good condition.
£1,500–1,700 / €2,250–2,500 / $2,800–3,100 ⊞ MW
The SRX600 of 1986 was the successor to the SR500 and was virtually a brand new motorcycle with a hi-tech specification.

1987 Yamaha XS650C, 653cc, overhead-camshaft parallel twin, 75 x 74mm bore and stroke, 5-speed gearbox, disc front and drum rear brakes, screen, short megaphone silencers, US custom model, good condition.
£1,350–1,500 / €2,000–2,200 / $2,500–2,750 ⊞ NLM

Dirt Bikes

◄ **1946 BSA Trials,** 348cc, overhead-valve single, 71 x 88mm bore and stroke, alloy head and barrel, 4-speed foot-change gearbox, rigid frame, telescopic front forks, alloy mudguards, Lyta-type alloy tank.
£2,000–2,400 / €3,000–3,600 $3,700–4,400 ⌁ PS
This is probably an ex-factory BSA trials mount. These machines were ridden by the likes of Bill Nicholson.

1949 Triumph Trophy, 498cc, ex-works/Bob Manns, fully restored.
£9,200–11,000 / €13,800–16,500 / $17,000–20,400 ⌁ B(Kn)
In 1995, this Trophy, which had been in the same family ownership since 1959, was stripped for restoration. During the course of that restoration, various detailed modifications from standard were noted, including a reduced lower fork yoke, reinforced head stock, 21in front wheel, narrow foot brake pivots, narrow front stand/mudguard stay, and no ears on fork shroud but bosses for competition number plates. The engine internals revealed lipped roller main bearings, non-standard inlet manifold, lightened clutch, 10.5:1 compression pistons, large-section connecting rods and bigger valves. These discoveries suggested that the machine had a significant history. The previous owner was traced and revealed that it had been a works bike used by Bob Manns. Subsequent correspondence with Bob Manns confirmed that most of the modifications were developed while he used the bike. He indicated that the engine in the bike is the scrambler engine, tuned in the Triumph Experimental Shop, and prepared for the International Moto Cross at Brands Hatch in 1949. Manns was a member of the victorious English team and recalls that his bike ran on 50/50 petrol/benzole, and that the output was nearly 40bhp. Discovery of this important information regarding the bike's history inspired a detailed and meticulous restoration, carried out in the owner's spare bedroom.

▶ **1951 AJS Model 16M Trials Replica,** 348cc, overhead-valve single, 16bhp at 5,600rpm, alloy mudguards and tank.
£2,900–3,500 / €4,350–5,200 $5,400–6,500 ⌁ B(Kn)
While the Porcupine was establishing its credentials on the circuit in post-war competition, AJS was enjoying considerable success in trials, thanks to such notable riders as Gordon Jackson, Hugh Viney and Bob Manns. The achievements of AJS in the hugely popular ISDT events kept the marque's name in the public mind, while sister machines from Matchless ensured maximum publicity for AMC.

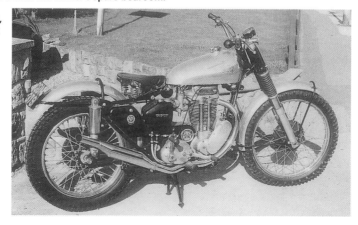

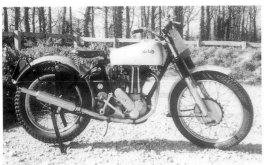

1951 Norton 500T, 490cc, overhead-valve vertical single, 79 x 100mm bore and stroke, 21bhp at 5,000rpm, 4-speed foot-change gearbox.
£3,250–3,600 / €4,900–5,400 / $6,000–6,600 ⊞ CotC

1951 Royal Enfield Bullet Trials, 346cc, overhead-valve single, 70 x 90mm bore and stroke, Albion 4-speed gearbox, swinging-arm frame, Royal Enfield telescopic front forks, high-level exhaust, unrestored.
£1,000–1,200 / €1,500–1,800 / $1,850–2,200 ⚲ CGC
The swinging-arm three-fifty Bullet made its debut in February 1948, when a trio of prototypes turned out in the Colmore Trial.

c1952 Matchless G3C, 348cc, overhead-valve single, rear-mounted magneto, rigid frame, telescopic front forks, alloy mudguards, genuine 'C' engine and frame.
£2,700–3,200 / €4,000–4,800 / $5,000–6,000 ⚲ CGC
The G3C (Competition) was expressly manufactured for trials use. For what was classed as a heavyweight single, it was a purposeful machine that carried the very minimum of excess weight.

1953 Francis-Barnett Falcon Model 65 Overseas, 197cc, Villiers 7E single-cylinder 2-stroke engine, 4-speed foot-change gearbox, 5in brakes, telescopic forks, swinging-arm frame, original specification, very good condition.
£990–1,100 / €1,500–1,650 / $1,800–2,000 ⚙ FBC

◄ **1955 Matchless G3LC,** 384cc, overhead-valve single, 69 x 93mm bore and stroke, 4-speed gearbox, 21in front and 19in rear wheels, rigid frame, Teledraulic front forks, alloy mudguards.
£2,600–2,900
€3,900–4,300
$4,800–5,300 ⊞ CotC
This was the first year of alloy hubs front and rear. This competition model has optional lighting equipment.

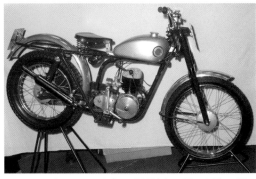

1956 Francis-Barnett Falcon 76 Trials, 197cc, Villiers 9E single-cylinder 2-stroke engine, piston-port induction, 4-speed foot-change gearbox, telescopic forks, swinging-arm frame.
£990–1,100 / €1,500–1,650 / $1,800–2,000 ⊕ FBC
When Francis-Barnett introduced its 'springer'-framed Falcon 76 for the 1956 season, the bike was produced in both trials and scrambles forms with 9E engine and four-speed gearbox.

1956 BSA B34 Trials, 499cc, overhead-valve single, all-alloy engine, Amal Monobloc carburettor, 4-speed wide-ratio gearbox, 21in front wheel, single sprung saddle, swinging-arm frame, alloy fuel and oil tanks.
£3,800–4,250 / €5,700–6,300 / $7,000–7,700 ⊞ NLM

1958 Matchless G3C, 348cc, overhead-valve single, 69 x 93mm bore and stroke, AMC wide-ratio 4-speed gearbox, 2-piece alloy primary chaincase, magneto ignition, restored to original specification.
£3,100–3,500 / €4,650–5,200 / $5,700–6,500 ⊞ MW

1959 Francis-Barnett Model 83 Trials, 249cc, AMC Mk25/C single-cylinder 2-stroke engine, 66 x 73mm bore and stroke, Norton Roadholder forks, Girling shocks, 21in front and 19in rear wheels.
£2,400–2,700 / €3,600–4,000 / $4,400–4,900 ⊞ VER

c1959 Matchless G3C, 348cc, overhead-valve single, Pykett alloy cylinder barrel, AMC 4-speed wide-ratio gearbox, small hubs, Teledraulic forks, Girling shocks, alloy mudguards, excellent condition.
£3,400–3,800 / €5,100–5,700 / $6,300–7,000 ⊞ BLM
This Matchless G3C was specially prepared for pre-'65 trials by specialist Peter Pykett during the late 1970s.

◄ **1960 AJS CS14 Competition,**
248.5cc, overhead-valve single,
69.85 x 64.85mm bore and stroke,
10:1 compression ratio, alloy head,
iron barrel, Amal Monobloc carburettor.
**£1,100–1,400 / €1,650–2,000
$2,000–2,400** ⚙ PS
The CS (scrambles) model was a
development of the Model 14
lightweight roadster. Features
included tuned engine, heavier-
gauge frame, modified sub-frame,
longer Girling shocks, Teledraulic
forks, 19in wheels, offset hubs,
knobbly tyres and alloy mudguards.

1960 Matchless G80CS, 498cc, overhead-valve single, 8.7:1 compression ratio, Amal Monobloc carburettor, full-width alloy hubs.
£14,000–16,800 / €21,000–25,000 / $26,000–31,000 ⚙ BB(L)
Associated Motor Cycles established a formidable reputation in off-road competition in the 1950s, winning the
British 500cc Moto-Cross Championship on four occasions. In the USA, desert race victories by riders such as
Walt Fulton and Bud Ekins ensured a healthy demand for AMC's Matchless G80CS and AJS 18CS 'scramblers'.
AMC had announced its post-war range of Matchless and AJS heavyweight singles in June 1945. Housed in
a rigid frame with Teledraulic front forks, the ruggedly-built overhead-valve engine drove via a four-speed
gearbox. Hairpin valve springs were adopted for 1949 and a swinging-arm frame introduced – the latter
initially for export only – models so-equipped being suffixed 'S'. The production scramblers also received the
new frame; the trials models, though, kept the rigid back end. The scrambles engine went all-alloy for 1950,
and subsequently received different cams and larger valves before being redesigned with short-stroke
dimensions (86 x 85.5mm bore and stroke in the five hundred's case) for 1956. A new duplex frame appeared
for 1960 and there were further engine improvements. AMC continued to develop its four-stroke scramblers
to the end of production in 1969, but by then the days of such heavyweight machines were at an end.
This machine was restored by Bud Ekins and was displayed at the New York Guggenheim Museum's *Art of
the Motorcycle* exhibition in 1998.

1961 Norman B4 C/S, 247cc, Villiers 32A single-cylinder
2-stroke engine, 4-speed gearbox, not registered,
'as new' condition.
£2,400–2,750 / €3,600–4,000 / $4,500–5,000 ⊞ VER
The B4 C/S ('S' for Springer) was an attractive little
trials mount, finished in black with a gold-lined deep
maroon tank.

1960s Rickman Triumph Metisse, 490cc, Triumph Tiger
100SS spec engine, single Amal Monobloc carburettor,
siamesed exhaust, CZ hubs, nickel-plated frame,
fully-prepared for pre-'65 scrambles.
£2,800–3,100 / €4,200–4,700 / $5,200–5,800 ⊞ BLM

Colour Review

1911 Premier TT Roadster, 499cc, side-valve single, magneto ignition, belt drive, spring forks, rigid frame, no gears or clutch, concours condition.
£5,900–6,500 / €8,800–9,700 / $10,900–12,000 ⊞ VER
In the early years of the 20th century, Premier (based in Coventry) claimed to be the largest bicycle factory in the world. It built motorcycles from 1908 to 1915, although after 1914 they were known as Coventry-Premier.

◄ **1922 Rudge Multi,** 499cc, inlet-over-exhaust single, 85 x 88mm bore and stroke, variable transmission, belt final drive, lighting equipment, fully restored, concours condition.
£7,200–8,000
€10,800–12,000
$13,300–14,800 ⊞ VER
The final year of production; this example was first registered in 1923.

1938 Rudge 500 Special, 493cc, pent-roof 4-valve single, twin-port head, 84.5 x 88mm bore and stroke, 4-speed foot-change gearbox, girder frame, rigid frame, concours condition.
£7,200–8,000 / €10,800–12,000 / $13,300–14,800 ⊞ PM

1938 Rudge Sports Special, 493cc, overhead-valve pent-roof 4-valve single, twin-port head, speedometer and rev-counter, fully restored.
£5,400–6,000 / €8,100–9,000 / $11,000–12,100 ⊞ BLM
The Sports Special was only offered in the period 1937–39 and was the performance version of the Standard Special model. It is quite rare.

► **1957 Sunbeam S7,** 489cc, overhead-camshaft inline twin, 4-speed foot-change gearbox, shaft final drive, plunger rear suspension, very original, older restoration.
£2,800–3,100
€4,200–4,650
$5,200–5,700 ⊞ CotC
Debuting in 1946, the S7 was a radical departure in terms of powertrain and styling from other more traditional British motorcycles of the era.

1915 Triumph Junior, 225cc, 2-stroke single, countershaft 2-speed gearbox, belt final drive, rocking-spring front fork, restored.
£2,350–2,600 / €3,500–3,900 / $4,350–4,800 ⊞ CotC

◄ **1917 Triumph Model H,** 550cc, side-valve single, belt drive, 3-speed hand-change Sturmey-Archer countershaft gearbox, magneto ignition, acetelyne lighting, excellent condition.
£5,000–5,500
€7,500–8,300
$9,200–10,200 ⊞ VER

► **1946 Triumph 3T,** 349cc, overhead-valve vertical twin, 55 x 73.4mm bore and stroke, 4-speed foot-change gearbox, excellent condition ex-factory specification.
£2,900–3,250
€4,400–4,900
$5,400–6,000
⊞ CotC

1956 Triumph T100, 498cc, overhead-valve vertical twin, 63 x 80mm bore and stroke, alloy head, iron barrel, swinging-arm frame, telescopic forks, nacelle, dualseat, original specification.
£3,150–3,500 / €4,700–5,200 / $5,800–6,400 ⊞ CotC

1960 Triumph 3TA Twenty-One, 349cc, overhead-valve parallel twin, unit construction, 4-speed foot-change gearbox, rear enclosure.
£2,600–2,900 / €3,950–4,400 / $4,800–5,250 ⊞ PM
The Twenty-One was the first of the modern unit-construction Triumph twins. It ran from 1957 until 1966.

1961 Triumph T120R Bonneville, 649cc, overhead-valve twin, 46bhp at 6,500rpm, 71 x 82mm bore and stroke, 9:1 compression ratio, twin Amal Monobloc carburettors, duplex primary chain, duplex frame, 18in wheels, 115mph top speed, restored to very high standard.
£7,200–8,000 / €10,800–12,000 / $13,300–14,800 ⊞ MW

1961 Triumph 5TA Speed Twin, 490cc, overhead-valve parallel twin, unit construction, 4-speed foot-change gearbox, rear enclosure.
£2,700–3,000 / €4,050–4,500 / $5,000–5,500 ⊞ CotC

1963 Triumph Tiger 90, 349c, overhead-valve unit vertical twin, 58.25 x 65.5mm, rev-counter, concours condition.
£3,000–3,300 / €4,500–5,000 / $5,500–6,100 ⊞ BLM

1969 Triumph T120 Bonneville, 649cc, overhead-valve unit-construction twin, 71 x 82mm bore and stroke, twin Amal Concentric carburettors, twin-leading-shoe front brake, fork gaiters, concours condition.
£4,500–5,000 / €6,700–7,500 / $8,300–9,200 ⊞ CotC

1976 Triumph Trident T160, 740cc, overhead-valve across-the-frame triple, 5-speed gearbox, electric start, front and rear disc brakes, unrestored.
£3,400–3,800 / €5,100–5,700 / $6,300–7,000 ⊞ CotC

◀ **1980 Triumph Bonneville 750,** 744cc, overhead-valve twin, left-hand gearchange, front and rear disc brakes, fully restored to concours condition.
**£4,050–4,500
€6,100–6,700
$7,500–8,300** ⊞ VER
This example is a UK model with the classic-style fuel tank. Non-standard front mudguard

▶ **1962 Velocette Venom Clubman,** 499cc, overhead-valve single, full-width hubs, dualseat, rearset footrests, fully restored, low mileage.
**£5,000–5,500 / €7,500–8,300
$9,200–10,200** ⊞ VER
The Venom Clubman was an improved and uprated Venom with GP carburettor, close-ratio gears and polished engine internals.

◀ **1951 Vincent-HRD Black Shadow,** 998cc, overhead-valve V-twin, 2-into-1 exhaust, dual front brakes, Girdraulic forks, cantilever frame, excellent condition.
**£21,000–23,000
€31,500–34,500
$38,800–42,500** ⊞ VER
The Black Shadow was the high-performance version of the Vincent V-twin range.

◄ **1951 BSA B34 Gold Star Competition,** 499cc, overhead-valve single, alloy head and barrel, 4-speed foot-change gearbox, rigid frame, telescopic forks, high-level exhaust, totally restored regardless of cost.
£4,150–4,600
€6,200–6,900
$7,700–8,500 ⊞ BLM

1956 Matchless 350 G3LC, 348cc, overhead-valve all-alloy single, 16bhp at 5,600rpm, 69 x 93mm bore and stroke, 4-speed Burman gearbox, band-type primary chaincase, fully restored.
£2,500–2,800 / €3,800–4,200 / $4,600–5,100 ⊞ CotC

1980 Suzuki PE175, 246cc, 2-stroke single, reed-valve induction, 5-speed gearbox, conical hubs, high-level exhaust, long-travel forks, monoshock rear suspension, fully restored, concours condition.
£1,100–1,200 / €1,600–1,800
$2,000–2,200 ⊞ MW
During the late 1970s and early 1980s, Suzuki produced a whole family of enduro machines: the PE175, 250 and 400. Later versions sported the company's patented 'Full Floater' monoshock rear suspension.

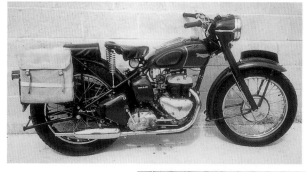

◄ **1954 Triumph TRW,** 499cc, side-valve twin, single Solex carburettor, 16.8bhp, 4-speed gearbox, telescopic front forks, rigid frame, 19in wheels, top speed 75mph, fully restored.
£2,700–3,000 / €4,050–4,500
$5,000–5,500 ⊞ BLM

► **1977 Gitane Champion Veloce,** 49cc, Minerelli P6 single-cylinder 2-stroke engine, 6-speed gearbox, cast-alloy wheels, disc front brake, fairing, monoshock rear suspension, concours condition.
£900–1,000
€1,350–1,500
$1,650–1,850 ⊞ MW
The Testi company (1951–83) built the range of Gitane machines, including the Champion Veloce, which was marketed in Britain during the mid–late 1970s by the Alan Taylor organization.

◄ **c1916 Indian V-Twin Race Bike,** 998cc, side-valve V-twin, leaf-spring front suspension, rigid frame, drum rear brake, front-mounted magneto.
£40,500–45,000
€61,000–67,000
$75,000–83,000 ⊞ AtMC
In 1915, the side-valve Powerplus engine of Charles Gustafson Senior superseded the Hedstrom 100 design. Whereas the 100 engine employed plain bearings on both ends of the crankshaft, the Powerplus featured roller bearings on the timing (off-side) and a plain bearing on the left (drive side).

1954 AJS 7R, 348cc, overhead-camshaft single, 74 x 81mm bore and stroke, magneto, 10:1 compression ratio, Burman close-ratio 4-speed gearbox, fitted with later tank, seat, fork gaiters and flyscreen.
£10,000–11,000 / €15,000–16,500 / $18,500–20,300 ⊞ MW

► **1957 Itom Mark 7 Competition,** 49cc, 2-stroke single, 3-speed twistgrip gearchange, full-width alloy hubs, telescopic forks, swinging-arm frame, fully restored and race-ready.
£2,000–2,200
€3,000–3,300
$3,700–4,100 ⊞ NLM
The first Itom was a cyclemotor, which was designed in 1944. Based in Turin, the marque soon built an excellent reputation for its 50cc and later 65cc models, all powered by its own single-cylinder, piston-port two-stroke engines.

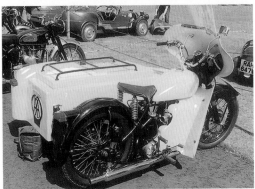

◄ **1960 Ducati 125 Monza,** 124cc, bevel-driven overhead-camshaft single, 55.2 x 52mm bore and stroke, unit construction, 4-speed gearbox, telescopic forks, swinging-arm rear suspension, twin shocks, fairing, alloy rims.
£2,150–2,400 / €3,200–3,550 / $4,000–4,450 ⊞ MW

1965 Bultaco TSS 250, 244cc, water-cooled single-cylinder 2-stroke, 6-speed gearbox, Oldani front brake, Girling rear shocks, fairing.
£3,150–3,500 / €4,700–5,200 / $5,800–6,450 ⊞ MW

◄ **1959 BSA M21 and AA sidecar,** 591cc, side-valve single, 82 x 112mm bore and stroke, telescopic front forks, plunger rear suspension, Avon handlebar fairing, leg shields, box sidecar.
£1,800–2,000 / €2,700–3,000 / $3,350–3,700 ⊞ MW

► **1960s BSA Café Racer,** 646cc, tuned BSA A10 engine, Amal Concentric Mk1 carburettor, siamesed exhaust, twin-leading-shoe front brake, Ariel rear hub, alloy mudguards, clip-ons, rearsets, fork gaiters, fibreglass racing fuel tank and single racing seat.
£2,900–3,200
€4,350–4,800
$5,350–5,900 ⊞ MW

1974 Japauto 1000VX, 950cc, Honda overhead-camshaft CB750 engine with big-bore kit, 90bhp, 4-pipe exhaust, cast-alloy wheels, triple disc brakes, top speed 135mph.
£4,100–4,500 / €6,150–6,750 / $7,600–8,400 ⊞ MW

1961 Francis-Barnett Trials 85, 249cc, AMC single-cylinder 2-stroke engine, 66 x 73mm bore and stroke, 4-speed foot-change gearbox, full cradle frame, swinging-arm suspension, Norton forks, optional lighting equipment.
£1,600–1,800 / €2,400–2,700 / $3,000–3,300 ⊕ FBC

1961 Triumph T20 Trials Cub, 199cc, overhead-valve unit single, 63 x 64mm bore and stroke, distributor, high-level exhaust, single seat, largely standard specification for year.
£1,500–1,650 / €2,250–2,550 / $2,800–3,100 ⊞ CotC
The T20C Trials Cub was introduced for 1957 with swinging-arm frame, lower gearing, larger wheels, improved front forks, crankcase shield, longer prop stand and alloy mudguards. For 1958, fork gaiters arrived. Then, in 1959, there was a new cylinder barrel with deeper fins and a crankcase cutaway for a larger sprocket. The T20T replaced the T20C for 1961. This was followed by the TR20 trials model for 1962.

1961 Matchless G3C, 347cc, overhead-valve all-alloy single-cylinder engine, Amal Monobloc carburettor, alloy wheel rims, trials model with optional lighting kit, very good condition.
£2,700–3,000 / €4,000–4,400 / $5,000–5,500 ⊞ MW

1963 James M2ST Commando, 247cc, Villiers 32A engine, ex-works/Brian Povey.
£3,700–4,400 / €5,500–6,600 / $6,800–8,100 ⋩ AGr
It was World Champion road racer Bill Lomas who developed James' original trials model Commando, which became an instant clubman's winner when it arrived in 1953. The 197cc machine was fitted with a 400 x 19in rear tyre and oil-damped forks. Within a couple of seasons, James introduced a rear suspension for trials and, by 1958, with engines tending towards a capacity of 250cc, James was forced by its parent company to fit AMC's recently-announced 250cc two-stroke. This engine series failed to work as well as the Villiers motors that James had traditionally fitted for many years. Eventually, under pressure from their retained team riders, both the James and Francis-Barnett teams reverted to Villiers' popular and efficient 250cc motor, which, by 1962, was available with a choice of alloy cylinder conversions. This ex-works machine was ridden by Brian Povey, a typical feature being the low, wide handlebars, which aided his trademark 'body lean' riding style.

1966 Greeves Anglian Trials, 246cc, Villiers 37A single-cylinder 2-stroke engine, Amal Concentric carburettor, conical hubs, alloy mudguards.
£5,700–6,800 / €8,500–10,200
$10,500–12,600 ⋩ B(Kn)
Based at Thundersley in Essex, Greeves gained a reputation for sporting success out of all proportion to its resources. The company's unorthodox trademarks of a cast beam 'downtube' and rubber-in-torsion leading-link forks proved adaptable to almost all forms of motorcycle, from humble commuter to clubman's road racer, but it was the firm's off-road products that really put it on the map. This machine is the actual works development Anglian, owned from new and for many years by Bert Greeves himself, and ridden by some of the biggest trials stars of its day, including Don Smith, who used it to win the 1967 European Trials Championship, Malcolm Rathmell, Arthur Browning, Martin and Arthur Lampkin, Dick Clayton and Paul England. It incorporates a number of special features, including altered frame geometry and factory fitted Griffon swinging arm and conical hubs. Campaigned originally with Greeves' 'banana' leading-link forks that superseded the rubber-in-torsion type for trials use, it was subsequently updated in period with Ceriani telescopic forks.

◀ **1966 Greeves Model 24T Anglian Trials,** 246cc, Villiers 32A 2-stroke single-cylinder engine, Amal 626 Concentric carburettor, Ceriani front forks, alloy tank, alloy rims, fully restored 2001–02.
£4,800–5,700 / €7,200–8,600 $8,900–10,650 ➚ B(Kn)
This machine is a genuine ex-works Anglian, which was ridden for the factory by Bill Wilkinson, who won the Scottish Six Days Trial riding a similar works machine in 1969. Its original logbook is signed by Derry Preston-Cobb, sales director of Invacar Ltd, the parent company of Greeves Motorcycles.

1966 Matchless G85CS, 497cc, overhead-valve single, 86 x 85.5mm bore and stroke, 12:1 compression ratio, magneto ignition, 41bhp at 6,500rpm, 21in front and 18in rear wheels.
£10,200–12,200 / €15,300–18,300 / $18,800–22,500 ➚ AGr
For many years, AMC, parent company of AJS, Francis-Barnett, James, Matchless and Norton, produced off-road models for competition, in a specification that required a considerable amount of work by the purchaser before being suitable for competitive racing. In the early 1960s, and with the commercial writing on the wall, AMC finally awoke. The resultant G85CS was a superb manifestation of that wake-up call. Raced with great verve and success by Chris Horsfield, Vic Eastwood and David Nichol, the red and silver 'Matchies' were always in contention.

▶ **c1968 BSA B44/B50 Scrambler,** 441cc, overhead-valve single, 79 x 90mm bore and stroke, alloy barrel, oil-in-tube frame, shuttle-valve front forks, conical rear hub, 20in front and 18in rear wheels with knobbly tyres.
£950–1,150 / €1,400–1,650 / $1,750–2,100 ➚ B(Kn)
BSA introduced the B44GP in 1965, essentially as a purpose designed motocross bike. This B44-engined machine has been prepared in a B50MX frame, a new model developed in 1971 for moto-cross use and powered by a 500cc engine.

1969 Jawa 500DT Type 680 Speedway, 498cc, chrome-plated frame, restored 2000.
£640–760 / €960–1,150 / $1,200–1,400 ➚ B(Kn)
The forerunner of the Jawa marque was the ESO company, which was formed in 1949. In 1966, the ESO name was dropped and the firm's DTS speedway model became the Jawa 500DT (Dirt Track). This chromium-plated two-valve model was used by former world champion Barry Briggs in the Golden Greats series.

1972 BSA B50MX, 499c, overhead-valve unit single, 84 x 90mm bore and stroke, 10:1 compression ratio, 34bhp at 6,200rpm, energy transfer ignition.
£2,150–2,400 / €3,200–3,600 / $4,000–4,400 ⊞ BLM
This model was sold in the USA as the Triumph TR5MX.

1972 Bultaco Sherpa 250, 247cc, 2-stroke single, alloy head, cast-iron barrel, cradle frame, twin-shock rear suspension, conical hubs.
£900–1,000 / €1,350–1,500 / $1,700–1,900 ⊞ MW
The Sherpa was the first successful Spanish trials bike and was developed with assistance from trials champion Sammy Miller. It was introduced in late 1964, and for the next two decades, it was at or near the top in the 'feet-up' sport.

1972 Bultaco Sherpa 325, 325cc, 2-stroke single, unit construction, conical hubs, full cradle frame, twin-shock rear suspension, leading-axle, long-travel forks, original, unrestored.
£800–900 / €1,200–1,350 / $1,500–1,650 ⊞ BLM

1973 Cotton 220 Trials, 220cc, Minarelli single-cylinder 2-stroke engine, 5-speed gearbox, single-downtube frame, twin-shock rear suspension, full-width alloy hubs.
£1,100–1,300 / €1,650–1,900 / $2,000–2,400 ⋊ PS
During the 1950s and 1960s Cotton offered a succession of Villiers powered trials and scrambles mounts. However, after Manganese Bronze acquired Villiers, no more engines were made available, so Cotton switched to Italian Minarelli power, first 170cc, then 200cc and finally 220cc.

1976 Honda TL125, 124cc, overhead-camshaft single, 5-speed gearbox, full cradle frame, full-width hubs, twin-shock rear suspension, in need of cosmetic restoration.
£540–600 / €750–900 / $920–1,100 ⋊ PS
The TL125 was Honda's first serious attempt at a 125 trials mount.

1978 DMW Trials, 247cc, 2-stroke single, 4-speed gearbox, full cradle frame, conical hubs, Ceriani-type front forks, restored.
£1,000–1,200 / €1,500–1,800 / $1,850–2,200 ⋊ B(Kn)
In 1977, DMW produced a small batch of trials machines under the direction of Mike Parkes. These were powered by a DMW-made variant of the Villiers 3TA trials engine.

◄ **c1999 MRD Rickman Triumph Metisse,** 649cc, 1967 Triumph TR6 Trophy unit-construction engine, siamesed exhaust, Rickman nickel-plated frame kit, alloy fuel tank, Lucas chrome headlamp.
£6,000–6,600 / €9,000–9,900 / $11,000–12,200 ⊞ BLM
This machine has only recently been manufactured by the MRD concern, which has continued production of the classic Rickman Metisse chassis.

Military Bikes

As a war machine, the motorcycle replaced the horse as an important means of communication, while in sidecar form it established itself as a functional and extremely mobile light assault vehicle and transport.

During WWI, the British led the way with Douglas 350s, P & M's, Royal Enfield V-twins, Rudge Multis and Triumph 550s. Following America's entry into the conflict, these were joined by a fleet of Harley-Davidsons, Indians and Excelsiors. Other pioneer military motorcycles included the Belgian FN, German NSU and Austrian Puch.

When Germany marched into Poland in September 1939, many countries in Europe had been on a virtual war footing for several months. For example, Norton had forsaken its traditional challenge for Grand Prix honours during 1939, concentrating instead on military contracts.

The machine Norton was building was the 490cc Model 16H side-valve single. This was basically a 1937 civilian model with little more than a crankcase shield, pillion seat or rear carrier rack, a pair of canvas pannier bags, provision for masked lighting, and an overall coat of khaki paint. The company also built the very similar Big Four with larger 634cc displacement. Some 100,000 16Hs were built for wartime service.

Many military motorcycles were little more than tarted-up civilian models, but modern warfare was to display a need for more specialized machinery. In addition, each country found it had particular motorcycle requirements: the British concentrated mainly on simple singles, the Germans complex horizontal twins, while the Americans opted for heavyweight V-twins. Even so, there were many other interesting developments.

In Britain, where the staple diet in military bike hardware was usually a side- or overhead-valve

single, there were several types that didn't follow this line. Douglas built a prototype flat-twin, James and Royal Enfield small-displacement two-strokes, Triumph various overhead-valve twins, while AMC constructed a prototype with a 990cc V-twin engine.

Germany was known for big flat-twins, and there were large numbers of BMWs and Zündapps using this engine format, but there were also many other designs. Most of these were two-strokes – from Ardie, DKW, TWN (the German Triumph), and Zündapp. Victoria produced a four-stroke single, the 342cc KR35WH.

But it was NSU that really come up with something different. This was the extraordinary Kettenkrad, which was really a small, tracked personnel carrier that just happened to have a motorcycle front fork. This unique machine was powered by a liquid-cooled overhead-valve four-cylinder Opel engine. NSU also built a 122cc two-stroke, and 250 OS and 601 OSL motorcycles. The last two machines used overhead-valve single-cylinder engines and four-speed gearboxes.

From Italy came names that were well known on the race ciruit: Benelli, Bianchi, Gilera and Moto Guzzi. Of the most interest were the Gilera Marte, with a 499cc side-valve engine and shaft final drive, and the Moto Guzzi Alce, with typical horizontal single-cylinder engine. The Italians also took their *motocari* (motorcycle trucks) to war including the Gilera Gigante VT in 500 and 600cc guises and Guzzi's Triacle.

The most interesting of the American military bikes were not the hordes of Harley-Davidson and Indian V-twins, but the unusual Crosley side-valve 580cc twin, the Harley-Davidson XA flat-twin (modelled on the BMW 12) and the Indian 841 with tranverse V-twin and shaft final drive.

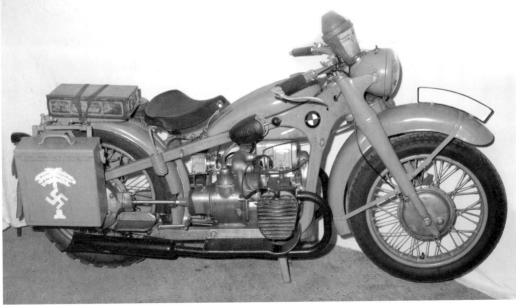

c1939 BMW R12, 745cc, side-valve flat-twin, hand-change gearbox, shaft final drive, full military equipment, including panniers, ammunition box, gas mask canister, 'coal scuttle' helmet and *Panzerfaust* anti-tank weapon.
£3,500–4,200 / €5,300–6,300 / $6,500–7,800 ✗ B(Kn)

◀ **c1940 Norton 16H,** 490cc, side-valve single, 79 x 100mm bore and stroke, 4-speed foot-change gearbox, girder forks, rigid frame, 14bhp at 4,500rpm, 65mph, completely restored in 1990 to authentic military specification.
£2,900–3,400 / €4,350–5,200 / \$5,300–6,300 ⚒ B(Kn)

1942 Indian 741B, 500cc, side-valve V-twin, 3-speed gear change.
£4,700–5,600 / €7,000–8,400 / \$8,700–10,400 ⚒ B(Kn)
A smaller Indian V-twin model, the 37cu in (600cc) Scout, joined the existing 1000cc Powerplus in 1920, to be followed by a 45cu in (750cc) variant in 1927. Introduced in April 1928, the 101 Scout featured a revised 750cc side-valve engine in a new frame, and this sporting machine proved an immense success for the firm, so much so that its replacement in 1931 by a heavier Chief-framed model was greeted with dismay. Introduced in 1934, the Sport Scout went some way towards retrieving the Scout's reputation, featuring a lighter frame and European-style girder forks; 30.5cu in (500cc) and 45cu in Scouts, designated Model 741B and 640B respectively, were produced for the Allied forces during WWII's early years, before the US Army switched to the Jeep.

1942 Harley-Davidson WLA45, 742cc, side-valve V-twin, 69.85 x 96.83mm bore and stroke, 4.32:1 compression ratio, 3-speed hand-change gearbox, 23bhp at 4,600 rpm, top speed 65mph.
£4,900–5,500 / €7,300–8,100 / \$9,000–10,000 ⊞ RRM
The Harley-Davidson WL model was adopted by the American and Allied forces during WWII for solo escort, despatch and general police duties. Some 80,000 were produced.

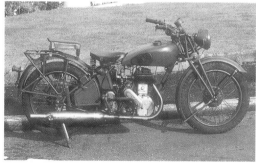

c1945 Norton 16H, 490cc, side-valve single, 79 x 100mm bore and stroke, 4.9:1 compression ratio, magneto ignition, 4-speed foot-change gearbox.
£1,500–1,700 / €2,250–2,500 / \$2,800–3,100 ⊞ PM

c1950s Condor A-580-I, 578cc, side-valve flat-twin, 70 x 75.2mm bore and stroke, 6:1 compression ratio, 20bhp at 4,400rpm, 4-speed foot-change gearbox, drum brakes, shaft final drive, top speed 75mph.
£2,400–2,700 / €3,600–4,000 / \$4,400–4,900 ⊞ RRM
The first series of A-580 machines was delivered to the Swiss Army in 1948, with telescopic front forks and a rigid frame. During the mid-1950s, an improved model, the A-580-I arrived with plunger rear suspension and a revised exhaust. The 580 series remained in service until 1977, by which time a total of 4,420 had been delivered.

1950 Triumph TRW, 499cc, side-valve vertical twin, 63 x 80mm bore and stroke, 6:1 compression ratio, 4-speed foot-change gearbox, telescopic front forks, rigid frame.
£3,100–3,500 / €4,650–5,200 / $5,700–6,300 ⊶ WCMC
During the latter years of WWII, the British military authorities prepared a specification for the ideal military motorcycle, which led to the Edward Turner-designed prototype TRW twin in 1944. However, the production machine did not enter series production until the beginning of the 1950s. Thousands were built for both British and foreign forces, and the model remained in production until the early 1960s.

c1962 Bianchi MT61, 318cc, overhead-valve 4-stroke, unit construction, telescopic front forks.
£570–680 / €850–1,000 / $1,050–1,250 ⚒ B(Kn)
Founded in the late 1890s, Bianchi made little impact outside Italy before WWII despite an innovative approach that saw a team of unit-construction, twin-overhead-camshaft three-fifties entered in the 1926 Isle of Man TT. In the post-war period, the company's road range consisted mainly of lightweights, the mainstay of production being 175cc models like the Tonale. Featuring a unit-construction, overhead-camshaft engine, duplex loop frame and full-width alloy hubs, the Tonale must have seemed light years ahead of its British contemporaries. A 250cc version of this Bianchi single powered the Sprint racer, while a further stretched – to 318cc – version went into the firm's MT61 military offering, which was introduced in 1961 for use by the Italian Army.

1964 Triumph TRW, 499cc, side-valve twin, 4-speed gearbox, siamesed exhaust, telescopic forks, rigid frame, pillion seat, unrestored.
£1,350–1,500 / €2,000–2,200 / $2,500–2,750 ⊞ BLM

1974 Condor A-350, 340cc, Ducati overhead-camshaft unit-construction single-cylinder engine, Dell-Orto VHB carburettor, 5-speed gearbox, duplex cradle frame, Mazocchi suspension, full-width Grimeca brake hubs, 12 volt electrics, top speed 90mph.
£720–800 / €1,100–1,250 / $1,300–1,450 ⊞ NLM

1972 Moto Guzzi Nuovo Falcone, 498cc, unit-construction horizontal single, 88 x 92mm bore and stroke, foot-change gearbox, tubular frame, twin rear shocks, enclosed telescopic forks, 26bhp at 4,800rpm, top speed 80mph.
£2,100–2,400 / €3,150–3,500 / $3,900–4,300 ⊞ BLM

▶ **1974 Moto Guzzi Nuovo Falcone,** 498cc, overhead-valve horizontal single, 88 x 82mm bore and stroke, Dell'Orto VHB carburettor, heel-and-toe gearchange.
£1,900–2,150 / €2,850–3,150 / $3,500–3,900 ⊞ NLM

Mopeds

1941 Rudge Autocycle, 98cc, 2-stroke vertical single.
£520–620 / €780–930 / $960–1,150 ⚡ B(Kn)
Formed by the acquisition in 1894 of the Rudge Cycle Company Ltd by the Whitworth Cycle Company, Rudge-Whitworth built its first motorcycle in 1911. This 3.5hp single-cylinder model proved outstandingly successful: in 1911, Victor Surridge's machine became the first five-hundred to exceed 60mph, while Rudge-mounted Cyril Pullin won the Isle of Man Senior TT in 1914. In the 1920s, Rudge became famous for the four-valves-per-cylinder engine, its first production motorcycle so-equipped appearing in 1924, and the company persevered with the layout until motorcycle manufacture ceased at the outbreak of WWII. This was not quite the end of the story of Rudge two-wheelers, however, as the Rudge Autocycle continued to be made by Norman in Kent. Powered by the 98cc Villiers engine, the Autocycle first appeared in 1940 in two versions, Standard and De Luxe, the latter enjoying the convenience of engine enclosure.

1949 Francis-Barnett Powerbike 56, 98cc, Villiers 2F engine, single-speed transmission, rubber-band suspension.
£440–530 / €660–790 / $810–970 ⚡ B(Kn)
The downturn in the motorcycle market in the early 1920s prompted Francis-Barnett to switch from producing expensive, high-quality machines to more utilitarian models. The first of these, introduced in 1923, were the triangulated, pin-jointed, straight-tube frame models whose novel method of construction gave rise to the 'Built like a Bridge' advertising slogan. Experience in the production of pressed-steel car components resulted in yet another innovatory model the following decade, the partially-enclosed Cruiser. After WWII, the firm became part of AMC and concentrated on two-stroke lightweights. The semi-enclosed Powerbike autocycle first appeared in 1939 and resumed production after WWII.

c1950 BSA Winged Wheel, 35cc, 2-stroke single-cylinder engine.
£120–140 / €180–210 / $220–260 ⚡ CGC

c1950 Whizzer Autocycle, 138cc, single-cylinder engine with inclined cylinder, pedal starting, belt final drive.
£2,600–3,100 / €3,900–4,600 / $4,800–5,700 ⚡ BB(L)
Introduced in the USA in 1939, the Whizzer was also produced in Belgium and Luxembourg for the European market. The 138cc side-valve Whizzer was firstly a clip-on engine for use in any suitable bicycle, drive being transmitted to the rear wheel by means of a belt-driven friction roller beneath the bottom bracket. After WWII, by which time the design had been refined to incorporate belt drive to the rear wheel, the Whizzer could be purchased as a complete machine with Schwinn-designed frame.

c1954 Vincent-HRD Firefly Cyclemotor, 48cc, 2-stroke horizontal single.
£500–600 / €750–900 / $920–1,100 ⚡ B(Kn)
Vincent took over the production of electrical component manufacturer Miller's Cyclemotor in 1953. Known as the Firefly, the engine was designed to fit beneath a conventional pedal cycle's bottom frame bracket and drove the rear wheel via a roller. Vincent soon offered a complete machine with a frame manufactured by the Sun company. The Firefly outlasted its more famous big V-twin brothers, remaining in production until 1958.

1955 Mobylette Model AV85, 49cc, 2-stroke single, front and rear suspension, adjustable seat, rear carrier, concours condition.
£540–600 / €810–900 / $1,000–1,100 ⊞ MW
This series was nicknamed 'The Blue'.

1961 Peugeot Model BB3 Sport, 49cc, 2-stroke single, beam frame, swinging-arm rear suspension, telescopic forks, full-width drum brakes, twist-grip gear-change, very rare, 'as new' condition.
£630–700 / €950–1,050 / $1,150–1,300 ⊞ MW

1964 Lambretta Lambretino, 48cc, 2-stroke single, alloy head, cast-iron barrel, original, unrestored.
£220–250 / €330–380 / $400–440 ⊞ MAY
Lambretta's moped never sold in the expected quantities. It was very much an Italian copy of the successful NSU Quickly.

1974 Garelli Tiger Cross, 49cc, 2-stroke single, duplex frame, alloy head and barrel, chrome-plated bore, 4-speed foot-change gearbox, full-width hubs, concours condition.
£720–800 / €1,100–1,250 / $1,300–1,450 ⊞ MW
Popular in the mid-1970s as a 'Sixteener Special', the Tiger Cross was built with low-level exhaust, flat handlebars and new roadster styling as the Rekord.

1978 De Blazi Kari-Bike, 49cc, 2-stroke single, fold-down handlebars and seat, stainless steel mudguard, cast-alloy wheels, front and rear suspension, excellent condition, with original bike cover.
£670–750 / €1,000–1,100 / $1,250–1,400 ⊞ NLM
The De Blazi moped was marketed in the UK by Britax.

1962 Ducati 48 Piuma, 48cc, 2-stroke single, 38 x 42mm bore and stroke, 3-speed twist-grip gear-change, 18in wheels, swinging-arm rear suspension.
£140–160 / €210–250 / $260–310 ⚙ B(Kn)
The Piuma ran from 1961 until 1968 and was Ducati's first two-stroke machine.

1964 NSU Quickly S, 49cc, 2-stroke single, piston-port induction, swinging-arm rear suspension, leading-link front forks, dualseat.
£115–135 / €170–200 / $210–250 ⚙ B(Kn)
Another motorcycle manufacturer with its roots in the bicycle industry, NSU built its first two-wheeler in 1900. Down through the years it made a large number of different models, ranging from 50cc to the large-capacity V-twin, but its most successful creation was the Quickly moped. Introduced in 1953, this achieved over 1.1 million sales. This three-speed Quickly S was one of the last made.

1976 NVT ER2L Easy-Rider Prototype, 49cc, 2-stroke automatic transmission.
£270–320 / €400–480 / $500–600 ⚙ CGC
After the collapse of Norton Villiers Triumph in the mid-1970s, Dennis Poore formed a new company known as NVT Ltd. Its brief was to create some order out of the chaos, primarily by reacquiring Norton's intellectual rights (and Commando spares stocks) from the liquidator; and generating revenue by assembling and selling 50cc Franco Morini-engined Easy-Rider mopeds. NVT's range comprised five models, four with single- or two-speed automatic transmission, plus a four-speed version to compete with the 'fag end' of the rapidly shrinking FSIE market. Each model utilized a massive, tubular frame that contained the fuel. With front and rear suspension that gave greater movement than any competitor, and wider section tyres, the Easy-Rider rapidly gained a useful niche in the market, despite moped sales being generally in decline. This Easy-Rider belonged to the late Tony Denniss from new. In 1975 Tony was closely involved with development of NVT's new moped and personally completed a few hundred miles aboard this hand-built prototype.

Police Bikes

◄ **1952 Gilera Saturno 500 Carabinieri,** 499cc, overhead-valve single, 84 x 90mm bore and stroke, 18bhp at 4,500rpm, 4-speed foot-change gearbox, girder forks, top speed 75mph.
£4,900–5,500 / €7,400–8,200 / $9,000–10,000 ⊞ NLM
The Saturno was built in a large number of guises for civilian and service use, plus various sporting roles, including road racing and motocross. The police/military model was based on the civilian Turismo.

1955 Terrot 500RG STA, 499cc, overhead-valve semi-unit-construction single, alloy head, cast-iron barrel, dry-sump lubrication, pillion seat, panniers, crashbars.
£1,850–2,100 / €2,800–3,100 / $3,400–3,800 ⊞ MW
The Terrot five-hundred was widely used by the provincial French police services, and was very British in its style and design – apart from unit construction of its gearbox and clutch assemblies.

1964 Velocette LE, 192cc, side-valve flat twin, foot-change gearbox, shaft final drive, conventional kickstart, 12 volt electrics, restored.
£810–900 / €1,200–1,350 / $1,500–1,650 ⊞ MAY

1971 Moto Guzzi V7, 703.7cc, 90-degree V-twin, 4-speed foot-change gearbox, dry car-type clutch, shaft final drive, telescopic front forks, swinging-arm rear suspension, drum brakes, unrestored, poor condition.
£1,250–1,400 / €1,900–2,100 / $2,300–2,600 ⊞ NLM

1982 Moto Guzzi 850T3 Police, 844cc, V-twin, 5-speed foot-change gearbox, shaft final drive, triple Brembo disc brakes, cast-alloy wheels, restored with all police equipment, 'as new' condition.
£3,700–4,400 / €5,500–6,600 / $6,800–8,100 ➹ COYS

1993 Moto Guzzi V50, 490cc, overhead-valve 90-degree V-twin, 5-speed gearbox, shaft final drive, triple disc brakes, cast-alloy wheels, full fairing, panniers, rear seat compartment, siren and additional lighting equipment.
£1,400–1,600 / €2,100–2,400 / $2,600–2,900 ⊞ NLM

Racing Bikes

1920 N.U.T. Factory Entry 1920TT, 500cc, JAP V-twin engine, Burman gearbox, Brampton front forks.
£13,500–15,000 / €20,200–22,500 / $25,000–27,500 ⊙ T&DC
Based in Newcastle-upon-Tyne, this marque took its name from the initials of its home city. Virtually all the engines used by the marque were specially built and prepared by the JAP factory.

c1925 Moto Guzzi C2V Twin Spark, 498cc, restored, near concours condition.
£11,200–13,400 / €16,800–20,000
$20,700–24,800 ➚ BB(L)
Although Moto Guzzi's Normale roadster, in tuned form, had proved capable of winning races, its inlet-over-exhaust valve gear limited further development, prompting a switch to the superior overhead-valve layout of the Corsa 2V. Guzzi's first purpose-built racer, and first machine to feature the marque's classic red finish, the 500cc C2V (two-valve) retained the Normale's horizontal-single engine and over-square bore and stroke dimensions of 88 x 82mm, but was considerably more powerful, its 17bhp maximum output being good for a top speed of 75mph. The C2V made its race debut in the 1923 Giro d'Italia long-distance race and remained a catalogued model for a further four years, being dropped in 1927.

1926 Chater Lea Brooklands Racer, 349cc, overhead camshaft, exposed valve gear, converted to foot-change gearbox, restored.
£8,300–9,900 / €12,500–15,000 / $15,300–18,300 ➚ B(Kn)
Following the record-breaking successes of Dougal Marchant's Blackburne-engined, overhead-camshaft Chater Lea, the company produced its own design of power unit in 1925. This was A. C. Woodman's famous 'face cam' engine, which used two contoured plates at the top of a vertical gear-driven shaft to operate the rocker arms. A second oil pump was used to lubricate the valve gear, which was fully enclosed. Factory records confirm that the engine in this machine was supplied new to Ron Hopkins in 1926. Hopkins, together with P. J. Ashton riding his trusty Chater Lea in solo and sidecar form, established Class D records at Brooklands in 1928, achieving 80.87mph in four hours, as well as achieving five-, six- and eight-hour records.

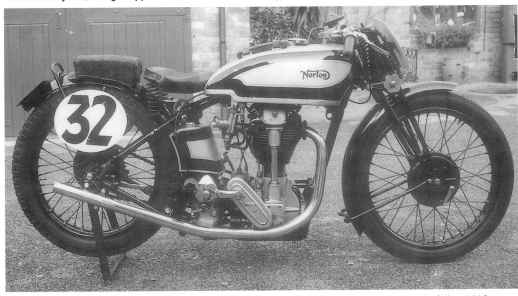

1933 Norton Model 40 International, 490cc, overhead-camshaft single, foot-change gearbox, girder forks, rigid frame, drum brakes, original specification, racing history.
£15,300–17,000 / €23,000–26,000 / $28,300–32,000 ⊞ VER

◀ 1935 Excelsior
Manxman ER12, 349cc,
overhead-camshaft single,
75 x 79mm bore and
stroke, Amal TT carburettor,
4-speed close-ratio foot-
change gearbox, alloy rims,
girder forks, rigid frame,
completely restored.
£10,800–12,000
€16,200–17,900
$20,000–22,000 ⊞ EXM

1948 Moto Guzzi Gambalunga, 498cc, fully restored, concours condition.
£27,300–33,000 / €41,000–49,000 / $51,000–61,000 ⚲ BB(L)
Moto Guzzi's first successful customer racer was the pre-war Condor, introduced in 1938 and revamped for
1946 as the Dondolino. A more highly-developed version produced by Giulio Carcano for factory tester and
budding racer Ferdinando Balzarotti resulted in the legendary Gambalunga. Its soubriquet arose from the
engine's long-stroke configuration, a break from Guzzi's customary practice, although normality soon returned
when, in 1948, the traditional 88 x 82mm bore and stroke dimensions were reinstated. Also making its debut
on the Gambalunga was Guzzi's own design of leading-link front fork which later would find its way on to
the firm's Grand Prix machines. This Gambalunga was sold new to Enrico Lorenzetti. He had already achieved
some notable successes as a privateer riding Moto Guzzis, winning the 1947 Italian Grand Prix, and later the
following year the Swiss and Ulster GPs, these last two events probably on this very machine. He went on to
become World 250cc Champion in 1952 riding for Moto Guzzi.

1949 AJS 7R, 348cc, overhead-camshaft 2-valve vertical single, 74 x 81mm bore and stroke, hairpin valve springs, enclosed
valve gear, cam drive by chain with Weller tensioner, 32bhp, Burman close-ratio 4-speed gearbox, top speed 100mph.
£11,200–12,500 / €16,900–18,600 / $20,800–22,900 ⊞ VER
The 7R, soon nicknamed the 'Boy Racer', was designed by Philip Walker.

c1949 Moto Guzzi Dondolino, 498cc, restored to correct specification, excellent condition.
£21,500–25,800 / €32,000–38,000 / $40,000–48,000 ➤ BB(L)
After WWII, Moto Guzzi's first successful customer racer, the pre-war Condor, was revamped for 1946 as the Dondolino, gaining a more powerful 33bhp engine and shedding a few pounds to tip the scales at 282lb in race trim. A larger 260mm front brake was new for 1947. The pre-war V-twin was the works team's favourite mount in the 500cc class during the late 1940s, although a Dondolino customer-bike ridden by Enrico Lorenzetti proved good enough to win the 1946 Swiss Grand Prix. The Dondolino remained in production until 1951.

1949 Velocette KTT MkVIII, 349cc, double-overhead-camshaft single, 10.9:1 compression ratio, 4-speed close-ratio gearbox, swinging-arm frame, girder forks, alloy rims, megaphone, top speed 110mph, excellent condition.
£20,700–23,000 / €31,000–34,000 / $39,000–43,000 ⊞ VER

◄ **1953 MV Agusta 125 Competitzione,** 124cc, overhead-camshaft single, hairpin valve springs, close-ratio gearbox, full-width hubs, rev-counter, alloy wheel rims.
£5,400–6,000
€8,100–9,000
$10,000–11,000 ⊞ MW

◄ **1954 BSA CB32 Gold Star,** 348cc, overhead-valve single, close-ratio RRT2 gearbox, duplex frame, 8in front brake, restored by Len Harfield, fitted kickstart and speedometer, excellent condition.
£7,100–8,500 / €10,600–12,700 / $13,200–15,800 ⋌ CGC
BSA's most talented engineers worked on the new post-war Goldie. Bert Hopwood redesigned Val Page's original M24 engine into two units: the 350cc B32 and 500cc B34. Roland Pike was responsible for transforming the humdrum touring single into a firebreathing race winner, and accomplished scrambler Bill Nicholson developed the swinging-arm frame fitted from 1953 onwards.

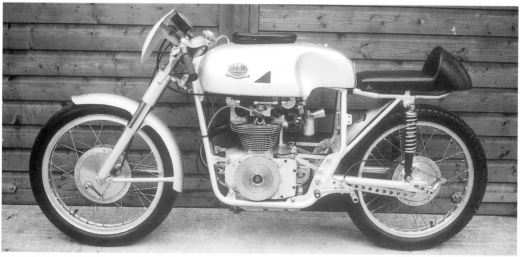

c1956 FB Mondial, 203cc, double-overhead-camshaft vertical single, gear-driven camshafts, hairpin valve springs, outside flywheel, Dell'Orto SS1 carburettor, full-width alloy hubs, duplex frame, alloy rims.
£20,700–23,000 / €31,000–35,000 / $39,000–43,000 ⊞ MW

c1957 Norton 30M Manx, 499cc, double-overhead-camshaft 2-valve single, Lucas racing magneto, laid-down gearbox, twin leading-shoe front brake, Isle of Man tank, concours condition.
£18,000–20,000 / €27,000–30,000
$33,000–37,000 ⊞ MW

Cross Reference
See Colour Review (pages 82–85)

▶ **1957 Norton 30M Manx,** 499cc, double-overhead-camshaft single, laid-down Norton gearbox, dry clutch, twin-leading-shoe front brake, alloy fuel and oil tanks, silencer for classic racing events.
£12,600–14,000 / €18,900–21,000 / $23,300–26,000 ⊞ MW

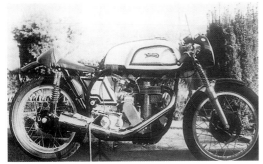

1958 Norton Model 30M Manx, 499cc, double-overhead-camshaft single, Molnar crank, QUB cam drive 'lighthouse', original matching-number crankcases, Featherbed frame, Roadholder forks, spare 2- and 6-gallon tanks, racing spares including fairings and pistons.
£13,800–16,600 / €21,000–25,000 $25,800–31,000 ⚒ B(Kn)
No other racing motorcycle is comparable to the Manx Norton. Other machines are faster – though few handle better – more modern, more colourful, but the Manx is still capable of extending a good rider. For a racing machine to remain current in the top flight of racing for over ten years and in top clubman use to the end of the 1960s was remarkable, let alone being able to lap the TT course at over a 'ton'. This was due to patient factory development of the motor and to the remarkable Featherbed frame which remained improved, but largely unchanged, into the 1960s, and was equally successful on road machines in an era when a road bike was expected to echo its maker's racing machines. This example is believed to have a works frame and yokes, and is, unusually, an 88mm-bore model.

> A known continuous history can add value to and enhance the enjoyment of a motorcycle.

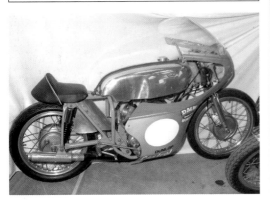

c1964 DMW Hornet Mk1, 247cc, Villiers Starmaker 2-stroke engine, telescopic forks.
£3,500–4,200 / €5,200–6,200 / $6,500–7,800 ⚒ B(Kn)

1965 Greeves Silverstone RCS, 246cc Greeves Challenger single-cylinder 2-stroke engine, leading link front fork, 5-speed Albion gearbox.
£4,200–4,800 / €6,300–7,200 / $7,800–8,900 ⊞ MW

1960 Maserati 50/T2, 48cc, 2-stroke single, twistgrip 3-speed gear-change, alloy head, cast-iron barrel, engine supported at rear of crankcase and cylinder head, telescopic forks, swinging-arm rear suspension.
£3,100–3,700 / €4,650–5,600 / $5,700–6,800 ⚒ CGC
Maserati built not only cars, but also motorcycles and even spark plugs!

1963 Honda CB72, 247cc, single-overhead-camshaft parallel twin, 4-speed gearbox, full-width hubs, twin-leading-shoe front brake, hydraulic steering damper, factory race kit, alloy rims, megaphones.
£1,600–1,800 / €2,400–2,700 / $3,000–3,300 ⊞ MW

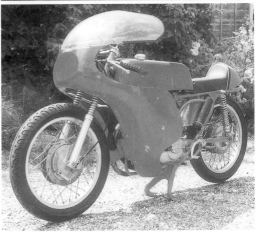

1965 Ducati Vic Camp Mach 1, 248cc, single-overhead-camshaft single, wet-sump lubrication, 30mm Amal Concentric Mk1 carburettor, 30bhp, 5-speed gearbox, alloy rims, fairing, top speed 110mph.
£2,250–2,500 / €3,400–3,750 / $4,150–4,600 ⊞ MW
Ducati specialist Vic Camp converted many Mach 1s for racing during 1964 to 1967.

c1966 Cotton Telstar, 247cc, Villiers Starmaker single-cylinder 2-stroke engine, duplex cradle frame, Armstrong leading-link front forks, 4-speed gearbox, standard specification apart from Norton Dominator front brake.
£3,500–3,850 / €5,200–5,800 / $6,500–7,200 ⊞ MW

1966 Ducati Monza Racer, 248cc, overhead-camshaft single, bevel-driven, 5-speed gearbox, unit construction, tuned engine, 32mm carburettor, later Mk3 front end (double-sided front brake and 35mm Marzocchi front forks), fibreglass tank, seat and fairing, alloy rims.
£2,150–2,400 / €3,200–3,600 / $4,000–4,400 ⊞ MW

1967 Matchless GB500 Prototype, 497cc, overhead-valve single.
£4,250–5,100 / €6,400–7,600 / $7,900–9,400 ⋌ B(Kn)
During the 1960s, anyone wishing to start a career in the five-hundred class was faced with purchasing and maintaining an expensive Manx Norton or Matchless G50. This state of affairs prompted brothers Peter and Philip Green to manufacture an inexpensive, over-the-counter, clubman racer. They formed Dynamic Balancing Engineers to manufacture the GB500. This used an overhead-valve Matchless G85CS motocross unit tuned by ex-AMC race mechanic Jack Emmott. The motor incorporated a forged 9.5:1 piston while retaining the standard 7R-type crankpin, con-rod and flywheels.

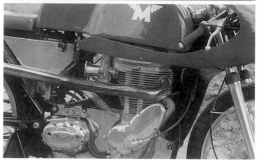

The magneto was bolted to the back of the timing chest, simplifying engine removal, while an Amal Concentric carburettor and high-level megaphone exhaust system helped the motor produce a claimed 49bhp at 7,000rpm. Bolted to Dural engine plates, the Matchless G85CS/BSA RRT2 engine-gearbox unit formed a structural member of the frame, which was constructed from aircraft-quality T45 tubing. The shortened R. E. Humphries front fork was fitted with a Dural top yoke, while braking was looked after by an 8in Jim Robinson twin-leading-shoe unit at the front and a 6in British Hub item at the rear. The Greens moulded their own fibreglass 4-gallon fuel and 4.5-pint oil tanks. All-up weight was a creditable 240lb, around 40lb lighter than a standard Manx Norton. The Greens had hoped that their prototype would be the first of a short production run, but their plans came to nought, and this remains the sole example. The machine was raced originally by 'works' rider Terry Sparrow, but its subsequent racing career remains unknown.

◀ **1968 Aermacchi 350 Ald d'Oro,** 349cc, overhead-valve horizontal single, dry clutch, outside flywheel, factory short-stroke engine, 5-speed gearbox, Fontana front brakes, Ceriani GP front forks, Girling rear shock absorbers.
£7,200–8,000
€10,800–12,000
$13,300–14,800 ⊞ MW

c1970s Benelli Four Replica, 250cc, across-the-frame-four, 4-pipe exhaust with meggaphones, Oldani front and Grimeca rear drum brakes, Ceriani front forks, alloy rims, fairing.
£4,000–4,400 / €6,000–6,600 / $7,400–8,200 ⊞ MW
This machine is a replica of the 1960s Benelli 250 Grand Prix racing four, as ridden by Tarquinio Provini.

c1972 Seeley Kuhn Commando Mk4, 745cc, 5-speed needle-roller gearbox, Manx 3-plate clutch, Seeley 'short' front forks, Lockheed brakes, Norton 'slimline' oil tank, fully restored to original specification.
£5,200–6,200 / €7,800–9,300 / $9,600–11,500 ⋏ B(Kn)

◀ **1972 Seeley Suzuki T500,** 492cc, Suzuki T500 twin cylinder 2-stroke engine, Seeley frame, front and rear disc brakes, expansion-chamber exhausts.
£5,000–5,500 / €7,500–8,300 $9,200–10,200 ⊞ MW

▶ **1976 Yamaha TZ350,** 347cc, water-cooled 2-stroke twin, 6-speed gearbox, front and rear disc brakes, cantilever monoshock rear suspension, wire wheels.
£2,450–2,700 / €3,700–4,100 $4,500–5,000 ⊞ MW
This machine was built by Dennis Trollope, using a Spondon chassis. John McEntree rode it in 1977 in British short-circuit events and the Manx GP. Then it was sold to Arthur Buxton in 1978, and he rode it in the British Clubmans Championships.

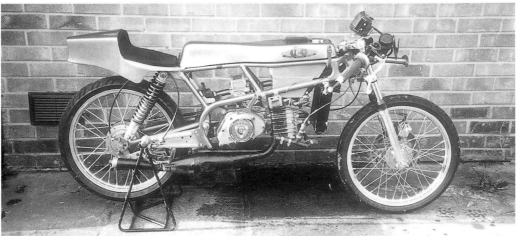

1979 UFO Kreidler, 49cc, Van Veen Kreidler liquid-cooled disc-valve 2-stroke single-cylinder engine, 18bhp, 6-speed gearbox, dry clutch, electric water pump, top speed 100mph.
£5,000–5,500 / €7,500–8,300 / $9,200–10,200 ⊶ CFRC

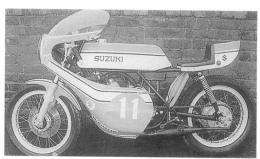

c1980 Terry Shepherd Suzuki, 349cc, liquid-cooled 2-stroke twin, close-ratio gear cluster, FEMSA ignition, Krober rev-counter.
£1,150–1,350 / €1,750–2,100 / $2,200–2,600 ⚲ B(Kn)
This three-fifty Suzuki-based racer is one of 40 manufactured by well-known racer/tuner Terry Shepherd. The engine used T20 crankcases topped by Shepherd's own water-cooled heads and barrels, incorporating Yamaha TZ350 pistons, con-rods and crankshaft.

1984 Ducati TTF2, 600cc, Ducati Pantah V-twin engine, belt-driven overhead camshafts, 5-speed gearbox, Marzocchi forks, triple disc brake, monoshock rear suspension.
£4,000–4,500 / €6,000–6,700 / $7,400–8,300 ⊞ MW
During the early 1980s several replicas of the works Ducati TTF2 machines raced to four world championships by Englishman Tony Rutter were built. This is one of them.

◄ **1991 Norton NRS 588 Rotary,** 588cc, liquid-cooled twin-rotor rotary engine, 136bhp at 9,800rpm, 9.2:1 compression ratio, Keihin flat-side carburettors, 6-speed gearbox, wet clutch, White Power inverted front forks, top speed 176mph.
£34,000–38,000 / €51,000–57,000 $63,000–70,000 ⊞ MW
This machine is an ex-JPS team bike.

1994 Norton Duckhams Rotary, 588cc, liquid-cooled twin-rotor rotary engine.
£16,600–20,000 / €25,000–30,000 $31,000–37,000 ⚲ AGr
This machine is a former Norton factory display bike, built as a third machine for the Duckhams-backed team.

1994 Norton Duckhams Rotary, 588cc, liquid-cooled twin-rotor rotary engine.
£43,000–52,000 / €65,000–78,000 $80,000–96,000 ⚲ AGr

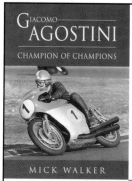

Restoration Bikes

1915 New Hudson Model D, 211cc, 2-stroke single, Druid front forks, rigid frame, belt final drive, partly restored, engine running, fitted with incorrect 3-speed Albion gearbox.
£750–900 / €1,100–1,300 / $1,400–1,650 ✗ B(Kn)

c1919 Diamond Model D, 296cc, Villiers 2-stroke single-cylinder engine, outside flywheel, acetylene headlight, barn find.
£2,000–2,400 / €3,000–3,600 / $3,700–4,450 ✗ B(Kn)

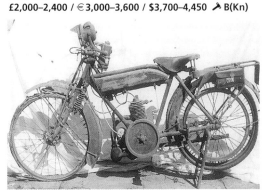

1921 ABC, 398cc, transversely-mounted overhead-valve unit-construction, flat-twin, 4-speed gearbox, cradle-type frame, leaf-spring suspension, in need of complete restoration.
£1,900–2,300 / €2,850–3,400 / $3,500–4,200 ✗ B(Kn)

c1921 Alldays 2¾hp Matchless, 2-stroke single, belt drive.
£1,300–1,550 / €1,950–2,300 / $2,400–2,850 ✗ B(Kn)

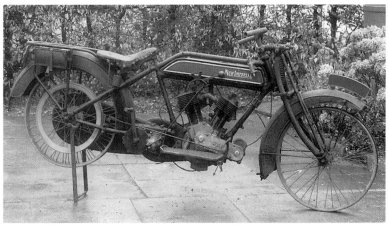

◀ **1921 New Imperial,** 999cc, side-valve JAP V-twin engine, front-mounted magneto, all-chain drive, caliper rear brake, girder forks, largely complete apart from rubber components including tyres.
£4,650–5,600
€7,000–8,400
$8,600–10,400 ✗ B(Kn)

▶ **1922 Lea-Francis 3½hp,** 496cc, V-twin, caliper brakes, several components missing, in need of complete restoration.
£3,450–4,150
€5,150–6,200
$6,400–7,700 ✗ B(Kn)
Although more famous for motor car manufacture, Lea-Francis also built motorcycles between 1911 and 1926. These were generally powered by V-twin engines from either M.A.G. (Motosacoche) or JAP. During WWI these motorcycles were produced under contract for military purposes.

1925 Brough Superior SS80 8/30, 980cc, side-valve twin engine, 85.7 x 85mm bore and stroke, Sturmey Archer hand-change gearbox.
£16,900–20,300 / €25,300–30,000 / $32,000–38,000 ➹ CGC

► **1928 Sun Tourer,** 147cc, Villiers single-cylinder 2-stroke engine, some parts missing.
£350–420 / €520–620 / $650–780 ➹ B(Kn)
Sun was originally a Birmingham cycle manufacturer, but it began building motorcycles in 1911. It used a variety of engines, including JAP, Vitesse, Blackburne and Villiers. Sun was acquired by Raleigh in 1961, and only bicycles were manufactured after this date.

1932 Sunbeam Model 9, 493cc, overhead-valve single-cylinder engine, 80 x 98mm bore and stroke.
£2,000–2,200 / €3,000–3,300 / $3,700–4,100 ➹ B(Kn)
The overhead-valve Model 9's frame and cycle parts, which had much in common with those of Sunbeam's larger side-valve models, evolved slowly. Changes to the Model 9's engine were confined mainly to its top-end. The early flat-tankers featured a straight-ahead exhaust port, a peculiarity that necessitated the adoption of a bifurcated downtube. Later on in the 1920s, Sunbeam followed the trend to twin-port heads before reverting to a single-port design in 1934. Pushrod enclosure had arrived by 1930, to be followed a couple of years later by partial enclosure of the rocker gear.

1935 Sunbeam Model 9A, 596cc, overhead-valve single, 88 x 98mm bore and stroke, drum brakes, all-chain-drive.
£2,000–2,400 / €3,000–3,600 / $3,700–4,450 ➹ B(Kn)
Sunbeam began experimenting with overhead valves on its factory racers in the early 1920s, and these appeared on production models in 1924. The new five-hundred roadster was known as the Model 9, while its race bike counterpart, which could top 90mph, was accordingly designated the Model 90. The John Greenwood design was advanced for its day, with a specification that included a crankshaft supported by three ball-bearings, dry-sump lubrication and primary drive enclosed in a cast-alloy chaincase. Power was transmitted by a single-row chain to a three-speed, 'cross-over-drive' gearbox with offside power take-off. The last gained four speeds as part of an extensive redesign for 1932, at which time an over-bored, 596cc version of the Model 9 – the 9A – became available for the first time.

Restored values

The cost of a professional restoration will have an influence on, but no direct relation to, a motorcycle's market value. A restored motorcycle can have a market value lower than the cost of its restoration.

◄ **1939 Triumph Model 2H,** 249cc, overhead-valve single.
£1,600–1,900 / €2,400–2,850 / $3,000–3,600 ➹ B(Kn)

1949 Scott Flying Squirrel, 596cc, liquid-cooled 2-stroke, parallel twin, Dowty pneumatic front forks.
£2,750–3,300 / €4,100–4,900 / $5,100–6,100 ✗ B(Kn)

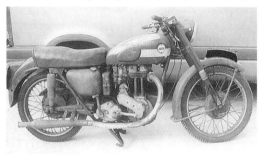

1954 Ariel NH Red Hunter, 346cc, overhead-valve single, 72 x 85mm bore and stroke, iron head and barrel, swinging-arm frame, telescopic forks, complete but unused since 1970s.
£800–960 / €1,200–1,400 / $1,500–1,800 ✗ B(Kn)

1954 New Hudson Autocycle, 98cc, engine running, in need of tyres, saddle, lights and control cables.
£125–150 / €190–220 / $230–270 ✗ B(Kn)
New Hudson returned briefly to the manufacture of two-wheelers in 1940 with the Autocycle. This had a Villiers HDL engine, pedal transmission and rigid front forks. Production resumed in 1946, by which time New Hudson was owned by BSA. Post-war developments included the adoption of pressed-steel girder blade-type forks in 1949 and the Villiers 2F engine the following year. Deletion of the 2F power unit brought an end to Autocycle production in 1958.

1957 MZ 250, 247cc, 2-stroke piston-port single, 16in wheels, drum brakes, very early model, not missing any known parts.
£190–230 / €280–330 / $350–420 ✗ CGC

1952 Ducati 98TL, 98cc, overhead-valve unit single, 49 x 52mm bore and stroke, 5.8bhp at 7,500rpm, 4-speed gearbox, 17in wheels, telescopic forks, swinging-arm frame, top speed 60mph.
£1,100–1,200 / €1,600–1,800 / $2,000–2,200 ⊞ NLM

1954 MV Agusta Pullman, 123.5cc, 2-stroke single, 53 x 56mm bore and stroke, 6bhp at 5,200rpm, 4-speed gearbox, 15in wheels.
£720–800 / €1,100–1,250 / $1,350–1,500 ⊞ NLM

1955 Parilla 125, 124cc, 2-stroke single, piston-port induction, unit construction, 4-speed foot-change gearbox, telescopic forks, swinging-arm frame, full-width drum brakes.
£720–800 / €1,100–1,250 / $1,350–1,500 ⊞ NLM

c1957 New Hudson Autocycle, 98cc, suitable for spares or restoration.
£25–35 / €38–45 / $46–55 ✗ B(Kn)

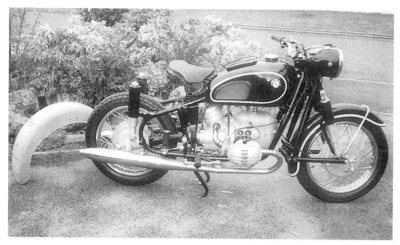

◄ **1958 BMW R60**, 594cc, overhead-valve flat-twin, recently restored, very little work needed to complete.
£2,400–2,900
€3,600–4,300
$4,450–5,300 ⚙ **B(Kn)**

► **1958 Mondial 125 Sport**, 124cc, overhead-valve unit single, 4-speed foot-change gearbox, rocking heel-and-toe gear lever, telescopic forks, swinging-arm frame, complete.
£810–900 / €1,200–1,350
$1,500–1,650 ⊞ **NLM**

Dealer prices

Miller's guide prices for dealer motorcycles take into account the value of any guarantees or warranties that may be included in the purchase. Dealers must also observe additional statutory consumer regulations, which do not apply to private sellers. This is factored into our dealer guide prices. Dealer motorcycles are identified by the ⊞ icon; full details of the dealer can be found on page 167.

► **1958 Moto Guzzi Lodola**, 174cc, overhead-camshaft single, unit construction, 62 x 57.8mm bore and stroke, 9bhp at 6,000rpm, 4-speed foot-change gearbox, top speed 70mph, complete, but unused for many years.
£540–600 / €810–900
$1,000–1,100 ⊞ **NLM**
The Lodola was the last of Carlo Guzzi's own designs, but even though it had an overhead-camshaft engine (later superseded by a 235cc pushrod unit), it was more tourer than sportster.

c1958 New Hudson Autocycle, 98cc, Villiers 2F single-cylinder 2-stroke engine, complete.
£210–250 / €315–375 / $390–460 ⚙ **B(Kn)**
This was the last year of production.

1959 Ducati 85T, 85cc, overhead-valve unit single, 45.5 x 52mm bore and stroke, 8:1 compression ratio, wet-sump lubrication, 17in wheels, complete.
£315–350 / €470–520 / $580–650 ⊞ **MW**

◀ **1961 Laverda 200 Twin,** 199.5cc, overhead-valve twin, 52 x 47mm bore and stroke, unit construction, 4-speed gearbox, wet-sump lubrication, alloy head and barrel with detachable cast-iron liners, primary drive by gears, final drive by chain, top speed 63mph.
£630–700 / € 950–1,050 $1,150–1,300 ⊞ NLM
The Laverda 200 Twin made its debut at the 1961 Milan Show.

1962 BSA C15, 247cc, overhead-valve single, alloy head, cast-iron barrel, distributor, 4-speed gearbox, full-width hubs, complete, but with non-standard Amal Concentric carburettor.
£510–570 / € 760–850 / $940–1,050 ⊞ BLM

1962 Norman B4 Sports, 249cc, Villiers 2T piston-port 2-stroke twin-cylinder engine, missing several components, including mudguards, carburettor, engine casing, side panels and rear light.
£270–300 / € 400–440 / $500–550 ⚲ NORM

▶ **1964 Moto Morini Tresette Sprint,** 172.4cc, overhead-valve single, 60 x 61mm bore and stroke, unit construction, 4-speed gearbox, full-width brake hubs, swinging-arm rear suspension, complete, but needing restoration.
£1,100–1,200 / € 1,600–1,800 $2,000–2,200 ⊞ NLM

1965 Norton Atlas, 745cc, overhead-valve vertical twin, 73 x 89mm bore and stroke, 49bhp at 6,800rpm, AMC 4-speed gearbox, top speed 118mph, some incorrect parts, unrestored.
£2,000–2,400 / € 3,000–3,600 / $3,700–4,450 ⚲ PS
Introduced in 1962, the Atlas was basically the 650SS with a larger bore size. Although this gave increased torque, it also meant more vibration.

1978 Yamaha RD250E, 247cc, 2-stroke twin, 54 x 54mm bore and stroke, 6-speed gearbox, complete.
£140–170 / €210–250 / $260–310 ⚲ **B(Kn)**
Yamaha's final shot at the air-cooled quarter-litre twin, the RD250C arrived in 1976, looking identical to the simultaneously introduced RD400 apart from cast-alloy wheels. The RD250E for 1978 was given electronic ignition and the four hundred's cast wheels.

1979 Moto Morini 3½ Strada, 344cc, overhead-valve 72-degree V-twin, 68 x 57mm bore and stroke, 6-speed foot-change gearbox, cast-alloy wheels, disc front brake, drum rear brake, missing front mudguard, rev-counter, cables and other smaller parts.
£900–1,000 / €1,350–1,500 / $1,650–1,850 ⊞ **NLM**

Scooters

1922 Kenilworth Scooter, 142cc, 4-stroke single-cylinder engine, forward-mounted magneto, all-chain drive, caliper brakes, tubular frame, footboards, valanced mudguards.
£1,800–2,000 / €2,700–3,000 / $3,350–3,700 ⊞ **VER**

▶ **1949 Brockhouse Corgi,** 98cc, Excelsior Spryt single-cylinder 2-stroke engine, 50 x 50mm bore and stroke, 6in wheels.
£900–1,000 / €1,350–1,500 $1,650–1,850 ⚲ **T&DC**
The Corgi was based on the Welbike, a lightweight foldable paratroop scooter built by Excelsior during WWII. Post-war, Brockhouse Engineering took over production.

1950 Bernadet BM250, 248.8cc, 2-stroke, 67 x 70mm bore and stroke, 9bhp, top speed 55mph.
£2,250–2,500 / €3,350–3,750 / $4,150–4,600 ⊞ MW
The Bernadet company existed from 1897 until 1956,
but this scooter was only made during the years
immediately following WWII.

1952 Rumi Scoiattolo, 124cc, 2-stroke horizontal twin,
6bhp at 4,800rpm, Dell'Orto 15S carburettor, 3-speed
gearbox, top speed 50mph.
£2,700–3,000 / €4,050–4,500 / $5,000–5,500 ⊞ NLM
The Scoiattolo was introduced at the Milan Show in
1951, and although it ran through to 1957, it was
never built in large numbers.

c1950s Peugeot S157, 150cc, 2-stroke single, twistgrip
gear-change, 10in wheels, twin saddles, spare wheel.
£900–1,000 / €1,350–1,500 / $1,650–1,850 ⊞ MW

1955 Rumi Formichino, 124cc, 2-stroke horizontal twin, 42 x 45mm bore and stroke, 6.5bhp at 6,000rpm, 3-piece cast-alloy structural sections, 4-speed foot-change gearbox, multi-plate wet clutch, top speed 56mph.
£3,600–4,000 / €5,400–6,000 / $6,700–7,400 ⊞ NLM
The Formichino was designed by Donnino Rumi, son of the company's founder, Achille Rumi.

1957 Maico Maicoletta, 247cc, 2-stroke single, 67 x 70mm bore and stroke, electric start, 4-speed gearbox, disc-type wheels, restored.
£1,000–1,200 / €1,500–1,800 / $1,850–2,200 ⚒ H&H
The Maicoletta was built in two engine sizes, 247 and 277cc, the latter achieved by increasing the bore size to 71mm.

1957 Lambretta LDA 150, 149cc, 2-stroke single, 6bhp at 4,750rpm, 57 x 58mm bore and stroke, twistgrip gear-change, kickstart, top speed 50mph, concours condition.
£1,500–1,700 / €2,300–2,550 / $2,850–3,150 ⊞ MW
This model preceded the famous Li series. For 1957, the front was redesigned to add a sleek cowling over the handlebars, which incorporated the speedometer and horn, while the headlamp was mounted in the legshields.

◀ **1958 Triumph (TWN) Contessa,** 198cc, 2-stroke split single, 9.5bhp, 4-speed gearbox, 12 volt electrics, electric starter, 10in wheels, top speed 62mph.
£900–990 / €1,350–1,500
$1,650–1,800 ⊞ BLM
Built in the German Triumph works (which split from the British company in 1929) to become TWN (Triumph Werke Nürnberg), the Contessa had an engine based on the Coronet motorcycle unit; the scooter was launched at the Brussels Show in January 1955. After 1958, TWN ceased two-wheel production (it switched to office equipment). Thereafter, rival Hercules acquired the Contessa design, renaming it the Viscount and replacing the engine with a 200cc Sachs unit.

▶ **1962 Lambretta Li2 150,** 148cc, fan-cooled 2-stroke engine single, 57 x 58mm bore and stroke, 6.5bhp, twistgrip gear-change, top speed 53mph, concours condition.
£1,700–1,900 / €2,550–2,800
$3,150–3,500 ⊞ MAY
The Li Series 2 arrived in 1959, and the most notable difference from the Series 1 was the repositioned headlamp, which moved from the legshields to the handlebars.

Sidecars

1909 Moto Rêve and Sidecar, 298cc, V-twin, belt final drive, acetylene lighting including sidecar.
£3,000–3,600 / €4,500–5,400 / $5,500–6,600 ✈ BRIT
In the early part of the 20th century, the Swiss Moto Rêve concern was a leading manufacturer of motorcycles and a supplier of proprietary engines to other manufacturers. The former were powered by V-twin engines of 298, 403 and 497cc, although by 1909 a parallel twin had been developed. In 1912, a branch factory was established in England, producing motorcycles under the Alp brand, of 3 and 3½hp ratings in both V- and upright twin form, while an economy model was powered by a 199cc English Precision engine; the last Alp, produced in 1917, had a 348cc two-stroke unit. Moto Rêve continued to produce motorcycles in Switzerland until 1925, its last machine powered by a 346cc overhead-valve single of advanced design.

► **1913 Scott Motorcycle and Sidecar,** 532cc, liquid-cooled 2-stroke parallel twin-cylinder engine.
£15,500–18,600 / €23,300–28,000
$28,600–34,000 ✈ B(Kn)

1912 Matchless V-twin and Sidecar, 631cc, side-valve engine, fully restored.
£11,700–13,000 / €17,500–19,500
$21,600–24,000 ⊞ VER

◄ **1920 Indian Powerplus and Princess Sidecar,** 990cc, side-valve V-twin.
£11,800–14,200 / €17,700–21,300
$21,800–26,200 ✈ BB(S)

1921 Matchless Model H and double-adult Sidecar, 996cc, MAG V-twin engine, hand-change gearbox, rear suspension, sidecar hood.
£8,150–9,800 / €12,200–14,700 / $15,100–18,100 ✈ CGC
The Model H spring-frame sidecar combination was for several years the most expensive model in the Matchless range.

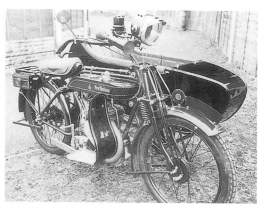

1922 New Hudson Standard Sidecar Combination,
594cc, side-valve single, 'through-the-tank' gear-change,
Druid forks, 2 owners from new.
£6,800–8,200 / €10,300–12,300 / $12,700–15,200 ⚲ B(Kn)
**This outfit was supplied as a complete sidecar
combination ex-works.**

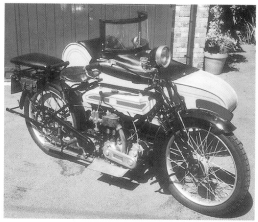

1923 Triumph Model SD Gloria and Sidecar, 550cc,
side-valve single, forward-mounted magneto, chain final
drive, drum front/caliper rear brake, good original condition.
£6,000–6,700 / €9,000–10,000 / $11,100–12,400 ⊞ VER

1923 James V-twin and Sidecar, 800cc,
side-valve V-twin, hand-change gearbox,
fully-enclosed rear chain in aluminium case,
kickstart, acetylene lighting, concours condition.
**£9,900–11,000 / €14,800–16,500
$18,300–20,300** ⊞ MW

1925 Henderson and Swallow Sidecar, 1301cc, 28bhp at
3,400rpm, centrally-sprung trailing-link forks, twin-downtube frame.
£16,600–18,500 / €24,900–27,800 / $31,000–34,000 ⊞ VER
**The Model K was introduced in 1920, and was the first all-new
Henderson produced in Chicago after the company's take-over
by the Schwinn concern.**

1925 Triumph Model P and Sidecar, 494c, side-valve
vertical single, double-barrel carburettor, forward-mounted
magneto, all-chain drive.
£4,050–4,500 / €6,100–6,700 / $7,500–8,300 ⊞ VER
**Many thousands of Model Ps were sold, but it did not
enjoy the best of reputations for quality or reliability;
it was being built very much to a budget.**

1926 BSA S26 and Sidecar, 493cc, side-valve single,
hand-change gearbox, kickstart, magdyno, electric lighting,
girder forks, rigid frame, older restoration fitted with more
practical 1928 BSA drum brakes.
£2,600–2,900 / €3,900–4,300 / $4,800–5,300 ⊙ VMCC

▶ **1929 Harley-Davidson Model J and Sidecar,** 998cc,
V-twin engine, 3-speed gearbox, pumped lubrication.
**£10,100–12,100 / €15,100–18,100
$18,700–22,400** ⚲ B(Kn)

◀ **1937 BMW R12 and Sidecar,** 745cc, side-valve flat-twin, 78 x 78mm bore and stroke, 18bhp at 3,400rpm, pillion saddle, sidecar spare wheel.
£5,400–6,000 / €8,100–9,000
$10,000–11,100 ⊞ MW
The R12 was built between 1935 and 1942, and pioneered the use of the telescopic front fork. It was also widely chosen by both civilian owners and the German military for sidecar use. A total of 36,008 R12s were built. This single-carburettor version was produced exclusively for the German Army between 1937 and 1942.

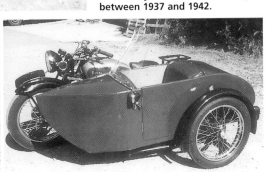

1937 Royal Enfield KX and Period Sidecar, 1140cc, side-valve V-twin, 85.5 x 99.25mm bore and stroke, hand-change gearbox, drum brakes, single carburettor, chain-driven magneto.
£6,300–7,000 / €9,400–10,500 / $11,700–13,000 ⊞ CotC

1938 Brough Superior SS80 and Brough Sidecar, 982cc, 'castle' front forks, restored, little recent use.
£12,400–14,900 / €18,600–22,300 / $23,000–27,600 ⚲ B(Kn)

c1938 Ariel 4G Square Four and Steib Sidecar, 995cc, overhead-valve 4-cylinder engine, 65 x 75mm bore and stroke, iron heads and barrels, 4-speed foot-change gearbox, girder forks.
£5,100–5,700 / €7,600–8,500
$9,400–10,500 ⚲ AOM

1941 Harley-Davidson Knucklehead and Sidecar, 1200cc, V-twin engine, concours condition.
£12,400–14,900 / €18,600–22,300 / $23,000–27,600 ⚲ BB(L)
Introduced in 1936, the Knucklehead was Harley-Davidson's first series-production overhead-valve model. It was built in both 999cc (61cu in) and 1200cc (74cu in) engine sizes.

◄ **1950 Moto Guzzi Astore and Parri Sidecar,** 498.4cc, overhead-valve horizontal single, 88 x 82mm bore and stroke, 5.5:1 compression ratio, 19bhp at 4,300rpm, 4-speed foot-change gearbox.
£10,800–12,000 / €16,200–18,000
$20,000–22,200 ⊞ NLM
The Astore was built between 1949 and 1950, and essentially was a lower-compression version of the more well-known Falcone. Fitted with coachbuilt Parri-style single seat sidecar.

► **1950 Velocette MAC and Period Sidecar,** 349cc, overhead-valve single, 68 x 96mm bore and stroke, 4-speed foot-change gearbox, rigid frame, telescopic forks, drum brakes, pillion saddle.
£2,500–2,750 / €3,700–4,100
$4,600–5,100 ⚙ Velo
Even though it was only a three-fifty, the MAC was still capable of pulling a single-seat sidecar – thanks to the generous amount of torque from its long-stroke, single-cylinder engine.

◄ **1951 BSA M21 AA and AA Patrol Sidecar,** 591cc, side-valve single, 82 x 112mm bore and stroke, 4-speed foot-change gearbox, telescopic forks.
£1,600–1,900 / €2,400–2,850
$2,950–3,500 ⚒ B(Kn)
The AA's new machines in 1951 were liveried in the traditional corporate colour scheme of yellow and black, with AA badges on the sidecar and petrol tank panels. The capacious sidecar box contained most tools to enable roadside repairs to be carried out, along with selected commonly required spares. The road patrols had significantly less weather protection than today's rescue services but leg shields provided some rider comfort for the cold winter months.

1952 Motobécane Model U2C and sidecar, 175cc, overhead-valve 4-cylinder engine, unit construction, enclosed valve gear, 4-speed foot-change gearbox, single-seat sidecar with tubular chassis and aluminium body.
£2,350–2,600 / €3,500–3,900 / $4,350–4,800 ⊞ MW

1955 AJS Model 20 and sidecar, 498cc, overhead-valve vertical twin, alloy heads, iron barrels, 4-speed Burman gearbox, full-width alloy hubs, 'Jampot' rear shock absorbers, excellent condition.
£2,900–3,200 / €4,350–4,800 / $5,400–6,000 ⊞ MW

1957 BSA A10 Golden Flash and Watsonian Monaco Sidecar, 646cc, overhead-valve pre-unit parallel twin, 70 x 84mm bore and stroke, 4-speed foot-change gearbox, 19in wheels, telescopic forks, swinging-arm frame.
£4,000–4,500 / €6,000–6,700 / $7,500–8,300 ⊞ PM

Auction prices

Miller's only includes motorcycles declared sold. Our guide prices take into account the buyer's premium, VAT on the premium, and the extent of any published catalogue information relating to condition and provenance. motorcycles sold at auction are identified by the 🔧 icon; full details of the auction house can be found on page 167.

◀ **1957 Norton Model 19 and Watsonian Monaco Sidecar,** 597cc, overhead-valve single, 82 x 113mm bore and stroke, 4-speed foot-change gearbox, Roadholder forks, swinging-arm frame, full-width alloy hubs.
£2,100–2,500 / €3,150–3,750
$3,900–4,600 🔧 B(Kn)

▶ **1960 BMW R60 and Steib-pattern Sidecar,** 594cc, overhead-valve flat-twin, 72 x 73mm bore and stroke, Earles front forks, Denfold dualseat, chrome rear carrier, replica Steib single-seat sidecar.
£4,300–4,800 / €6,500–7,200
$8,000–8,900 ⊞ MW

◀ **1962 Triumph 6T Thunderbird and Watsonian Monarch Sidecar,** 649cc, overhead-valve pre-unit twin, 71 x 82mm bore and stroke, alloy head, cast-iron barrel, 4-speed foot-change gearbox, headlamp nacelle, siamesed exhaust, all correct tinware, 24,000 miles recorded.
£2,900–3,250
€4,400–4,900
$5,400–6,000 ⊛ VMCC

Specials

c1929 Ariel V-twin Special, 600cc, JAP side-valve V-twin engine, 85.7 x 104mm bore and stroke, Ariel single-cylinder frame and cycle parts.
£2,650–3,200 / €4,000–4,800 / $4,900–5,900 ⚒ CGC

1951 Ariel Square Four Special, 995cc, Earles-type front forks, oil cooler, 12 volt electrics, alloy rims, one-off fairing and seat, indicators.
£2,050–2,450 / €3,050–3,650 / $3,800–4,550 ⚒ CGC

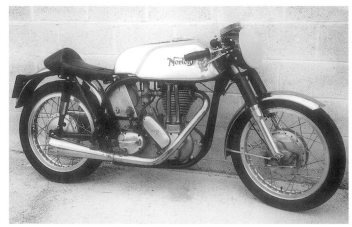

◀ **c1954 Norton ES2 Café Racer,** 490cc, overhead-valve single, 79 x 100mm bore and stroke, alloy cylinder barrel and head, tuned engine, Amal Mk1 Concentric carburettor, 4-speed AMC gearbox, early wideline Norton frame, full café racer conversion with Manx-style alloy fuel and oil tanks, alloy rims, twin-leading-shoe Dominator front brake, sweptback exhaust header pipe with megaphone, clip-ons and flyscreen.
£2,700–3,000 / €4,000–4,500 $5,000–5,500 ⊞ BLM

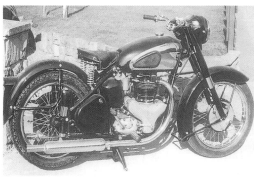

c1959 Norton Café Racer, 490cc, Norton overhead-valve ES2 single-cylinder engine, laid-down Norton gearbox, Featherbed frame, twin-leading-shoe front brake, Dominator full-width hubs, alloy rims, racing tank and seat, clip-ons, megaphone silencer.
£1,150–1,350 / €1,700–2,000 / $2,100–2,500 ⚒ B(Kn)

c1956 BSA B31/A10 Special, 646cc, A10 twin-cylinder engine, B31 single-cylinder frame, very good condition.
£1,700–2,050 / €2,550–3,050 / $3,150–3,800 ⚒ B(Kn)

1959 Tribsa Special, 499cc, 1950s Triumph all-alloy Tiger 100 pre-unit engine, single Amal Concentric Mk1 carburettor, BSA primary chaincase, 1959 BSA frame, fork gaiters, indicators, megaphone silencers.
£2,700–3,000 / €4,000–4,500 / $5,000–5,500 ⫘ WCMC

◀ **1959 Tribsa Special,** 499cc, Triumph pre-unit twin-cylinder engine, one-piece balanced crankshaft, E3134 camshafts, gas-flowed cylinder head, twin Amal Concentric carburettors, BSA frame, chrome BSA Rocket Gold Star fork yokes, Norton Roadholder fork leg assemblies, twin chrome Jaeger instruments, Triumph twin-leading-shoe front brake.
£3,600–4,000 / €5,400–6,000 $6,700–7,400 ⊞ BLM

▶ **1960s Beezton Café Racer,** 654cc, 1955 Norton Dominator 88 Wideline frame, 1971 BSA A65 unit engine, SRM timing-side needle-roller-bearing conversion, Boyer Brandsen electronic ignition, Robinson 4-leading-shoe front brake, racing tanks, seat, high-level exhaust.
£4,600–5,500 / €6,900–8,200 $8,500–10,200 ⋗ B(Ba)

1960s Matchless Drag Bike, twin 497cc Matchless overhead-valve single-cylinder engines, extended rigid frame, AMC full-width alloy hubs, Teledraulic front forks.
£2,700–3,000 / €4,000–4,500 / $5,000–5,500 ⊞ OxM

◀ **1964 BSA C15 Café Racer,** 247cc, racing tank, dual racing seat, rear-set footrests, clip-ons, fork gaiters, Gold Star silencer, alloy rims, chrome headlamp, lightweight mudguards.
£1,450–1,600 / €2,200–2,450 / $2,700–3,000 ⊞ BLM

▶ **c1964 Norton Manx/Dominator/ Commando Special,** 745cc, Commando twin-cylinder engine, 73 x 89mm bore and stroke, 1964 Dominator frame, alloy fuel and oil tanks, Manx-type rear swinging arm, Manx top yoke and mudguards, 8-leading-shoe CMA front drum brake, Manx rear wheel, sweptback exhaust pipes, short megaphone silencers.
£4,850–5,800 / €7,300–8,700 $9,000–10,700 ⋗ B(Kn)

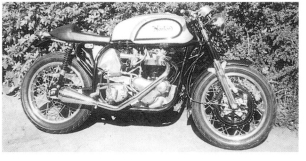

1968 Vincent Egli, 998cc, ex-race bike converted for road use, Black Shadow specification engine, twin Amal Concentric Mk1 carburettors, Fritz Egli chassis, alloy tank, Ceriani front forks, 8-leading-shoe front drum brake, rear disc brake.
£12,600–14,000 / €18,900–21,000 / $23,300–26,000 ⚙ **VOC**

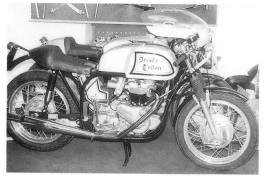

1970s Dresda Triton, 649cc, Triumph T120 Bonneville pre-unit engine, Amal Concentric Mk1 carburettors, Triumph gearbox, Norton Dominator slimline frame, Roadholder forks, full-width brakes, 5-gallon tank, racing seat.
£4,000–4,500 / €6,000–6,700 / $7,400–8,300 ⊞ **MW**

c1970 Ducati Sebring Café Racer, 340cc, overhead-camshaft unit single, wet-sump lubrication, 5-speed gearbox, Benelli 2C front brake, 32mm Marzocchi front forks, racing tank, 1974 Desmo 250 seat, alloy rims, clip-ons, rear-sets.
£2,050–2,300 / €3,100–3,450 / $3,800–4,200 ⊞ **MW**

◄ **1976 Japauto 1000 VX,** 950cc, Honda CB750 4-cylinder engine, Japauto big-bore kit, fairing, cast-alloy wheels, triple disc brakes.
£5,000–5,500 / €7,500–8,200 $9,200–10,200 ⊞ **MW**
Japauto was a Paris dealership that gained a lot of success (and publicity) for a series of Honda-engined specials built in the 1970s. This particular bike is a road-going replica of the firm's race-winning endurance machines.

▶ **c1980 Moto Guzzi Le Mans Special,** 900cc, rebuilt 1999 at a cost of £2,700 / €4,000 / $5,000, little use since, new barrels, pistons, valves and balanced crank, Carillo rods, PR3 cams, ported cylinder heads, uprated timing chain and tensioner, deep sump, twin Dell'Orto carburettors, stainless-steel Keihan exhaust, 42mm Marzocchi forks, 320mm Brembo front brake discs with 4-pot calipers, Koni Dial-a-Ride shocks, stainless steel braided brake hoses.
£2,550–3,050 / €3,850–4,600 $4,700–5,600 ⚑ **B(Kn)**

Memorabilia

A signed photograph of Steve
Spray, in John Player Special leathers,
mounted on board, c1995, 37 x 25in
(94 x 63.5cm).
£210–250 / €310–370
$390–460 ✗ AGr

▶ A Norton plastic electric wall
clock, from the former Norton factory
at Shenstone, Warwickshire, c1992,
13in (33cm) square.
£250–300 / €380–450
$460–550 ✗ AGr

A two-piece graphic on soft board,
depicting a John Player Norton Rotary
racing motorcycle, c1995, 48 x 72in
(122 x 183cm).
£170–200 / €250–300
$310–370 ✗ AGr

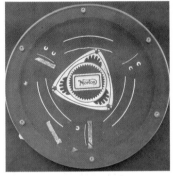

A Norton perspex display case,
containing a sectioned epitrochoid
rotor, c1995, 15in (38cm) diam.
£190–220 / €280–330
$350–410 ✗ AGr

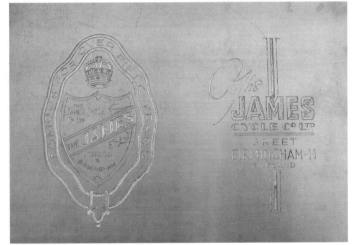

◀ A brass printer's plate, inscribed
'The James Famous For Over Fifty
Years', and 'The James Cycle Co Ltd,
Greet, Birmingham 11, England',
embossed with the James logo,
mid-20thC, 6 x 8in (15 x 20.5cm).
£140–165 / €210–250
$260–310 ✗ AGr

A New Imperial Cycles Ltd Registered Office inscribed
brass plate, 1900–50, 6 x 10in (15 x 25.5cm).
£210–250 / €310–370 / $390–460 ✗ AGr

A John Player Special Team photograph, including Steve
Spray and Brian Crighton, c1995, 17 x 24in (43 x 61cm).
£200–240 / €300–360 / $370–440 ✗ AGr

A 'Sprocket' cartoon drawing, depicting the Norton management discussing the rotary engine, 1990s, 5¾ x 8¼in (14.5 x 21cm).
£230–270 / €340–400 / $420–500 ⚒ AGr

▶ J. Montgomery, an acrylic painting on canvas, depicting an early Scott twin-cylinder racing motorcycle, signed, 1950s, 19 x 30in (48.5 x 76cm), framed.
£45–55 / €70–80 $85–100 ⚒ CGC

◀ J. Montgomery, an acrylic painting on canvas, depicting two flat-tank vintage motorcycles, signed, 1950s, 19 x 30in (48.5 x 76cm).
£55–65 €85–100 $100–120 ⚒ CGC

◀ J. Montgomery, an acrylic painting on canvas, depicting a Rudge Multi, signed, 1950s, 19 x 30in (48.5 x 76cm).
£45–55 / €70–80 / $85–100 ⚒ CGC

J. Montgomery, an acrylic painting on canvas, depicting a 'Garden Gate' plunger-framed Manx Norton, excellent condition, late 1940s, signed, 1950s, 19 x 30in (48.5 x 76cm).
£80–95 / €120–140 / $150–180 ⚒ CGC

An autograph book, comprising 280 A4 pages with signatures of Mike Hailwood, Barry Sheene, Phil Read, Kork Ballington, Randy Mamola, Joey Dunlop, Will Hartog, Ron Haslam, Rolf Biland, Tom Herron, Pat Hennen, George O'Dell, Rolf Steinhausen, Jock Taylor, and many other British and foreign riders.
£1,650–1,950 / €2,500–2,900 / $3,000–3,600 ⚒ B(Kn)

◀ A Mini-Motor double-sided advertising sign, 1950s.
£100–120 €150–180 $185–220 ⚒ CGC

Decter Brown, three framed and glazed posters for Thruxton National Motorcycle Racing on 21 April, 4 May and 23 June, 1960s.
£310–370 / €460–550 / $570–680 ⚒ CGC

▶ A New Hudson double-sided enamel sign, 1920s–30s, 15¾ x 19¾in (40 x 50cm).
£310–370 €460–550 $570–680 ⚒ H&H

A Raleigh Motorcycles enamel sign, inscribed 'Raleigh – The Record Breaker', minor wear to mounting holes, 1930s, 19¾ x 15⅜in (50 x 40cm).
£120–140 / € 180–210
$220–260 ➚ H&H

◄ **A black and white print,** entitled 'The Great Escape', featuring Steve McQueen, c2000, 33½ x 26in (85 x 66cm), framed and glazed.
£110–130 / € 165–195
$200–240 ➚ H&H

A Motor Cycling Club Petrol Consumption Test bronze medal, by Mappin & Webb, awarded 12th September 1908, in original stamped box.
£35–42 / € 50–60
$65–78 ➚ B(Kn)

An Auto-Cycle Club timekeeper's official programme, from the first race for the International Cycle Tourist Trophy, 28 May 1907, the notes with entrant numbers against a nett and gross timed figure, possibly the original timings taken by A. V. Ebblewhite as he waited at the line, some wear.
£940–1,100 / € 1,400–1,650 / $1,750–2,100 ➚ B(Kn)

A Motor Cycling Club London to Edinburgh gold medal, awarded to H. R. G. Slingo, dated May, 1913, in original Harrods presentation box.
£210–250 / € 310–370
$390–460 ➚ B(Kn)

A gold and enamel OMCC 12-Hour Reliability Trial Indian Medal, awarded May 1913, in original presentation box.
£250–300 / € 380–450
$460–550 ➚ B(Kn)

Sets/pairs

Unless otherwise stated, any description which refers to 'a set' or 'a pair' includes a guide price for the entire set or the pair, even though the illustration may show only a single item.

◄ **A Motor Cycling Club London–Edinburgh–London Side Car Cup silver trophy,** by Mappin & Webb, awarded to H. R. G. Slingo in 1913, hallmarked, makers' stamp, 1913, 8in (20.5cm) high.
£80–95 / € 120–140
$150–180 ➚ B(Ba)

► **Five silver Oxford Motor Cycle Club awards,** presented for trials, runs and hillclimbs, 1913–14.
£80–95 / € 120–140
$150–180 ➚ B(Kn)

A Motor Cycling Club Devon Trial Motor Bicycle & Side Car silver trophy, awarded to H. R. G. Slingo on 1 and 3rd August 1914, hallmarked, 10¼in (26cm) high.
£105–125 / €160–190 $195–230 ↗ B(Ba)

A Sunbeam Motorcycle Club 200-Mile Trial enamelled medal, awarded to L. Gorham, 1929, in original box.
£125–150 / €185–220 $240–280 ↗ B(Ba)

A Castrol postcard, depicting Norton works riders Freddie Frith and Jimmie Guthrie, 1930s, 4 x 6in (10 x 15cm).
£11–15 / €18–22 / $24–28 ⊞ S&D

Two Grindlay-Peerless sales brochures, a duotone 4-page folder with skirt dated November 1930 and a Tiger range duotone 4-page folder with skirt dated 1932.
£35–40 / €50–60 / $65–75 ↗ H&H

Three Coventry Eagle sales brochures, a black and white catalogue dated 1931, duotone brochures with 8 page foldouts for 1932 and 1934, 11½ x 8¼in (29.5 x 210cm), large A4.
£50–60 / €75–90 / $90–105 ↗ H&H

An Excelsior brochure and Excelsior Motorcycles handbook, brochure comprising 20 duotone pages, 1937, 11½ x 8¼in (29.5 x 210cm), handbook 1933–34, large A4.
£55–65 / €80–95 $100–120 ↗ H&H

▶ **A Vespa dealership poster,** French,1950s, 37½ x 24in (95 x 61cm), framed and glazed.
£110–130 / €165–195 $200–240 ↗ CGC

A selection of 40 motorcycle sales brochures, including BSA, Triumph, Royal Enfield, James, Velocette and Norton, 1950s.
£240–290 / €360–430 / $450–540 ⚲ H&H

◀ **Rod Walker,** a watercolour, depicting Jim Redman during the 1965 TT cornering the 6-cylinder 250cc Honda that won the event three years running, commissioned 1989 to celebrate Honda's 30th appearance at the event, signed, 1968, 15½ x 20in (39.5 x 51cm), framed and glazed.
£210–250 / €320–380 $390–460 ⚲ H&H

Two posters, Motorcycle Racing at Thruxton International 500-mile Grand Prix 11 May, Commonwealth Trophy Meeting 2 September, 1968, 19¾ x 15in (50 x 38cm), framed and glazed.
£45–50 / €70–80 / $85–100 ⚲ CGC

A Piaggio Service Station sign, 1970s.
£135–150 / €200–220 $250–280 ⌺ MAY

Rod Organ, a painting of 500cc Motocross Championship winner Graham Noyce, commissioned by the late Brian Coombes, c1976.
£350–420 / €520–620 $650–780 ⚲ B(Ba)

A Quadrophenia film review poster, 36¼ x 25½in (92 x 65cm), framed and glazed.
£28–32 / €40–50 / $50–60 ⚲ H&H

▶ **John Player Special original artwork for a poster,** depicting the rotary racing machine No. 20 ridden by Trevor Nation, under tissue, 1989, 28 x 40in (71 x 101.5cm).
£470–560 €700–840 $850–1,000 ⚲ AGr

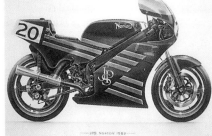

A Denso Spark Plugs sponsor's calendar poster for 1995, signed by Ian Simpson and Phil Borley.
£150–180 / €220–260 / $280–330 ⚲ AGr

V. R. Williamson, oil on canvas portrait of Jim Moody riding the Duckhams rotary, signed and dated 1995.
£960–1,150 / €1,450–1,700 / $1,800–2,150 ⚲ AGr

Key to Illustrations

Each illustration and descriptive caption is accompanied by a letter code. By referring to the following list of Auctioneers (denoted by *), dealers (•), Clubs, Museums and Trusts (🚲), the source of any item may be immediately determined. Inclusion in this edition no way constitutes or implies a contract or binding offer on the part of any of our contributors to supply or sell the goods illustrated, or similar articles, at the prices stated. Advertisers in this year's directory are denoted by †.

If you require a valuation, it is advisable to check whether the dealer or specialist will carry out this service and if there is a charge. Please mention *Miller's* when making an enquiry. A valuation by telephone is not possible. Most dealers are willing to help you with your enquiry; however, they are very busy people and consideration of the above points would be welcomed.

AGr 🔨 Andrew Grant, St Mark's House, St Mark's Close, Cherry Orchard, Worcester WR5 3DL Tel: 01905 357547 www.andrew-grant.co.uk

AOM 🚲 Ariel Owners Motor Cycle Club, Andy Hemingway, 80 Pasture Lane, Clayton, Bradford, Yorkshire BD14 6LN andy_hemingway@yahoo.com

AtMC ⊞† Atlantic Motorcycles, 20 Station Road, Twyford, Berkshire RG10 9NT Tel: 0118 9342266 www.classicbikesatlantic.co.uk

B(Ba) 🔨 Bonhams, 10 Salem Road, Bayswater, London W2 4DL Tel: 020 7313 2700 www.bonhams.com

B(Kn) 🔨† Bonhams, Montpelier Street, Knightsbridge, London SW7 1HH Tel: 020 7393 3900 www.bonhams.com

BB(L) 🔨 Bonhams & Butterfields, 7601 Sunset Boulevard, Los Angeles CA 90046, USA Tel: 323 850 7500

BB(S) 🔨 Bonhams & Butterfields, 220 San Bruno Avenue, San Francisco CA 94103, USA Tel: 415 861 7500

BGB 🚲 Benelli Motobi Club GB, Val Peace, 85 Ballamaddrell, Port Erin, Isle of Man IM9 6AU

BJ 🔨 Barrett-Jackson Auction Company, LLC, 3020 N Scottsdale Road, Scottsdale, Arizona, USA Tel: 480 421 6694 www.barrett-jackson.com

BLM ⊞† Bill Little Motorcycles, Oak Farm, Braydon, Swindon, Wiltshire SN5 0AG Tel: 01666 860577 www.classicbikesuk.com

BRIT 🔨 British Car Auctions Ltd, Classic & Historic Automobile Division, Auction Centre, Blackbushe Airport, Blackwater, Camberley, Surrey GU17 9LG Tel: 01252 878555

CFRC 🚲 Classic 50 Racing Club, Chris Alty, 14a Kestrel Park, Ashurst, Skelmersdale, Lancashire WN8 6TB Classic50Racing@aol.com

CGC 🔨 Cheffins, 8 Hill Street, Saffron Walden, Essex CB10 1JD Tel: 01799 513131 vintage@cheffins.co.uk www.cheffins.co.uk

CMT 🚲 Cotswold Motorcycle & Three Wheeler Club, 82 Hampton Street, Tetbury, Gloucestershire GL8 8LE

CotC ⊞† Cotswold Classics, Unit 30, Ullenwood Court, Ullenwood, Nr Cheltenham, Gloucestershire GL53 9QS Tel: 01242 228622 tim@cotswold-classics.co.uk www.motorcyclesclassic.com

COYS 🔨 Coys of Kensington, 2–4 Queens Gate Mews, London SW7 5QJ Tel: 020 7584 7444 www.coys.co.uk

EWC 🚲 Exeter Motorcycle & Three Wheeler Club, No 1 Bourne Rise, Pinhoe, Exeter, Devon EX4 8QD

EXM 🚲 Excelsior Manxman Tel: 01273 842433

FBC 🚲 Francis-Barnett Owners Club, Club Secretary Sue Dorling, Clouds Hill, 5 Blacklands Road, Upper Bucklebury, Nr Reading, Berkshire RG7 6QP Tel: 01635 864256

H&H 🔨 H & H Classic Auctions Ltd, Whitegate Farm, Hatton Lane, Hatton, Warrington, Cheshire WA4 4BZ Tel: 01925 730630 www.classic-auctions.co.uk

ILO 🚲 International Laverda Owners Club, New Membership and Club Archive c/o John Faulkner, Hill Farm, Dorton, Aylesbury, Buckinghamshire HP18 9NJ Tel: 01844 238 269 evenings until 11pm editor@iloc.org.uk/ www.iloc.org.uk/

IMC 🚲 Indian Motorcycle Owners Club, c/o John Chatterton, (Membership Secretary), 183 Buxton Road, Newtown, Disley, Stockport, Cheshire SK12 2RA Tel: 01663 747106

IMOC 🚲 Italian Motorcycle Owners Club (GB) www.italianmotorcycles.co.uk

LDM 🚲 The London Douglas Motorcycle Club Ltd, Reg Holmes, 48 Standish Avenue, Stoke Lodge, Patchway, Bristol BS34 6AG www.douglasmotorcycles.co.uk

MAY ⊞† Mayfair Motors, PO Box 66, Lymington, Hampshire SO41 0XE Tel: 01590 644476 mayfair@enterprise.net

MW ⊞† Mick Walker, 10 Barton Road, Wisbech, Cambridgeshire PE13 1LB Tel: 01945 461914 www.mickwalker.co.uk

NIO 🚲 New Imperial Owners Association, Mrs J. E. Jarvis, Lyndhurst House, Victoria Road, Hayling Island, Hampshire PO11 0LU

NLM ⊞† North Leicester Motorcycles, Whitehill Road, Ellistown, Leicestershire LE67 1EL Tel: 01530 263381 stuart@motomorini.co.uk www.motomorini.co.uk

NORM 🚲 Norman Cycles Club, 8 St Francis Road, Cheriton, Folkestone, Kent CT19 4BJ www.normancycles.co.uk

OxCH ⊞ Oxford Classic Honda, Unit 2, The Old Thames Water Workshop, Sandford, Oxford OX4 4YU Tel: 01865 771166 www.classichondamotorcycles.co.uk

OxM ⊞† Oxney Motorcycles, Rolvenden,
Cranbrook, Kent TN17 4QA
Tel: 01797 270119
www.oxneymotorcycles.co.uk

PAN ⚙ Panther Owners Club, Graham & Julie
Dibbins, Oakdene, 22 Oak Street,
Netherton, Dudley, West Midlands
DY2 9LJ
www.pantherownersclub.com

PM ⊞† Pollard's Motorcycles, The Garage,
Clarence Street, Dinnington,
Sheffield, South Yorkshire S31 7HA
Tel: 01909 563310

PS 🔧 Palmer Snell, 65 Cheap Street,
Sherborne, Dorset DT9 3BA
Tel: 01935 812218

RRM ⊞ RR Motor Services Ltd, Bethersden,
Ashford, Kent TN26 3DN
Tel: 01233 820219

S&D ⊞ S&D Postcards, Bartlett Street Antique
Centre, 5–10 Bartlett Street, Bath,
Somerset BA1 2QZ Tel: 07979 506415
wndvd@aol.com

T&DC ⚙ Taunton & District British & Classic
Motorcycle Club, 3 Vickery Close,
Curry Rivel, Langport, Somerset
TA10 0PY

Velo ⚙ Velocette Owners Club, William
Greenwood (Secretary), 7 Townsend
Road, Harpenden, Hertfordshire
AL5 4BQ Tel: 01582 713880
billwgreenwood@aol.com
www.velocetteowners.com

VER ⊞† Verralls (Handcross) Ltd, Caffyns Row,
High Street, Handcross, Haywards Heath,
West Sussex RH17 6BJ
Tel: 01444 400678 www.verralls.com

VJMC ⚙ Vintage Japanese Motorcycle Club,
PO Box 515, Dartford, Kent DA1 5WB
www.vjmc.com

VMCC ⚙† The Vintage Motor Cycle Club, Allen
House, Wetmore Road, Burton-on-Trent,
Staffordshire DE14 1TR
Tel: 01283 540557 hq@vmcc.net
www.vmcc.net

VOC ⚙ Vincent HRD Owners Club, Paul Adams
(Information Officer), 1 St Georges Road,
Footscray, Sidcup, Kent DA14 5JN
Tel: 020 8300 3118

WCMC ⚙ Wells Classic Motorcycle Club, 51 St
Cuthberts Avenue, Wells, Somerset BA5 2JS

WMC ⚙ Whitchurch MCC, 50 Ravenhead Drive,
Whitchurch Park, Bristol, Somerset
BS14 9AU

Index to Advertisers

Bibliography

Bacon, Roy; *British Motorcycles of the 1930s*,
Osprey, 1986
Bacon, Roy; *Honda The Early Classic Motorcycles*,
Osprey, 1985
Bacon, Roy; *BSA Twins & Triples*, Osprey, 1980
Rhodes, Ivan; *Velocette*, Osprey 1990
Bacon, Roy; Hicks, Roger; McDiarmid, Mac; Tipler,
John & Walker, Mick; *The Encyclopaedia of
Motorcycles*, Silverdale, 2001
Rhodes, Ivan; *Velocette*, Osprey 1990
Walker, Mick; *BMW Twins The Complete Story*,
Crowood, 1998
Walker, Mick; *Laverda Twins & Triples The Complete
Story*, Crowood, 1999
Walker, Mick; *Moto Guzzi Twins The Complete
Story*, Crowood, 1998
Walker, Mick; *MV Agusta Fours The Complete Story*,
Crowood, 2000

Walker, Mick; *Gilera The Complete Story*,
Crowood, 2000
Walker, Mick; *British Racing Motorcycles*, Redline, 1998
Walker, Mick; *Italian Racing Motorcycles*,
Redline, 1999
Walker, Mick; *German Racing Motorcycles*,
Redline, 1999
Walker, Mick; *European Racing Motorcycles*,
Redline, 2000
Walker, Mick; *Hamlyn History of Motorcycling*,
Hamlyn, 1997
Walker, Mick; *The Manx Norton*, Redline 2000
Walker, Mick; *The AJS 7R*, Redline 2001
Walker, Mick; *Japanese Grand Prix Racing
Motorcycles*, Redline 2002
Webster, Mike; *Classic Scooters*, Parragon, 1997
Wherrett, Duncan; *Vincent*, Osprey 1994
Woollett, Mick; *Norton*, Osprey, 1992

Glossary

We have attempted to define some of the terms that you will come across in this book. If there are any other terms or technicalities you would like explained or you feel should be included in future editions, please let us know.

ACU – Auto Cycle Union, which controls a large part of British motorcycle sport.

Advanced ignition – Ignition timing set to cause firing before the piston reaches centre top, variation is now automatic.

Air-cooling – Most motorcycle engines rely on air-cooling, their cylinder barrels and heads being finned to dissipate heat.

Air intake – The carburettor port that admits air to mix with fuel from the float chamber.

AMCA – Amateur Motor Cycle Association, promoters of British off-road events.

APMC – The Association of Pioneer Motor Cyclists.

Auto Cycle Club – Formed in 1903, this was the original governing body of motorcycle sport. In 1907 it became the Auto Cycle Union.

Automatic inlet valve – Activated by the engine suction; forerunner of the mechanically-operated valve.

Balloon tyres – Wide-section, low-pressure tyres, fitted to tourers for comfort.

Beaded-edge tyres – Encased rubber beads in channels on wheel rim.

Belt drive – A leather or fabric belt running from the engine or gearbox to the rear wheel.

BHP – A measure of engine output; the amount of power required to lift 33,000lb to a height of 1ft in a minute equals 1bhp.

BMCRC – British Motor Cycle Racing Club, formed in 1909. Also known as Bemsee.

BMF – British Motorcycle Federation.

Bore/stroke ratio – The ratio of an engine's cylinder diameter to its piston stroke.

Caliper – A clamping device containing hydraulically-operated pistons that forms part of a disc brake.

Cam – Device for opening and closing a valve.

Camshaft – The mounting shaft for the cam; can be in low, high or overhead position.

Carburettor – Used to produce the air/fuel mixture required by the engine.

Chain drive – Primary form of drive from engine to gearbox and secondary gearbox to rear wheel.

Combustion chamber – Area where the fuel/air mixture is compressed and ignited, between the piston and cylinder head.

Compression ratio – The amount by which the fuel/air mixture is compressed by the piston in the combustion chamber.

Crankcase – The casing enclosing the crankshaft and its attachments.

Crankshaft – The shaft that converts the vertical motion of the piston into a rotary movement.

Cylinder – Contains the piston and is capped by the cylinder head. Upper portion forms the combustion chamber where the fuel/air mixture is compressed and burnt to provide power.

Cylinder head – Caps the top of the cylinder. In a four-stroke engine, it usually carries the valves and, in some cases, the camshaft(s).

Damper – Fitted to slow the movement in the suspension system, or as a crankshaft balance.

Displacement – The engine capacity or amount of volume displaced by the movement of the piston from bottom dead centre to top dead centre.

Distributor – A gear-driven contact that sends high-tension current to the spark plugs.

DOHC – Double overhead camshaft.

Dry sump – An engine lubrication system in which the oil is contained in a separate reservoir and pumped to and from the engine by a pair of pumps.

Earles forks – A front fork design incorporating long leading links connected by a rigid pivot behind the front wheel.

Featherbed – A Norton frame, designed by Rex and Crommie McCandless, of Belfast, used for racing machines from 1950; road machines from 1953.

FIM – Federation Internationale Motorcycliste, controls motorcycle sport worldwide.

Flat-twin – An engine featuring two horizontally-opposed cylinders.

Float – A plastic or brass box that floats upon the fuel in a float chamber and operates the needle valve controlling the fuel flow.

Flywheel – Attached to the crankshaft, this heavy wheel smooths intermittent firing impulses and helps slow running.

Friction drive – An early form of drive using discs in contact instead of chains and gears.

Gearbox – Cased trains of pinion wheels that can be moved to provide alternative ratios.

Gear ratios – Differential rates of speed between sets of pinions to provide faster or slower rotation of the rear wheel in relation to the engine speed.

GP – Grand Prix, an international race to a fixed formula.

High camshaft – Mounted high up in the engine to shorten the pushrods in an ohv arrangement.

IOE – Inlet over exhaust, a common arrangement with an overhead inlet valve and side exhaust valve.

Leaf spring – Metal blades clamped and bolted together, used in early suspension systems.

Magneto – A high-tension dynamo that produces current for the ignition spark; superseded by coil ignition.

Main bearings – Bearings in which the crankshaft runs.

Manifold – Collection of pipes supplying fuel/air mixture or removing exhaust gases.

MCC – The Motor Cycling Club, which runs sporting events; formed in 1902.

Moped – A light motorcycle of under 50cc with pedals attached.

OHC – See Overhead camshaft.

Overhead camshaft – An engine design in which the camshaft (or camshafts) is carried in the cylinder head.

OHV – See Overhead valve.

Overhead valve – A valve mounted in the cylinder head.

Pinking – A distinctive noise produced by an engine with over-advanced ignition or inferior fuel.

Piston – Moves up and down the cylinder, drawing in fuel/air mixture, compressing it, being driven down by combustion and forcing spent gases out.

Post-vintage – A motorcycle made after December 31, 1930, and before January 1, 1945.

Pressure plate – The plate against which the clutch springs react to load the friction plates.

Pushrods – Operating rods for overhead valves, working from cams below the cylinder.

Rotary valve – A valve driven from the camshaft for inlet or exhaust and usually of a disc or cylindrical shape; for either two- or four-stroke engines.

SACU – Scottish Auto Cycle Union, which controls motorcycle sport in Scotland.

SAE – Society of Automotive Engineers. Used in a system of classifying engine oils such as SAE30, I0W/50, etc.

Shock absorber – A damper, used to control vertical movement of suspension, or to cushion a drive train.

Silencer (muffler) – Device fitted to the exhaust system of an engine in which the pressure of the exhaust gases is reduced to lessen noise.

Swinging arm – Rear suspension by radius arms, which carry the wheel and are attached to the frame at their forward ends.

Torque – Twisting force in a shaft; can be measured to determine at what speed an engine develops most torque.

Directory of Museums

BEDFORDSHIRE
Shuttleworth Collection
Old Warden Park, Biggleswade, SG18 9EA Tel: 01767
627288 enquiries@shuttleworth.org www.shuttleworth.org
A collection of vintage aircraft plus cars, motorcycles and
horsedrawn carriages from c1880 to 1945. Open daily
except Christmas to New Year week, April to October
10.00am–5.00pm, November to March 10.00am–4.00pm.

CHESHIRE
Mouldsworth Motor Museum
Smithy Lane, Mouldsworth, CW3 8AR Tel: 01928 731781
Collection of over 60 vintage, classic and sport cars,
motorcycles and early bicycles housed in 1930s Art Deco
building. Open Sundays Noon–5.00pm and Bank Holiday
weekends, also Wednesdays July and August.

CUMBRIA
Western Lakes Motor Museum
The Maltings, Brewery Lane, Cockermouth Tel: 01900 824448
Located in Jennings Castle Brewery beneath the walls of
Cockermouth Castle. Some 45 cars and 17 motorcycles
from Vintage to Formula 3.

DEVON
Combe Martin Motorcycle Collection
Cross Street, Combe Martin, Ilfracombe, EX34 0DH
Tel: 01271 882346
Around 100 classic and British motorcycles plus garage
memorabilia. Souvenir shop.

ESSEX
Battlesbridge Motorcycle Museum
Muggeridge Farm, Maltings Road, Battlesbridge, SS11 7RF
Tel: 01268 561700
An interesting collection of classic motorcycles and scooters
in a small informal 'museum'. Open most Sundays
11.00am–4.00pm, other times by appointment.

GLOUCESTERSHIRE
Cotswold Motoring Museum & Toy Collection
Old Mill, Bourton-on-the-Water, Nr Cheltenham, GL54 2BY
Tel: 01451 821 255 www.csma.uk.com
Collection of cars, motorcycles and caravans. Also large
collection of enamel signs, garage equipment and automobilia.
This is the home of the Brough Superior Company and of
"Brum", the small open 1920's car that has a television
series. Open 11th February to 31 October, 10.00am–6.00pm.

HAMPSHIRE
Sammy Miller Motorcycle Museum
Bashley Cross Road, New Milton, BH25 5SZ Tel: 01425 616446
info@sammymiller.co.uk www.sammymiller.co.uk/museum.htm
One of the finest collections of fully restored motorcycles in
Europe, including factory racers and exotic prototypes, plus
memorabilia. A living museum with over 300 rare and
classic motorcycles on display in 4 galleries. Open daily
10.00am–4.30pm.

National Motor Museum
Brockenhurst, Beaulieu, SO42 7ZN Tel: 01590 612345
www.beaulieu.co.uk/motormuseum
Collection comprising 250 vehicles from some of the
earliest examples of motoring to legendary World Record
Breakers like Bluebird and Golden Arrow. Open daily except
Christmas Day, May to September 10.00am–6.00pm,
October to April 10.00am–5.00pm.

ISLE OF MAN
Murray's Motorcycle Museum
Bungalow Corner, Mountain Road, Snaefell
Tel: 01624 861719
Collection of over 120 motorcycles from the turn of the last
century, including Hailwood's 250cc Mondial and Honda 125cc
and the amazing 500cc 4-cylinder roadster designed by John
Wooler. Open mid May to September daily 10.00am–5.00pm.

KENT
Canterbury Motor Museum
11 Cogans Terrace, Canterbury, CT1 3SJ Tel: 01227 451718
Interesting collection of veteran and vintage cars and
motorcycles, as well as memorabilia. Open any day by
prior appointment.

Norman Cycles Museum
Willesborough Windmill, Mill Lane, Hythe Road, Ashford
Tel: 01233 661866
Mopeds and cycles on display within the Barn. The Mill is
open 2.00pm–5.00pm Saturdays, Sundays and Bank
Holidays from April to September.

Ramsgate Motor Museum
West Cliff Hall, Ramsgate, CT11 9JX Tel: 01843 581948 or
01268 785002
A private collection of 65 classic cars dating from 1900 to
1970, 70 motorcycles, 30 bicycles plus memorabilia including
200 petrol globes. Open Easter to October, 10.30am–5.30pm.

LEICESTERSHIRE
Stanford Hall Motorcycle Museum
Stanford Hall, Lutterworth, LE17 6DH Tel: 01788 860250
enqiries@stanfordhall.co.uk www.stanford.hall
A collection of racing and vintage motorcycles dating from
1914 to the present day. Most in running order. Open
Sundays and Bank Holiday Mondays 1.30pm–5.00pm.

MIDDLESEX
London Motorcycle Museum
Ravenor Farm, Oldfield Lane South, Greenford, UB6 9LD
Tel: 020 8575 6644 thelmm@hotmail.com
www.motorcycle-uk.com/lmm
Unique collection of British motorcycles. Open weekends
and Bank Holidays, 10.00am–4.30pm.

NORFOLK
Caister Castle Car Collection
Caister-on-Sea, Nr Great Yarmouth Tel: 01572 787251
Private collection of cars and motorcycles dating back to
1893. Open daily mid May to September 10.00am–4.30pm,
closed Saturdays.

Norfolk Motorcycle Museum
Station Yard, Norwich Road, North Walsham, NR28 0PS
Tel: 01692 406266
Over 100 motorcycles from 1919 to the 1960s. Open daily
10.00am–4.30pm.

SCOTLAND
Moray Motor Museum
Bridge Street, Elgin, IV30 2DE Tel: 01343 544933
Collection of cars and motorcycles plus memorabilia and diecast
models. Open daily April to October, 11.00am–5.00pm.

Myreton Motor Museum
Aberlady, East Lothian, EH32 0PZ Tel: 01875 870288/
853117
Collection of over 50 cars, motorcycles, commercial vehicles
and WWII military vehicles. Also collection of period advertising,
posters and enamel signs.

SHROPSHIRE
Midland Motor Museum
Stanmore Hall, Stourbridge Road, Bridgnorth, WV15 6DT
Tel: 01746 762992
Collection of cars and motorcycles dating from 1920s to
1980s. Open daily 10.30am–5.00pm.

SOMERSET
Haynes Motor Museum
Sparkford, Yeovil, BA22 7LH Tel: 01963 440804
mike@haynesmotormuseum.co.uk
www.haynesmotormuseum.com
Haynes Publishing Company museum with collections of
vintage, veteran and classic cars and motorcycles. Some
250 cars and 50 motorcycles. Open daily March to October
9.30am–5.30pm, November to February 10.00am–4.30pm,
closed Christmas and New Years Days.

Lambretta Scooter Museum
77 Alfred Street, Weston-Super-Mare, BS23 1PP
Tel: 01934 614614

SURREY
A. R. E. Classic Bike Collection
285 Worplesdon Road, Guildford, GU2 6XN
Tel: 01483 232006
Around 50 mainly British bikes including memorabilia and
the workshop where restorations are carried out is open.
Phone for opening times.

WALES

Anglesey Transport & Agriculture Museum
Tacla Taid, Tyddyn Pwrpas, Newborough, Anglesey
Tel: 01248 440344
Display of 23 cars, 11 tractors, 20 motorcycles and
commercial vehicles. All with Anglesey connection.

Llangollen Motor Museum
Pentre Felin, Llangollen, LL20 8EE Tel: 01978 860324
Cars, motorcycles, model vehicles, signs and tools and
parts. Open March to October, Tuesday to Sunday,
10.00am–5.00pm.

Madog Car & Motorcycle Museum
Madog Street West, Porthmadog, Gwynedd, LL49 9DF
Tel: 07789 063030
Restored collection of British cars and motorcycles. Also
memorabilia. Open Whitsun to October, Monday to Friday,
10.00am–5.00pm.

WEST MIDLANDS

National Motorcycle Museum
Solihull Tel: 0121 704 2784
sales@nationalmotorcyclemuseum.co.uk
www.nationalmotorcyclemuseum.co.uk
Currently closed due to fire 16th September 2003. Museum
scheduled to re-open 1st December 2004.

WILTSHIRE

Atwell-Wilson Motor Museum
Stockley Lane, Calne, SN11 0NF Tel: 01249 813119
www.atwell-wilson.org www.atwell-museum.freeuk.com
Collection or cars, lorries, motorcycles, mopeds, pushbikes
and a large selection of vehicle manuals, archive material
and motoring memorabilia. Open Sunday to Thursday
11.00am–4.00pm.

YORKSHIRE

Craven's Collection of Classic Motorcycles
Brockfield Villa, Stockton-on-the-Forest, York, YO3 9UE
Tel: 01904 400493 richard@craven45.fsnet.co.uk
www.cravencollection.co.uk
A private collection of over 250 Vintage and Post-War
Classic Motorcycles. Also a vast collection of motoring
memorabilia. Suppliers to the TV series 'Heartbeat' and
'Emmerdale', etc. Open Easter Sunday and Monday and
1st Sunday of every month, 10.00am–4.00pm.

AUSTRALIA

The National Motorcycle Museum
33 Clarkson Street, Nabiac, NSW 2312 Tel: 02 6554 1333
www.nationalmotorcyclemuseum.com.au
Australia's largest collection of vintage, veteran and
interesting motorcycles. Open daily except Christmas Day
9.00am–4.30pm.

CANADA

Canadian Vintage Motorcycle Museum
Canadian Military Heritage Museum, 347 Greenwich Street,
Building #19, Brantford, Ontario museum@cvmg.ca
www.cvmg.ca/museum.htm
Collection of around 33 motorcycles along with items of
memorabilia with an emphasis on motorcycles with a
Canadian connection. Open April to September, Tuesday
to Sunday 10.30am–4.30pm, October to March Tuesday
to Friday 1.00pm–4.30pm, Saturdays and Sundays
10.30am–4.30pm.

Trev Deeley Motorcycle Museum
13500 Verdun Place, Richmond, BC Tel: 604 273 5421
www.trevdeeley.com/custom/collection.html
Over 250 motorcycles and memorabilia. Open Monday to
Friday 10.00am–4.00pm.

ITALY

Ducati Museum
Via Cavalieri Ducati, 3 Borgo Panigale (Bologna) – 40132
Tel: 39 051 6413111 www.ducati.com/heritage/museum
A collection of motorcycles spanning the history of Ducati.

USA

American Classic Motorcycle Museum
1170 US Hwy 64 West, Asheboro, NC 27203
Tel: 336 629 9564
Collection of over 30 antique and classic Harley-Davidson
motorcycles from 1936 to 1972 and an authentic 1948
Harley dealership/repair shop. Open Monday to Saturday,
contact for hours.

Bench Mark Works Motorcycle Museum
3400 Earles Fork Road, Sturgis, Mississippi 39769
Tel: 662 465 6444
Dedicated to pre-1970 BMW motorcycles.

Otis Chandler Museum of Transportation
1421 Emerson Ave, Oxnard, CA 93033 Tel: 805 486 5929
www.chandlerwheels.com
Over 100 motorcycles, automobiles including 1930s
American cars. Contact for opening times.

Indian Motorcycle Museum
Hall of Fame, 33 Hendee Street, Springfield, MA 01104
Tel: (413) 737 2624
Fine collection of American Indian motorcycles as well as
collections of bicycles, toy motorcycles and other motor-
powered items. Open March to November, Monday to
Sunday, 10am–4pm, December to February, Monday to
Sunday, 1–4pm, closed Thanksgiving, Christmas and
New Years.

Lone Star Motorcycle Museum
Texas Tel: 830 966 6103 awjohncock@ricc.net
www.lonestarmotorcyclemuseum.com
Collection of machines from around the world dating from
the 1910s to the 1980s. Open Friday 1.00pm–5.00pm,
Saturdays and Sundays, 10.00am–5.00pm, weekdays
by appointment.

Motorcycle Hall of Fame Museum
13515 Yarmouth Dr, Pickerington, Ohio 43147
Tel: 614 856 2222 info@motorcyclemuseum.org
A wide range of motorcycles and memorabilia on display
telling the stories and history of motorcycling and
honouring those who have contributed notably to the
sport. Open daily 9.00am–5.00pm, except Easter,
Thanksgiving, Christmas and New Year's Day.

National Motorcycle Museum & Hall of Fame
200 E. Main Street, PO Box 405, Anamosa, IA 52205
Tel: 319 462 3925 nationalmcmuseum@hotmail.com
www.nationalmcmuseum.org
A collection of motorcycles and memorabilia and pictures
of people who have made motorcycling what it is today.
Open May to October, Monday to Friday, 9.00am–5.00pm,
Saturday 9.00am–5.00pm, Sunday 10.00am–4.00pm,
November to April, Monday to Friday, 9.00am–5.00pm,
Saturday 10.00am–4.00pm, Sunday 11.00am–4.00pm.

Owls Head Transportation Museum
PO Box 277, Route 73, Owls Head, Maine 04854
Tel: 207 594 4418 info@ohtm.org www.ohtm.org
Antiques, classic and special interest auto, motorcycles,
aircraft, engines, bicycles and related vehicles. Open daily
except for Thanksgiving, Christmas, New Year's Day and
the first non-Easter Sunday of each April, April to October,
10.00am–5.00pm, November to March, 10.00am–4.00pm.

Rocky Mountain Motorcycle Museum
308 E. Arvada, Colorado Springs, CO 80906
Tel: (719) 633 6329
Over 50 original and fully restored vintage and antique
motorcycles dating from 1913 to 1973. Period memorabilia,
Hall of Fame, photographs and art, motorcycle restoration.
Open Monday to Saturday, 10.00am–7.00pm.

Dan Rouit Flat Track Museum
309 West Rialto Street, Clovis, California Tel: 559 291 2242
dkrouit118y@comcast.net www.vft.org/rouit.htm
Flat trackers posters, programs, trophies, plaques, leathers,
helmets and pictures all displayed for the racing enthusiast.
Contact between 11.00am–7.00pm for opening times
information.

Solvang Motorcycle Museum
320 Alisal Road, Solvang, CA 93463 Tel: 805 686 9522
info@motosolvang.com www.motosolvang.com
Collection of vintage and rare motorcycles as well as
European race bikes. Open weekends 11.00am–5.00pm
and by appointment mid week.

Sturgis Motorcycle Museum & Hall of Fame, Inc
PO Box 602 Sturgis, South Dakota 57785 Tel: 605 347
2001 info@SturgisMuseum.com
www.sturgismotorcyclemuseum.org
A museum dedicated to the history of the legendary Sturgis
Motorcycle Rally. Open all year.

Directory of Motorcycle Clubs

If you wish to be included in next year's directory, or if you have a change of address or telephone number, please inform us by 25th April 2006.

ABC Owners Club, D. A. Hales, The Hedgerows, Sutton St Nicholas, Hereford HR1 3BU Tel: 01432 880726

AJS/Matchless Owners Club of England, North American Section, PO Box 317, Yardley, Pennsylvania PA 19067, USA Tel: 215 295 4003

AMC Owners Club, c/o Terry Corley, 12 Chilworth Gardens, Sutton, Surrey SM1 3SP

American Historic Racing Motorcycle Association, Lorie Smith, Membership Co-ordinator, PO Box 1648, Brighton MI 48116-1648, USA Tel: 814 778 2291 ahrmanatlmemship@aol.com www.ahrma.org/

Ancient Iron Motorcycle Club, PO Box 107, Holy City CA 95026, USA Tel: 408 997 2396 www.ancientironmc.com

Antique Motorcycle Club of America, Inc, Dick Winger, PO Box 310, W Sweetser IN 46987, USA Club hotline: 1 800 782-AMCA (2622) www.antiquemotorcycle.org

The Antique Motorcycle Club of Australia, Inc, Mal Grant (Secretary), PO Box 402, Gisborne, Vic 3437, Australia Tel: 03 5428 9390

Ariel Owners Motor Cycle Club, Andy Hemingway, 80 Pasture Lane, Clayton, Bradford, Yorkshire BD14 6LN andy_hemingway@yahoo.com

Arizona Confederation of Motorcycle Clubs, 1855 W Greenway Road, STE 115, PMB 112, Phoenix, Arizona 85023, USA www.azcmc.com

Bantam Enthusiasts Club, c/o Vic Salmon, 16 Oakhurst Close, Walderslade, Chatham, Kent ME5 9AN

Benelli Motobi Club GB, Val Peace, 85 Ballamaddrell, Port Erin, Isle of Man IM9 6AU

The BMW Club, 27 Syon Gardens, Newport Pagnall, Buckinghamshire MK16 0JU Tel: 01908 216623 vintage@bmwclub.org.uk www.bmwclub.org.uk

BMW Motorcycle Owners Ltd (Vintage), Craig Vechorik, PO Box 6329, Miss State MS 39762, USA vech@ra.msstate.edu

Bristol & District Sidecar Club, 158 Fairlyn Drive, Kingswood, Bristol, Gloucestershire BS15 4PZ

British Iron Association, Massachusetts Chapter, Dave Kendrick, 173 Boston Road, Sutton MA 01590, USA www.massbia.com

British Motor Bike Owners Club, c/o Ray Peacock Crown Inn, Shelfanger, Diss, Norfolk IP22 2DL

British Motorcycle Association (BMCA), c/o Amateur Motor Cycle Association Ltd, 28 Navigation Way, Mill Park, Cannock, Staffordshire WS11 7XU Tel: 01543 466282 amca.office@btinternet.com www.amca.uk.com

British Motorcycle Club of Guernsey, c/o Ron Le Cras, East View, Village De Putron, St Peter Port, Guernsey, Channel Islands GY1

British Motorcycle Owners Club, c/o Phil Coventry, 59 Mackenzie Street, Bolton, Lancashire BL1 6QP

British Motorcyclists Federation, Jack Wiley House, 129 Seaforth Avenue, Motspur Park, New Malden, Surrey KT3 6JU

British Two-Stroke Club Ltd, Mrs Lynda Tanner (Membership Secretary), 259 Harlestone Road, Duston, Northampton NN5 6DD

Brough Superior Club, Box 393, Cos Cob, Connecticut CT 06807, USA Tel: 203 661 0526

BSA Owners Club, Chris Taylor, PO Box 436, Peterborough, Cambridgeshire PE4 7WD christaylor@natsecbsaoc.screaming.net

The Canadian Motorcycle Association, PO Box 448, Hamilton, Ontario L8L 1J4 Tel: 905 522 5705 www.canmocycle.ca

Canadian Vintage Motorcycle Group, Membership: Phil and Isobel Johnston Tel: 519 389 3622 membership@cvmg.ca www.cvmg.on.ca

Christian Motorcyclists Association (UK), PO Box 113, Wokingham, Berkshire RG11 5UB www.bike.org.uk

Classic 50 Racing Club, Chris Alty, 14a Kestrel Park, Ashurst, Skelmersdale, Lancashire WN8 6TB Classic50Racing@aol.com

Classic Japanese Motorcycle Club (CJMC), Don Brown, 3139 Hawkcrest, Circle San Jose CA 95135-2224, USA Tel: 408 531 1157 doncjmc@aol.com www.netcom.com/~tickover/cjmc.html

Classic Kawasaki Club (Formerly The Kawasaki Triples Club), PO Box 235, Nottingham NG8 6DT

Classic Racing Motorcycle Club Ltd, John Davidson (Membership Secretary) Tel: 01142 873885 www.crmc.co.uk

Classic Wing Club, 710 South Rush Street, South Bend IN 46601, USA Tel: 219 234 9777 classicwing@mvillage.com www.classicwingclub.org

Cotton Owners Club, P. Turner, Coombehayes, Sidmouth Road, Lyme Regis, Dorset DT7 3EQ sales@specializedmarine.com

Cushman Motor Scooter Club of America, PO Box 661, Union Springs, Alabama AL 36089, USA Tel: 205 738 3874

Dot Motorcycle Club, c/o Dot Motorcycles, St George's House, 36 Ellesmere Street, Hulme, Greater Manchester M15 4JW Tel: 01618 345472 Dotclub@freenetname.co.uk www.dot-motorcycle-club.co.uk

Ducati Owners Club, Tanya Chambers (Membership Secretary), Westview, 26 Outgate, Ealand, Lincolnshire DN17 4JD Tel: 01724 710175 tanya@docgb.org www.docgb.org

Excelsior Talisman Enthusiasts, Ginger Hall, Village Way, Little Chalfont, Buckinghamshire HP7 9PU Tel/Fax: 01494 762166 the.powells@virgin.net

Exeter British Motorcycle Club, c/o Bill Jones, 7 Parkens Cross Lane, Pinhoe, Exeter, Devon EX1 3TA

Exeter Classic Motorcycle Club, c/o Martin Hatcher, 11 Newcombe Street, Heavitree, Exeter, Devon EX1 2TG

Federation of Sidecar Clubs, Jeff Reynard, 5 Ethel Street, Beechcliffe, Keighley, West Yorkshire BD20 6AN Tel: 01535 609355 www.sidecars.org.uk

Francis-Barnett Owners Club, Sue Dorling (Club Secretary), Clouds Hill, 5 Blacklands Road, Upper Bucklebury, Nr Reading, Berkshire RG7 6QP Tel: 01635 864256

Freedom Riders Motorcycle Club, Montgomery County, Pennsylvania, USA www.freedomriders.com

Gold Star Owners Club, Maurice Evans, 211 Station Road, Mickleover, Derby DE3 5FE

Goldwing Owners Club, Gary Ingram, 60 Purley Avenue, Cricklewood, London NW2 1SB

Greeves Riders Association, Dave & Brenda McGregor, 4 Longshaw Close, North Wingfield, Chesterfield, Derbyshire S42 5QR

Harley Davidson Riders Club of Great Britain, SAE to Membership Secretary, PO Box 62, Newton Abbott, Devon TQ12 2QE

The Harley Hummer Club, Inc, 4517 Chase Avenue, Bethesda MD 20814, USA www.harleyhummerclub.org

Harley Owners Group, H.O.G. Customer Services, PO Box 114, Twickenham, Middlesex TW1 1XQ Tel: 00 800 1111 2223 customerservices@hog-europe.com

Hedingham Sidecar Owners Club, Annette McEwan (Newsletter Editor), 10 Fairfield, Denholme, Bradford, Yorkshire BD13 4DH a.mcewan2@btinternet.com

Hesketh Owners Club, Peter White, 1 Northfield Road, Soham, Cambridgeshire CB7 5UE

Historic Police Motorcycles Tel: 020 8393 4958

Honda Monkey Club, 28 Newdigate Road, off Red Lane, Coventry, Warwickshire CV6 5ES

Honda Owners Club (GB), Membership Secretary, 61 Vicarage Road, Ware, Hertfordshire SG12 7BE Tel: 01536 412086 www.hoc.org.uk

Indian Motorcycle Club of America, PO Box 1743, Perris CA 92572-1743, USA

Indian Motorcycle Owners Club, c/o John Chatterton (Membership Secretary), 183 Buxton Road, Newtown, Disley, Stockport Cheshire SK12 2RA Tel: 01663 747106

International Laverda Owners Club, New Membership and Club Archive c/o John Faulkner, Hill Farm, Dorton, Aylesbury, Buckinghamshire HP18 9NJ 01844 238 269 evenings until 11pm editor@iloc.org.uk/ www.iloc.org.uk/

International Motorcyclists Tour Club, c/o Tricia Hannon, 14 Sandiway Bank, Thornhill, Dewsbury, West Yorkshire WF12 0SD

Italian Motorcycle Owners Club (GB), www.italianmotorcycles.co.uk

Jawa-CZ Owners Club, John Blackburn, 39 Bignor Road, Sheffield, Yorkshire S6 IJD

Jawa/CZ Register, 1548 Deerwood Drive, East Mobile AL 36618, USA Tel: 334 342 0726 jawa1@zebra.net www.jawaczregister.org

Kawasaki Riders Club, Gemma Court, 1 Concord House, Kirmington, Humberside DN39 6YP

Latin American Motorcycle Association, International Headquarters, 3519 West Fullerton Avenue, Chicago, Illinois 60647, USA Tel: 773 235 0195 intpresident@latinbikers.com www.latinbikers.com

Laverda Owners Club, c/o Ray Sheepwash, 8 Maple Close, Swanley, Kent BR8 7YN

LE Velo Club Ltd, Kevin Parsons, Chapel Mead, Blandford Hill, Winterborne, Whitechurch, Blandford, Dorset DT11 0AB www.leveloclub.org.uk

Leominster Classic MCC, Ron Moore, The Yew Tree, Gorsty, Pembridge, Herefordshire HR6 9JF

The London Douglas Motorcycle Club Ltd, Reg Holmes, 48 Standish Avenue, Stoke Lodge, Patchway, Bristol BS34 6AG www.douglasmotorcycles.co.uk

London Sidecar Club, 107 Silverweed Road, Walderslade, Chatham, Kent ME5 0RF

Maico Owners Club, c/o Steve Thompson, St Ives, Eden Road, Gordon, Berwickshire TD3 6JT

Marston Sunbeam Register, Ray Jones, 37 Sandhurst Drive, Penn, Wolverhampton, West Midlands WV4 5RJ

Military Vehicle Trust, PO Box 6, Fleet, Hampshire GU52 6GE www.mvt.org.uk

Morini Owners Club, 60 Watergate Lane, Leicester LE3 2XP

Morini Riders Club, 60 Watergate Lane, Leicester LE3 2XP

Moto Club du Lion, 1 Allee du Coteau, 77400 St Thibault des Vignes, France Tel: (33-1) 06 14 95 07 34 motoclublion@hotmail.com

Moto Guzzi Club GB, 43 Poplar Avenue, Bedworth, Nuneaton, Warwickshire CV12 9EW Tel: 024 7673 0678 pollyfoyle7@yahoo.com

MV Agusta Owners Club of GB, Mr Alan Elderton (Chairman), 108 Thundersley Park Road, South Benfleet, Essex SS7 1ES

MZ Riders Club, 12 Whitehorn Avenue, Barleston ST12 9EF www.mzridersclub.co.uk

National Autocycle & Cyclemotor Club, David Casper, NACC Chairman & Machine Registrar, 7 St Nicholas Road, Copmanthorpe, York YO23 3UX Tel: 01904 704373 registrar@buzzing.org

New Imperial Owners Association, Mrs J. E. Jarvis, Lyndhurst House, Victoria Road, Hayling Island, Hampshire PO11 0LU

Norman Cycles Club, 8 St Francis Road, Cheriton, Folkestone, Kent CT19 4BJ www.normancycles.co.uk

North American Kawasaki Triples Club (NAKTC), knyt@insightbb.com

North Devon British Motorcycle Owners Club, Andy Wye (Secretary), 32 Merrythorn Road, Fremington, Barnstaple, N Devon EX31 3AL Tel: 01271 379170 andylin@andbmocl.freeserve.co.uk www.ndbmoc.freeserve.co.uk

Norton Owners Club, Colin Coleman, 110 Skegby Road, Annesley Woodhouse, Nottinghamshire NG17 9FF Tel: 01623 439143 ukmembers@nortonownersclub.org www.nortonownersclub.org

NSU Motorcycle Register, Val Albert, 9811 Maury Road, Fairfax VA 22032, USA NTYF35A@mailinb1.prodigy.com

Oregon Vintage Motorcyclists, PO Box 14645, Portland OR 97293-0645, USA best@efn.org www.efn.org/~best/

Panther Owners Club, Graham & Julie Dibbins, Oakdene, 22 Oak Street, Netherton, Dudley, West Midlands DY2 9LJ www.pantherownersclub.com

Raleigh Safety Seven and Early Reliant Owners Club Incorporating Historic Raleigh Motorcycle Club, Mick Sleap, 17 Courtland Avenue, Chingford, London E4 6DU

Rolls Royce Vintage & Classic Motorcycle Club, Ken Birch, 111 Havenbaulk Lane, Littleover, Derby DE23 7AD

Rotary Owners' Club, c/o David Cameron, Dunbar, Ingatestone Road, Highwood, Chelmsford, Essex CM1 3QU

Royal Automobile Club, PO Box 700, Bristol, Gloucestershire BS99 1RB Tel: 01454 208000

Royal Enfield Owners Club, Sylvia and Mick Seager (Membership Secretaries), 30/32 Causeway, Burgh-Le-Marsh, Skegness, Lincolnshire PE24 5LT Tel: 01754 810119 mickseager@boltblue.com

Rudge Enthusiasts Club Ltd, Bloomsbury, 13 Lade Fort Crescent, Lydd-on-Sea, Romney Marsh, Kent TN29 9YG www.rudge.ndirect.co.uk

Scott Owners Club, Brian Marshall (Press Officer), Walnut Cottage, Abbey Lane, Aslockton, Nottingham NG13 9AE

Sidecar Register, c/o John Proctor, 112 Briarlyn Road, Birchencliffe, Huddersfield, Yorkshire HD3 3NW

South Wales Sunbeam MCC, Miss Kate Baxter, 17 Heol Gelynog, Beddau, Pontypridd, South Wales CF38 2SG

Spanish Motorcycle Owner's Group (SMOG), Ken McGuire Jr, PO Box 297, Cropsey Ville, New York 12052, USA

Sunbeam MCC Ltd, Ian McGill, 13 Victoria Road, Horley, Surrey RH6 9BN A club for all makes pre-1931

Sunbeam Owners Club, Stewart Engineering, Church Terrace, Harbury, Leamington Spa, Warwickshire CV33 9HL

Suzuki Owners Club, PO Box 7, Egremont, Cumbria CA22 2GE Tel: 07811 407 397 secretary@suzuki-club.co.uk www.suzuki-club.co.uk

Tiger Cub & Terrier Register, Mike Estall, 24 Main Road, Edingale, Tamworth, Staffordshire B79 9HY

Tour du Dauphine en Petrolettes, 38550 St Maurice, L'Exil, France

Trail Riders Fellowship, PO Box 196, Derby DE1 9EY www.trf.org.uk

Trident and Rocket 3 Owners Club, Mr Graham Redrup (Secretary), events@tr3oc.co.uk

Triumph Motorcycle Club, 6 Hortham Lane, Almondsbury, Bristol, Gloucestershire BS12 4JH

Triumph Owners MCC, Mrs M. M. Mellish (General Secretary), 4 Douglas Avenue, Harold Wood, Romford, Essex RM3 0UT

Velocette Owners Club, William Greenwood (Secretary), 7 Townsend Road, Harpenden, Hertfordshire AL5 4BQ Tel: 01582 713880 billwgreenwood@aol.com www.velocetteowners.com

The Veteran and Vintage Motor Cycle Club of South Australia, Inc, PO Box 8 Goodwood 5034, Australia vvmccsa@senet.com.au

Veteran Grass Track Riders Association (VGTRA), Carl Croucher, 4 Whitmore Street, Maidstone, Kent ME16 9JU

Veteran Vespa Club, Ashley Lenton, 3 Vincent Road, Croydon, Surrey CR0 6ED

Vincent HRD Owners Club, Paul Adams (Information Officer), 1 St Georges Road, Footscray, Sidcup, Kent DA14 5JN Tel: 02083 003118

Vintage Japanese Motorcycle Club, PO Box 515, Dartford, Kent DA1 5WB www.vjmc.com

Vintage Japanese Motorcycle Club, 24 Cathy Street, Merrimack NH 03054-2840, USA

The Vintage Motor Cycle Club, Allen House, Wetmore Road, Burton-on-Trent, Staffordshire DE14 1TR Tel: 01283 540557 hq@vmcc.net www.vmcc.net

Vintage Motor Scooter Club, c/o Ian Harrop, 11 Ivanhoe Avenue, Lowton St Lukes, Nr Warrington, Cheshire WA3 2HX

Vintage Motorcycle Enthusiasts, PO Box 4341, Seattle WA 98194, USA vme@micapeak.com

Vintage Road Racing Association, Mrs Manzi Warwick, VRRA (Membership Secretary), 1870 Spruce Hill Road, Pickering, Ontario, Canada www.nornet.on.ca/~tharris/vrra/

Virago Star Owners Club, John Bryning (President), River Green House, Great Sampford, Saffron Walden, Essex CB10 2RS

Washington Motorcycle Roadracing Association, PO Box 94323, Seattle, Washington WA 98124-5623, USA

Yamaha Riders Club, Alan Cheney, 11 Lodden Road, Farnborough, Hampshire GU14 9NR

Zl Owners Club, PO Box No 11817, Birmingham, West Midlands B43 6WZ

Zundapp Bella Enthusiasts' Club, Bill Dorling (Chairman), 5 Blacklands Road, Upper Bucklebury, Reading, Berkshire RG7 6QP Tel: 01635 864256

Zündapp Bella Motor Scooter Register, 632 Crawford Street, Flint MI 48507, USA

Index

Italic page numbers denote colour pages, **bold** numbers refer to information and pointer boxes

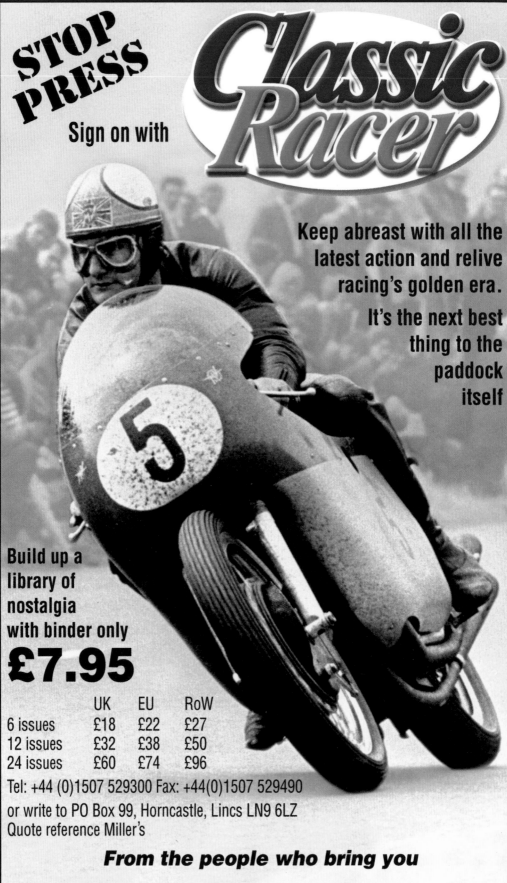